GROTIAN SOCIETY PAPERS

1968

GROTIAN SOCIETY PAPERS 1968

Studies in the History of the Law of Nations

EDITED BY

C. H. ALEXANDROWICZ

SPRINGER-SCIENCE+BUSINESS MEDIA, B.V. 1970

ISBN 978-94-017-5680-8 ISBN 978-94-017-5985-4 (eBook)
DOI 10.1007/978-94-017-5985-4

Originally published by Martinus Nijhoff, The Hague, Netherlands in 1970
Softcover reprint of the hardcover 1st edition 1970

TABLE OF CONTENTS

INTRODUCTION

Some years ago a group of lawyers believing in the need for renewed studies in the History of International Law formed the Grotian Society with the object of promoting interest in this branch of legal science which in recent times had come to be somewhat neglected. To achieve this purpose it was not sufficient to carry out research in this field. It is essential to bring the result of such research to the notice of a wide reading public, particularly in respect of those problems which are relevant to present day problems of international law.

In presenting this volume the Publishing House of Martinus Nijhoff at the Hague has testified to its belief in the work undertaken so far and the Grotian Society wishes here to express its indebtedness to their generous understanding and vision in making this work available to many lawyers and historians who might otherwise not readily find within one volume the result of much specialised research.

Formerly a collection of Grotian Papers had appeared through the courtesy of Professor T. S. Rama Rao, Editor of the Indian Year Book of International Affairs. This collection of papers received favourable reviews and it is therefore with hope and confidence that we look forward to the first publication in Europe of these Studies in the History of International Law.

The Grotian Society organised last January a Seminar on the History of the Law of Nations at Ditchley Park (Oxford). Papers were read at the Seminar by Mr. J. E. S. Fawcett (on the Role of the History of International Law in Decisions of International Tribunals); Dr. P. O'Higgins (on Historical Aspects of the Relationship between Municipal Law and Treaties); Mrs. E. Denza (on History of Diplomacy), Dr. K. R. Simmonds (on Gentili) and Professor C. H. Alexandrowicz (on Reversion to Sovereignty). Dr. Clive Parry, President of the Law

Faculty Board (Cambridge), addressed the meeting on problems of historical research.

Our special gratitude goes to all those who helped to make this seminar a success, particularly to Dr. Eli Lauterpacht, Fellow of Trinity College (Cambridge) and Secretary of the International Law Fund, Mr. G. Goddard, Vice-Chairman and Secretary-General of the Grotian Society and Dr. Simmonds, Director of the British Institute of International and Comparative Law which organised the Seminar jointly with the Grotian Society.

CHARLES HENRY ALEXANDROWICZ

Chairman of the Grotian Society,
Visiting Fellow, Centre of
International Studies, Cambridge

PROF. D. P. O'CONNELL
University of Adelaide

Territorial Claims In The Grotian Period

International lawyers have never been very explicit as to the legal significance to be attributed to conquest and annexation. As the Boer War controversy reminds us, annexation has been thought to be legally ineffective while hostilities continue; and within the European context the acquisition of territory has nearly always been provided for in the peace treaty following war, which, save in very few exceptional situations, was coincidental with the termination of hostilities. The only ambiguous situations, then, were those of colonial conquest where, as in the case of Burma, the entire State was extinguished so that no peace treaty could be negotiated; and since such cases are perhaps best characterized as cases of debellatio rather than of annexation we are left with very little historical material with which to examine the legal characteristics of forcible seizure of territory which did not take the form of cession by treaty.

Up to the French Revolution no war was fought in Europe without both sides asserting legal justification for their position, though the justification varied as legal concepts evolved. After the French Revolution nationalism constituted the principal justification for territorial conquest, and the Italian writers of the Risorgimento erected a complex legal edifice validating the unification of Italy on nationalist principles. The purpose of this paper is not to examine the legal basis of conquest over an extended period of European history, but rather to demonstrate from an examination of one short, but relatively autonomous period, the significance of legal notions – not necessarily international law notions – in territorial reconstruction. This is the half-century, roughly, from the termination of the Netherlands Revolt and the French Religious Wars to the Peace of Westphalia. The period is important for two reasons: first, the expansion of France to its "natural boundaries" began under Richelieu and Mazarin; and secondly medieval and feudal concepts of law were being transformed into concepts of territorial sovereignty from which rights to territory might be deduced. The period after the Peace of Westphalia is significantly different in character, and the French seizures of Strasbourg and Savoy were to be justified on principles which were unfamiliar to Richelieu and Mazarin. Examination of them must await another occasion.

During the period which has been selected for discussion France was the principal Power which gained territory, and it is therefore the French legal position which calls for examination. France acquired, in chronological order, the Dependencies of the Bishopric of Metz, so gaining a foothold in Lorraine; Pinerolo in the Marquisate of Saluzzo across the Alps in Italy; and the Provinces of Artois, Roussillon and Cerdagne. No French author of the period considered these acquisitions as other than the reunification in the French Crown of territories which had always been French: They did not argue in terms of power over territory, for the French Crown had lost such power in some instances for a long period, but in terms of the sovereign rights of the French Crown; and they did not think in terms of the *jus gentium* but in terms of the Fundamental Law of France.

Since it is upon the concept of the Fundamental Law that all the legal discussion turned, the examination must begin with this concept. It became explicit in French constitutional theory during the sixteenth century, and took on the character on an eternal principle governing the life of the nation. It implied that behind the institutions of government was something unalterable by established authority, and it assimilated traditional privileges and liberties to the laws of God and nature. A leading jurist of the reign of Louis XIII, Charles Loyseau, put is as follows:

> Il y a trois sortes de Loix qui bornent la puissance du Souverain, sans interner la Souveraineté. A sçavoir les loix de Dieu pour ce que le Prince n'est pas moins souverain pour estre sujet à Dieu; les regles de Justice naturelle et non positives, pour ce qu'il a eté dit cy-devant, que c'est le propre de la Seigneurie publique, d'estre exercée par Justice, et non pas à discretion: Et finalement les loix fondamentales de l'Etat, pour ce que le Prince doit user de sa Souveraineté selon la propre nature, et en la forme et aux conditions qu'elle est établie.[1]

The Fundamental Law included the Salic Law, which governed the succession to the French throne, and also the territories of the French

[1] *Oeuvres: Les traitez des seigneuries* (1613) (1701 ed.), p. 8.

Crown. No French monarch had the competence to alienate French territory, any more than he had to alter the succession to the throne. The pressure of this concept upon contemporary thinking is illustrated by a letter which the Secretary of State, the Comte de Chavigny, wrote to the Baron de Pujol, Richelieu's secret agent in Spain, respecting a proposal of peace which involved the division of the Duchy of Savoy. He wrote:

Le project que vous m'avés envoyé est sy impraticable en deux articles, que je ne l'ay osé monstrer à S. Em. qui auroit très mauvaise opinion de vous, si vous ne sçavies que les lois fondamentales du royaume, telles qu'est la loy Salique, sont du tout inviolables, en sorte qu'il n'est pas en la puissance du roy d'y apporter changement; et si S. Em. croyoit que vous pussiés penser que le roy fust capable de consentir à ce que Madame sa soeur demeurast despouillée de ses Estats. Il y a certaines choses qui, blessant le droit de la nature, blesseroient tellement l'imagination de tous les hommes, qu'il ne fault point y penser.[2]

The early seventeenth century was an age of great legalism and historicity, and several important works were written in which an examination was made of the historical boundaries of France and of the legal status of territories not actually governed by the French Crown. The title of one of these is significant:

La recherche des Droicts du Roy, et de la Couronne de France: sur les Royaumes, Duchez, Comtez, Villes et Pais occupez par les Princes estrangers: appartenans aux Roys tres-chrestiens, par Conquestes, Successions, Achapts, Donations et autres Titres legitimes. Ensemble de leurs Droicts sur l'Empire, et des devoirs et homages deubs à leur Couronne, par divers Princes estrangers.[3]

It is to be noted that this author regards conquest as a root of French title, but repudiates the validity of seizures from France on the ground of violation of the Fundamental Law. Cardin Le Bret,[4] examining the French claim to the Three Bishoprics of Metz, Toul and Verdun, concedes that it originated in their conquest by Clovis, but asserts that the French rights therein derived from peaceful possession from that time until the "usurpation" by the Ottonian dynasty in the time of Hugh Capet. Why the "peaceful possession" of the territory by the Emperors was insufficient to validate their title as it appears to have been suf-

[2] Avenel, *Lettres, instructions diplomatiques et papiers d'Etat du cardinal de Richelieu* (1853077), vol. 6, p. 739.
[3] By Jacques de Cassan (1632).
[4] *De la souveraineté du Roy* (1632).

ficient to validate an earlier French title is not made clear, and Cardin Le Bret goes so far as to reject the possibility of an imperial title arising through prescription.

The argument of other French authors concerning prescription is scarcely less tendentious. Jean de Silhon, dealing with the same claim, states that peaceful and uncontested occupation is a root of title, but that the usurpation is contested whenever the origins of a nation's rights are disputed; and on this ground he argues that

Le Roy peut legitimement garder Mets, Thoul et Verdun, quand bien ces places auroient esté iniustement occupeés.[5]

Charles Hersent went further, and derived the French claim to the Three Bishoprics from the rights of the Gauls as mentioned in Caesar, Tacitus and Strabo

qui donnet pour borne à la Gaule, depuis appeleé France, les Mons Pyrenees, les Alpes, le Rhin, les deux Mers Oceanie et Mediterranee.[6]

In time this argument concerning the ancient frontiers of France was to be transformed into an argument concerning the natural frontiers of France, and on this argument was France's Rhine policy to be founded. But in the first half of the seventeenth century legal thought had not sufficiently escaped its medieval trammels for this notion to justify a policy of territorial expansion. During the nineteenth century, when the question of Alsace-Lorraine preoccupied France and Germany, German historians sought to vilify France by asserting that Richelieu had predatory designs on all the territories west of the Rhine, and French historians sought intellectual compensation for the loss of Alsace-Lorraine in lauding Richelieu's policy of French aggrandizement. In fact it is doubtful if Richelieu, cautious and legalistic as he was, had any designs whatever upon Alsace. His statements of policy concerning the Rhine are delphic. On one occasion he referred to the ambition of Henri IV "to make the Rhine the boundary of France, fortifying three or four places there." [7] In a general statement of policy addressed to the royal council in 1629 he proposed an advance to Strasbourg so as to acquire a sallyport into Germany. But he warned that such an advance implied "lots of time, great discretion

[5] *Le Ministre d'Estat avec le véritable usage de la politique moderne* (1631), p. 102.

[6] *De la souveraineté du Roy à Mets* (1632).

[7] *Mémoires*, pub. by Petitot in Collection des mémoires relatifs à l'histoire de France (1823), vol. I, p. 24.

and quiet and disguised conduct." [8] Clearly he was formulating, not a policy of action, but a long-term objective, and the objective would be validated by legal arguments. When, in 1633, several of the rulers of Alsace asked for French garrisons to fend off a Spanish threat down the Rhine, Richelieu seized this opportunity of extending France's area of manoeuvre, but he did nothing to supersede the rulers in their actual government and gave no indication of intending to extend French jurisdiction to their territories.[9]

One of the cornerstones of Richelieu's statesmanship was France's legal claims to territory, and though many of his contemporaries equated these with France's natural frontiers, his position was independent of a geographical premise. In 1641 he wrote to the Chancellor:

> Je vous ai demandé un abrégé des droits du roy sur Milan, sur Naples, sur Sicile, sur le Piermont et lieux adjacens; comme aussy ce que nous avons à dire pour nous deffendre des prétentions que les ennemies ont sur le duché de Bourgogne. Je vous prie de me les envoier promptement, parce que j'en ay besoin pour l'instruction de la paix.[10]

He was referring here to the instructions to be issued to the French delegation at the conference of Münster.

In the archives of the French Ministry is a full volume of documents on the legal situation of the Three Bishoprics of Metz, Toul and Verdun,[11] and it was a dispute concerning these that led France and the Habsburgs into fatal confrontation during the Thirty Years War. The Bishoprics had been transferred to France in the Treaty of Câteau Cambrésis in 1559. At that time the concept of territorial sovereignty had not matured sufficiently to make it clear that they were no longer imperial territory: if they were imperial territory then the King of France held them as fiefs of the Emperor; if they were not imperial territory the Emperor, and his vassal the Duke of Lorraine, had no authority therein. For three quarters of a century the ambiguous character of the Three Bishoprics was not adverted to. It became an issue only with the abstraction of territorial sovereignty which occurred late in the sixteenth century. Bodin wrote:

[8] Avenel, *op. cit.*, vol. 3, p. 179.
[9] O'Connell, *Richelieu* (1968), p. 292.
[10] Avenel, *op. cit.*, vol. 6, p. 877.
[11] *Archives du Ministère des Affaires Etrangères: Etat numérique des fonds de la correspondance politique de l'origine à 1871, Lorraine*, vol. 8. See generally Haussonville, *Histoire de la réunion de Lorraine à La France* (1859-9).

Republique est un droit gouvernement de plusieurs mesnages, et de ce que leur est commun, avec puissance souveraine.[12]

In Loyseau the concept of sovereignty assumes a more metaphysical character. It is

la forme qui donne l'estre à l'Estat, mesme l'Estat et la souveraintеté prise in concreto sont synonimes et l'Estat est ainsi appellé parce que la Souveraineté est le comble et le periode de la puissance, ou il faut que l'Estat s'arreste et s'establisse.[13]

Cardin Le Bret puts it thus:

Elle est une supréme puissance deferеé à un seul, qui luy donne le droict de commander absolument, et qui n'a pour but que le repos et l'utilité publique ... La souveraineté n'est non plus divisible, que le poinct en la Geometrie.[14]

This geometrical analogy instantly suggested that there could be no divisibility of sovereignty concerning French territory, and that therefore all French territory must be held by the Crown absolutely, a notion that prevailed in the drafting of the provisions of the Peace of Westphalia.

It so happened that the Bishopric of Metz had several feudal dependencies scattered deep in Lorraine. Two of these, Vic and Moyenvic, were fortresses dominating the road between Nancy and Strasbourg. Had these dependencies been included in the cession of the Three Bishoprics at Câteau Cambrésis? If they had, then, according to French theory, they were French territory. A commission set up by Richelieu to investigate certain alienations of land from the Bishopric of Metz reported that France had jurisdiction in Lorraine. This claim coincided with the succession to the Duchy of Lorraine of an intemperate and disaffected youth, Charles IV, who was also Duke of Bar. As Duke of Lorraine he was a feudatory of the Emperor; but the Duchy of Bar was a dependency of France, and Charles' succession thereto derived through his wife, a cousin whom he had married in order to preserve the integrity of the lands of Lorraine. This provoked a complicated dispute over the succession, involving Louis XIII's refusal to invest Charles in Bar, and Charles' refusal to do homage to Louis XIII.

Finding himself challenged in respect of both Bar and portions of

[12] *Six livres de la République* (1576), p. 1.
[13] *Op. cit.*, p. 8.
[14] *Op. cit.*, pp. I, 71.

Lorraine, Charles in 1628 ordered the Bishop of Verdun to excommunicate the workmen engaged on the construction of the fortress there, on the ground that they had demolished church buildings. This was to return the French challenge as forcibly as Charles could; for to assert Lorraine competence in Verdun implied a subversion of French authority there in favour of imperial authority, and thus to threaten the settlement of Câteau Cambrésis. To reinforce the threat Charles asked the Emperor to garrison Vic and Moyenvic, and this he did as a strategic counterpoise to the French intervention in the War of the Mantuan Succession in 1629.[15]

The great legal debate over the status of the Three Bishoprics, conducted by Richelieu in diplomatic correspondence and through commissions of lawyers, and by jurists who applied themselves to private but patriotic propaganda, is of particular interest in the history of territorial disputes. It crystallized for the first time the implications of territorial sovereignty; it linked the concept of sovereignty with that of the Fundamental Law; and it set in train historical and quasi-legal investigations which were to result in ever-expanding French territorial claims. It constitutes the point of transition from a medieval concept of territory to a more modern one, and it formed the background of concepts utilised by the French negotiators at the conference in Westphalia.

The territorial dispute known as the Mantuan Succession Question, is also of importance in the evolution of the legal concept of territory. In 1627 the Duke of Mantua died without immediate heirs. Among the claimants were the Duke of Guastalla, supported by Spain ,the niece of Charles Emmanuel the Duke of Savoy, and the Duke of Nevers, who was a Frenchman. The Spanish governor of Milan conspired with Charles Emmanuel to take advantage of the disputed inheritance to partition the Marquisate of Montferrat, a dependency of Mantua, between them. Both the Emperor and France reacted to this act of aggression. The first summoned the Aulic Council which decreed the sequestration of the Duchy and appointed John of Nassau as imperial commissioner pending the investing of an heir. To Richelieu this signified a revival of imperial authority in the Habsburg borderlands. There was no knowing how far these claims, once acquiesced in, would extend: Provence had been imperial territory. And the intensification

[15] Haussonville, *op. cit., passim.*

of imperial authority was seen by Richelieu as no more than Habsburg aggrandizement. He wrote:

L'Empereur, sous divers prétextes d'apparence spécieuse, mais de nulle solidité, prenoit le train de se rendre maître de l'Allemagne et la réduire en une monarchie absolue, anéantissant les lois anciennes de la république germanique, sur lesquelles est fondée l'autorité impériale.[16]

In essence the Thirty Years War was concerned with the question of Germany's unification under tighter imperial authority. France's fear of Habsburg power led her to support the princes of the Empire against the Emperor, and to sponsor their sovereignty. Whereas imperial policy was centripetal, French policy was centrifugal. It was French policy that triumphed at Westphalia, and the conversion there of imperial feudatories into sovereign States postponed German unification for two centuries. In this respect the French Mantuan policy is significant in the evolution of the sovereign State.

Following the imperial sequestration of Mantua Richelieu intervened in northern Italy, and in the course of action directed against Charles Emmanuel of Savoy, seized the town of Pinerolo. It so happened that this town was part of the Marquisate of Saluzzo, which Charles Emmanuel had refused to restore to France when negotiating the Treaty of Vervins at the end of the French Wars of Religion. The question of French rights in Pinerolo was to become one of the most intractable of the diplomatic issues of the Thirty Years War.

The War of the Mantuan Succession nominally ended in 1631 when it was agreed at Cherasco that the Duke of Nevers would be invested in the Duchy of Mantua upon hypothecating his revenues to compensate the other claimants, and France would vacate Pinerolo. The imperial occupation of Vic and Moyenvic in the meantime persuaded Richelieu that he must retain Pinerolo as a strategic counterweight, and he contrived this by a piece of diplomatic sleight of hand. Three months before the Treaty of Cherasco[17] was signed, Charles Emmanuel's successor as Duke of Savoy, Victor Emmanuel, had signed a secret treaty by which he undertook to retrocede Pinerolo to France. When the imperial and Spanish commissioners entrusted with the execution of the Treaty of Cheraso inspected the fortress at Pinerolo upon its evacuation by the French army they failed to detect the

[16] *Mémoires*, vol. 10, p. 159.

[17] Dumont, *Corps universel diplomatique du droit des gens (1726-31)*, vol. 6, p. 14.

presence of two hundred French troops hidden in the cellars, who, immediately after the commissioners departed, proceeded to take possession once again.

There followed a diplomatic furore in which the Pope was enjoined by the Emperor to impose canonical sanctions upon Louis XIII for breach of faith. Richelieu blunted the point of this onslaught by publishing a new treaty with Victor Emmanuel by which France was to be given Pinerolo as a gage for six months only. But a secret article confirmed the earlier treaty, so that France considered itself to have sovereignty over Pinerolo in perpetuity.[18] When this secret was penetrated by the Spaniards pressure was again applied to the Pope, who undertook to instruct Bichi the nuncio in Paris to raise the question of Pinerolo, along with other issues, with a view to a peace settlement. Louis XIII's reply to Bichi's overtures was dictated by Richelieu, who, as usual, took refuge in legal arguments. Pinerolo was under French sovereignty; Savoy had freely sold it; it had always been part of the domains of the Crown, which, pursuant to the Fundamental Law, were inalienable. Bichi was persuaded that there was more in the French legal position than appeared at first sight, and he reported that the inalienability of Pinerolo was a "ticklish question." [19]

Did the participants in the diplomatic and academic debates concerning the disputed territories consult *De jure belli ac pacis*? If they did, they received little guidance on the modes of acquiring territory. Grotius asserts that in virtue of the *jus gentium* one is to be understood as having captured a thing who retains it in such a way that the original possessor has lost probable expectation of regaining it, or so that the thing has escaped pursuit.[20] Applying this principle to the acquisition of territory by conquest, he says that occupation of territory is not equivalent to capture, for mere possession is not secure possession.[21] But the whole discourse must be placed within the limiting context of his proposition that, according to the law of nature, we acquire by a lawful war things which are either equal to that which was owed and could not otherwise lawfully be obtained, or inflict upon the guilty a loss that does not exceed an equitable measure of punish-

[18] *Ibid.*, p. 40.

[19] Leman, *Urbain VIII et la rivalité de la France et de la maison d'Autriche de 1631 à 1635* (1920), p. 57.

[20] III, 6. 3.

[21] III, 6. 4.

ment.[22] Grotius' statements could have been assimilated in the arguments of either party to the territorial disputes of the time without casting any light whatever on the historical enquiry on which those disputes turned.

As for prescription, Grotius begins by citing Vázquez [23] for the proposition that it is an institution of municipal law, and has no place between independent States. He then goes on:

> But if we admit this, a very serious inconvenience clearly follows, in that contests about kingdoms and the boundaries of kingdoms never come to an end with lapse of time. Such a condition, again, not only tends to disturb the minds of many and to occasion wars, but is contrary to the common sense of nations.[24]

Jean de Silhon repeats this argument almost verbatim, but excludes a derogation from the original French title to Metz on the ground that the French claim had never been abandoned. In this he had the support of Grotius who concluded that

> a king can acquire a right as against a king, and an independent state, not only by express agreement, but also by abandonment of ownership and the occupation which follows it or assumes a new force from it.[25]

Grotius' treatment of territorial change is cautious compared with that of Gentili, who states categorically that

> territories, places and buildings ... all remain in the power of the man who holds them at the time when peace is made, unless it has been otherwise provided by a treaty [26]

and, concerning prescription, argues:

> Is that which might once have been a just cause for war also just after the lapse of many years? If actions are prevented on this ground by the law, why should not the same thing be true of causes for war and these actions under arms? *Usucapio* and *praescriptio* were introduced for the public good, in order that suits might have some limit. Why should not wars also be limited? [27]

Gentili adverts to the French thesis of the Fundamental Law, citing François Hotman, who died in 1590: [28]

[22] III, 6. 1.
[23] *Illustrium controversarium aliarumque usu frequentium Libri* VI, II, li. 28.
[24] II, 4. 1.
[25] II, 4. 11.
[26] *De jure belli libri tres*, III, 17. 623.
[27] *Ibid.*, I, 22. 171.
[28] *De jure successionis Regiae in Regno Francorum.*

But there is still another difficulty; namely, since kingdoms and principalities are said to fall to successors, not like private estates by the intention of the former owners, but only by law and custom, the prescriptive right does not seem to have a place in connexion with them. For when one acts in one's own right, as every prince who succeeds to a throne may do, the prescriptive right does not stand in his way nor the negligence of his predecessors.

He then rejects the French argument:

To this difficulty, and with respect to the princes who say that they hold their kingdoms only by virtue of that law and custom, I cannot make a much more definite reply than this, which I stated in general terms at the beginning; namely, that it is absurd that a just pretext for arms and warlike contention should not cease to exist even after centuries.[29]

The debate revolves around the just war, and the issue as it presented itself to the seventeenth century mind was whether war to recover territory long held in violation of the principle that the sovereign could not alienate territory was just or not. Only property acquired in just war passed to the conqueror in virtue of *jus gentium*. Writers of the pre-Grotian period such as Ayala,[30] Belli,[31] and Suarez [32] on this ground excluded prescriptive title to territory taken unjustly, and traced the doctrine to Cicero,[33] through the Digest,[34] the Code,[35] and St. Thomas Aquinas.[36] Grotius in *De jure praedae*,[37] does not depart from this tradition, and adds nothing of significance, despite his implied claim to do so. Vittoria [38] argues against acquisition of territory by conquest, on the ground that it is disproportionate to the relief of a wrong, which alone justifies war; and Alciati, who died in 1550, contended that war between Christians gave no right of conquest, because then a war would not be just.[39] Sometimes the concept of *postliminium* is used, for example in Grotius [40] and Ayala,[41] in a way which could support the French thesis of Fundamental Law.

[29] I, 22, 178.
[30] *De jure et officiis bellici et disciplina militari. Libri*, I, 5. 1.
[31] *De re militari et bello tractatus*, II, 2. 5.
[32] *De caritate*. Disp. XIII, 7.
[33] *De officiis* I.
[34] XLIX, XV. 24, 28.
[35] VIII, liii, 36.
[36] *De regimine principum*, III.
[37] VIII, Corollary 2.
[38] *De bello*, I. 16.
[39] *Comment. in Digesta seu Pandectas juris civilis*, L, 16. 118.
[40] *De jure praedae*, VIII, Corollary 2.
[41] *Op. cit.*, 33.

In none of the territorial disputes of the period was the *jus gentium* mentioned, or the possibility of legal relations between the disputant princes adverted to. The problem was conceived as one of proprietary rights, and the extent of the Crown's domain was a matter of historical fact transformed into legal rights in virtue of the Fundamental Law. The latter, in its turn, was given a metaphysical basis by linking it with the sovereignty of the Crown, making it the index of the Crown's plenary competence to govern, and by assimilating it to the law of nature, thereby making it a criterion of the just war. It was this assimilation that gained universal currency for the Fundamental Law, and thereby made it relevant in the solution of a legal dispute between princes. All this is far removed from the concept of an international law of territorial sovereignty, but it is equally far removed from the medieval notion that territorial rights were derived from a universal feudal law.[42] The utilisation of a basic proposition of the French constitution as the norm of reference was an inevitable outcome of the abstraction of sovereignty and the fracture of the feudal construction, and a necessary preliminary to the formulation of a rule of international law.

It is clear that the Peace Treaties of Westphalia in 1648 represented the triumph of political and strategic considerations over the moralistic and legalistic justifications of territorial claims of the Richelieu period, and that they validated the novel concept of cession of territory in full sovereignty outside the framework of feudal law and within that of the *jus gentium*. It was political reality that stimulated the change in thought which underlay the Westphalian settlement, but what is interesting to the historian of ideas is that the change was not adumbrated by the theorists and pamphleteers, but effected by the statesmen and diplomats: Thought lagged a generation behind practice. Had Richelieu survived to conduct the four years of negotiations at Münster and Osnabrück it may be that he would not have been able to disengage himself sufficiently from the legalistic universe of his youth to make claims to territory on the basis of conquest and bargain alone. This was the achievement of Mazarin, whose own predatory instinct was reflected in a frankly acquisitive French policy.

On 20 January 1646, Mazarin instructed the French plenipotentiaries at Münster to seek to exchange Catalonia (then in French mili-

[42] Albertini, *Das politische Denken in Frankreich zur Zeit Richelieus* (1951), pp. 146 *et seq.*

tary occupation) against the Spanish Netherlands and Franche Comté.[42a] The justifications he offered for this policy were exclusively political and strategic:

Premièrement, l'acquisition des Pays-Bas forme à la ville de Paris un boulevard inexpugnable, et ce seroit alors veritablement que l'on pourroit appeler le coeur de la France et qu'il seroit place dans l'endroit le plus seur du Royaume, puisque l'on auroit estendu les frontières jusques à la Hollande, et du costé de l'Allemagne, qui est celuy d'où on peut aussy beaucoup craindre, jusqu'au Rhin par la retention de la Lorraine et de l'Alsace, et par la possession de Luxembourg et de la comté de Bourgogne (Franche Comté); en second lieu, ce seroit sortir avec tant de fruit et de reputation de la presente guerre que les plus malins seroient bien en peine d'y trouver à redire; tant de sang repandu et de tresors consummez ne pourroient estre tenus par les plus critiques que fort bien employez quand on verroit annexez à cette couronne tout l'ancien royaume d'Austrasie et des provinces entières, dont la seule possession a donné autrefois moyen à des princes particuliers de resister à la France, mais de la travailler au point que chacun.[43]

He added that such annexations would prevent the Emperor from assisting Spain; that the people of Belgium would welcome the change because it would relieve them of the evils of war; and that the French exchequer would be spared the cost of maintaining frontier fortresses.

Respecting the province of Alsace, the Duchy of Lorraine and the Three Bishopries, he casually waved aside the arguments that a decade earlier had been directed to establishing a residual French sovereignty thereover.

Il n'y auroit pas d'inconvénient à reconnaître l'Alsace et les Trois-Evêchés comme terres d'Empires appartenant au roi de France; le Roi auroit alors ses représentants dans les diettes de l'Allemagne.[44]

In other words, he was content at that stage for the King of France to remain a vassal of the Emperor respecting these territories, which would "belong" to him as property but not in sovereignty, because thereby he could claim a seat in the imperial diet. This was quite a machiavellian exploitation of the legal ambiguity which Richelieu had striven to resolve.

As the negotiations at Münster developed, so did Mazarin's designs expand. The plenipotentiaries were instructed to claim Breisach on the

[42a] *Archives du Ministère des Affaires Etrangères: Correspondance politique, Allemagne*, vol. 5, fol. 82.

[43] *Ibid.*, fol. 191.

[44] Letter of 3 Feb. 1646, *ibid.*, fol. 321.

German side of the Rhine.[45] He "hoped" that France would obtain other German territories, such as Philippsburg (belonging to the Electorate of Trier, which was under French protection and on behalf of the integrity of which France had declared war on Spain in 1635), Benfeld, Saverne, and "perhaps even two Black Forest towns."[46] On 30 June 1646 he wrote that if France possessed Belgium, Breisach and Alsace she would in future have to fight only in Italy: but the plenipotentiaries should try to secure Philippsburg as well. In any event, it was necessary to retain Pinerolo.[47]

On 25 September 1646 Mazarin reported to the Duke of Orleans, the King's uncle, that the Emperor had decided to cede to the King of France "plein souveraineté" over the Three Bishopries and their dependencies, and would abandon all his right to Pinerolo, Breisach, the two Alsaces and Sundgau, which "demeureront à la perpetuité à la France, tout cela moyennant l'argent qu'on donne aux archiducs et à l'Empereur" [48] (The Archdukes were suzerains of Alsace, and in return for their waiver of their rights they would be compensated in cash). It a later letter to Turenne he referred to the "alienation de l'Alsace, qui s'est faite en nostre faveur." [49]

The securalisation of political issues which was completed with dramatic suddenness between the issuing of the Edict of Restitution in 1629 and the French entry into the Thirty years war in 1635 represented the decisive point of transition from the medieval to the modern worlds. Inasmuch this change irrevocably fractured the feudal concept of territory and brought the concept of territorial reconstruction within the ambit of the *jus gentium* it is as fundamental to the evolution of international law as it was to the politics of diplomacy. Needless to say, the extent and nature of the change was not immediately obvious to everyone, and echoes of a feudal conception persist until the French Revolution: Pufendorf merely restates Grotius,[50] and utilises the concept of postliminium in a manner reminiscent of the Fundamental Law argument; [51] Textor [52] says the same, and Wolff [53] hardly advances the

[45] Letter of 14 April 1646, *ibid.*, fol. 1033.

[46] Letter of 2 June 1646, *ibid.*, vol. 6, fol. 407.

[47] *Ibid.*, fol. 657.

[48] *Archives du Ministère des Affaires Etrangères: Etat numérique des fonds mém. et doc. France*, vol. 22, fol. 169.

[49] Chéruel, *Lettres du Cardinal Mazarin* (1887), vol. 3, p. 233.

[50] *De jure naturae et gentium*, VIII, 6. 24.

[51] *Ibid.*, VIII, 6. 26.

[52] *Synopsis juris gentium*, CIII, 96.

[53] *Jus gentium methodo scientifico pertractatum*, SS. 282. 283, 284.

discussion; and it is not until Vattel that the literature accepts the concept of territorial cession.[54] Even his work is, however, internally contradicting in its echo of Grotius' doctrine,[55] and in its citation of the advice given to Henry IV concerning the Fundamental Law, in support of the concept of inalienability of the public domain.[56] His reconciliation of the concepts of inalienability and cession [57] is so tortuous that it is clear that he, and international law, had come to the parting of the ways, but this was a whole century after political reality had rendered the Fundamental Law obsolescent. It is, perhaps, not until the publication of Meermann's work in 1774 [58] that the concept of territorial cession as a result of war was finally accepted, and not until Martens' work on the eve of the French Revolution that it gained universal currency.[59]

[54] *Le droit des gens*, I, 21, 257. III, 12. 197.
[55] *Ibid.*, I, 7. 91, 92, 93.
[56] *Ibid.*, I, 21, 260.
[57] *Ibid.*, I, 21, 263.
[58] *Von dem Recht der Eroberung nach dem Staats- und Völkerrecht.*
[59] *Précis du droit des gens*, VIII, 4. 282a.

Elizabeth Evatt

British Institute of International and Comparative Law

The Acquisition of Territory in Australia and New Zealand

Introduction

It is the purpose of this paper to examine and compare the circumstances of the British acquisition of sovereignty over Australia and New Zealand in the late 18th and early 19th centuries, and to see how far British practice accorded with or was influenced by contemporary practice and contemporary theories of international law relating to acquisition of territorial sovereignty.

The Acquisition of Territory: General Principles

In this study we are concerned with only two of the possible means by which a State may acquire territorial sovereignty, namely cession and occupation.[1] Cession involves the transfer of territory by treaty from one sovereign to another sovereign. Its counterpart in municipal law is transfer of property in land.

Occupation also has a private law analogy. Roman law recognised, as a principle of private law, that property not owned by any person (*res nullius*) could be brought into ownership by occupation (*occupatio*) which involved both the intention to assert ownership (*animus*) and some overt act of physical control (*factum*).[2] By analogy this rule of private law was extended to cover the acquisition by a State of sovereign rights over uninhabited territory.[3]

[1] On acquisition generally, see Jennings, *The Acquisition of Territory in International Law* (1963), O'Connell, *International Law*, Vol. 1 (1965), pp. 465 *et seq*.

[2] Justinian, *Institutes*, II. 1. 12; *Digest*, 41. I. 3.

[3] *E.g.*, Grotius, *De Iure Belli ac Pacis*, 1646 (Carnegie, London, 1925) II, III. 4. 1 & 2; Vattel, *The Law of Nations*, 1758 (Carnegie, Washington, 1916) I. XVIII, s. 204, 205, p. 84; see, generally, H. Lauterpacht, *Private Law Sources and Analogies of International Law*, (1927) ss. 41-44, p. 99 *et seq*.

The problem for early jurists was whether this principle could be extended to cover territory inhabited by relatively uncivilised native tribes.

Both Australia and New Zealand were inhabited by such tribes at the time of the British settlement, though the difference between aborigines and the Maoris is marked. Over the centuries, since the first European voyages of discovery, there have been differences of opinion as to the status of such territories, differences which have been considered at length by Lindley in his book *The Acquisition and Government of Backward Territory in International Law*.[4] On the one hand such territory could be regarded as *territorium nullius, i.e.*, territory not subject to any sovereign and capable of being acquired by occupation. On the other hand, if the native population were to be regarded as having sovereign rights in its territory, then such territory could only be acquired by cession, conquest or prescription. Lindley has outlined the opinions of international law publicists on this question,[5] showing how the earlier views of such writers as Vittoria, Grotius,[6] Pufendorf and others against regarding backward territory as *res nullius* came to be replaced, particularly in the 19th century by the view that "denies that International Law recognizes any rights in primitive peoples to the territory they inhabit, and, in its most advanced form demands that such peoples shall have progressed so far in civilization as to have become recognized as members of the Family of Nations before they can be allowed such rights." [7]

It is interesting at this point to refer to Vattel who was writing in the middle of the 18th century, about twenty years before the beginning of settlement in Australia. In his opinion:

> "Every nation is therefore bound by the natural law to cultivate the land which has fallen to its share, and it has no right to extend its boundaries or to obtain help from other nations except in so far as the land it inhabits can not supply its needs." [8]

It is the corollary of this in Vattel's view, that if native tribes do not

[4] (London, 1926). The term "backward territory" is described in the Preface.

[5] *Ibid.*, pp. 10-23. Fauchille, *Traité de Droit International*, Tome 1, 2 (1925) s. 547, p. 697 has also divided opinions of jurists between those recognising sovereignty and those acknowledging mere ownership.

[6] *Mare Liberum*, 1633 (Carnegie, New York, 1916) Ch. II, pp. 13-14; see also *op. cit.* note 3, II, XXII, 9 & 10.

[7] *Op. cit. supra*, at p. 20; see also O'Connell, *op. cit. supra*, p. 470.

[8] Vattel, *op. cit.*, I. VII. s. 81, pp. 37-38.

cultivate their territory, then, when "the Nations of Europe, which are too confined at home, come upon lands which the savages have no special need of and are making no present and continuous use of, they may lawfully take possession of them and establish colonies in them." [9]

This view recognising native rights only in so far as actual use is made of the land is entirely consistent with Vattel's theory concerning effective occupation which will be referred to below.[10]

Lindley has also examined in some detail State practice from earliest times,[11] showing how it accorded more with the views of the earlier writers and concluding that:

> "On the whole, the European States, in establishing their dominion over countries inhabited by people in a more or less backward stage of political development, have adopted as the method of such extension, Cession or Conquest, and have not based their rights upon the Occupation of *territorium nullius*." [12]

An instance of this apparent contradiction between theory and practice, which will be referred to in more detail later, is the Treaty of Waitangi under which the Maori chiefs of New Zealand purported to cede their sovereignty to Great Britain. It has been argued that this Treaty could not be recognised as valid in international law since the Chiefs had no status or capacity to enter into such a transaction.[13] This argument results in the labelling of both New Zealand and Australia as "*terrae nullius*," and their acquisition as "occupation," despite the very different circumstances of the two countries and the different approach in practice by Great Britain.

Australia is in fact one of the rare examples of a large tract of inhabited territory acquired peaceably by occupation without any consent being sought from the native population.[14] There is a practical explanation for this, for although a State might prefer to obtain some

[9] *Op. cit.* I. XVIII, s. 209, p. 85; at II. VII, s. 97, p. 142-3, he suggests that States may not otherwise assume sovereignty over backward tribes.

[10] *Infra.* p. 5 MS.

[11] *Op. cit.* pp. 24-44.

[12] *Ibid.* pp. 17, 43-44; see also O'Connell, *op. cit.* p. 469; *contra* Keller, Lissitzyn and Mann, *Creation of Rights of Sovereignty through Symbolic Acts 1400-1800* (1938) pp. 150-151, concluding that any such arrangements were only a "device to secure undisturbed enjoyment of lands."

[13] See *infra*, p. 17 (MS.), and notes 118, 119.

[14] Lindley, *op. cit.* pp. 40-41; see also *Cooper* v. *Stuart* (1889) 14 A.C. 286, 291.

form of consent where there is an organised community with a recognised chief, this was impossible in the case of Australia, inhabited by scattered unorganised tribes.

These introductory comments serve to indicate that, although it may be convenient to refer to a particular acquisition as occupation or cession, these categories should not be applied too rigidly.

One further preliminary point which should be referred to is that in applying the principles of international law to the acquisition of Australia and New Zealand, it is the law, so far as it can be ascertained, contemporary with the events described, which must be considered.[15] The period covered by this survey extends from 1600 - 1850; the sources or evidences of the relevant legal principles are to be found in the writings of jurists, in State practice, and in judicial and arbitral decisions.

I THE ACQUISITION OF AUSTRALIA

A. Discovery and Symbolic Claim

(1) Historical Outline

The discovery of Australia dates back to the early 17th century when Dutch navigators visited the West and North coasts. But the earliest claims to possession of Australian territory by discoverers of which written records remain where those made by Abel Tasman in 1642 and Captain Cook in 1770.

(a) Abel Tasman. In 1642 the Governor General of the Dutch East Indies, Antonio Van Diemen sent Abel Tasman to discover a route around the South Coast of Australia (*Terra del Zur*) to Peru and Chile. He carried with him additional instructions with these directions: [16]

> All continents and islands, which you shall discover, touch at and set foot on, you will take possession of on behalf of Their Mightinesses the

[15] Award of Huber in the *Island of Palmas*, case, 1928, 2. R.I.A.A. 831, 845, "a juridical fact must be appreciated in the light of the law contemporary with it."

[16] "Instructions for Skipper Commander Abel Jans Tasman . . . for the discovery and exploration of the unknown and known Southland, of the South-east coast of Nova Guinea, and of the islands circumjacent," Aug. 13, 1642: J. E. Heeres (ed.) *Abel Janszoon Tasman's Journal of his Discovery of Van Diemen's Land and New Zealand in 1642* (Amsterdam, 1898) Appendix E, p. 131 at p. 136.

States General of the United Provinces, the which in uninhabited regions or in such countries as have no sovereign, may be done by erecting a memorial-stone or by planting our Prince-flag in sign of actual occupation, seeing that such lands justly belong to the discoverer and first occupier; but in populated regions or in such as have undoubted lords, the consent of the people or the king will be required before you can enter into possession of them, the which you should try to obtain by friendly persuasion and by presenting them with some small tree planted in a little earth, by erecting some stone structure in conjunction with the people, or by setting up the Prince-flag in commemoration of their voluntary assent or submission; . . .

Tasman first sighted the South West coast of Van Diemen's Land (now called Tasmania) on November 24, 1642. On December 3 a landing was made in what is now Prince of Wales Bay, and a Prince-flag was planted as a symbol of the taking of possession.[17]

(b) Captain Cook. In 1768, when Cook embarked on the first of his great voyages of discovery in the Pacific, his first purpose was to make astronomical observations of Venus from the island of Tahiti. But there was at that time great interest and curiosity about the Southern Continent which was supposed to exist in the South Pacific between New Holland (as Australia was then called) and South America.[18] In the secret additional instructions from the Admiralty dated July 30, 1768, Cook was instructed, after completion of his task at Tahiti:

to proceed to the Southward in order to make discovery of the Continent above mentioned . . . [then] . . . to the Westward between the Latitude before mentioned and the Latitude of 35° until you discover it, or fall in with the Eastern side of the land discover'd by Tasman and now called New Zealand . . . [If you discover the Continent mentioned] . . . You are also with the consent of the Natives to take possession of convenient situations in the country in the name of the King of Great Britain or: if you find the country uninhabited take possession for His Majesty by setting up proper marks and inscriptions, as first discoverers and possessors . . .

You will also observe with accuracy the situation of such islands as you may discover in the course of your voyage that have not hitherto been discovered by any Europeans and take possession for His Majesty and make Surveys and Draughts of such of them as may appear to be of consequence.[19]

[17] *Ibid.* pp. 15 *et seq.* (translation of the Journal).

[18] See A. Dalrymple, *An Account of the Discoveries made in the South Pacifick Ocean, previous to 1764* (London, 1767) p. 88 *et seq.*

[19] Additional instructions to Captain Cook for his first voyage, July, 1768: Beaglehole, ed. *The Journals of Captain James Cook on His Voyages of Discovery*, Vol. I *The Voyage of the Endeavour, 1768-1771* (1955) p. cclxxxii.

Following these instructions Cook reached the North Island of New Zealand on October 7, 1769. After circumnavigating and charting both islands he proceeded westwards, reaching the East coast of New Holland on April 19, 1770 at Latitute 37°58′S. Long. 210°39′W., a place named by him Point Hicks.[20] Due to the sharp falling away of the land to the South and West, Cook expressed some doubt as to whether Tasman's Van Diemen's Land was part of the coast which he had discovered.[21] He continued North and made the first landing on the East Coast at Botany Bay on April 29, 1770. The Endeavour stayed there a few days, during which the English colours were displayed and an inscription cut in a tree.[22] Cook then continued up the East coast inside the Barrier Reef until he came to Cape York, the northernmost point. At Possession Island, two miles from the mainland (Lat.10½°S.) on August 22, 1770 he formally took possession of all the coastline discovered by him:

> Having satisfied my self of the great probability of a passage, thro' which I intended going with the Ship, and therefore may land no more upon the Eastern coast of *New Holland*, and on the Western side I can make no new discovery the honour of which belongs to the Dutch Navigators, but the Eastern coast from the Latitude of 38° South down to this place, I am confident, was never seen or viseted by any European before us; and Notwithstand[ing] I had in the name of His Majesty taken possession of several places upon this Coast, I now once more hoisted English Coulers, and in the Name of His Majesty King George the Third took possession of the whole Eastern Coast from the above Latitude down to this place by the name of *New South Wales*, together with all the Bays, Harbours, Rivers and Islands, situate upon the said Coast; after which we fired three Volleys of small Arms, which were answered by the like number from the Ship.[23]

On a later voyage, sailing under similar instructions, Captain Cook discovered Norfolk Island and on October 11, 1773 he formally took

[20] *Ibid.* pp. 298-299.

[21] *Ibid.* p. 299. Despite the later visit by Cook to Van Diemen's Land in January 1777 this doubt was not settled until 1789-99.

[22] *Ibid.* pp. 304-305.

[23] *Ibid.* pp. 387-388. It is interesting to note that in the original manuscript, after the words "Dutch Navigators" appeared "and as such they may lay claim to it as their property"; the latter words were deleted, as well as a later comment that the lands discovered by Cook belonged to Great Britain. This respect for prior discoveries explains why Cook, on his visit to Tasmania in January 1777 failed to perform any symbolic annexation, this coast having been visited already by Tasman and Dufresne.

possession of it for Great Britain.[24] He also visited Tasmania, but no record was made of any claim.[25]

(2) Legal Status of Symbolic Acts: Inchoate Title

While bare discovery, in the sense of first sighting, has not for a long time been relied on by States as a basis of title to territory,[26] great importance has always been attached in practice to claims based on symbolic or ceremonial acts of possession by discoveries. Such acts often include flag raising or the reading of proclamations.[27] In nearly every dispute concerning territory each of the conflicting States has sought, where possible, to establish the earliest connection with the contested area by proof of symbolic acts of possession. Although in former times such acts were "generally regarded as being wholly sufficient *per se* to establish immediately a right to sovereignty," [28] such enormous territorial claims were put forward on the basis of discovery [29] that States who wished to enter into overseas expansion themselves sought to restrict the rights obtained through discovery, as they had done in the case of Papal Grants. This led to a change of emphasis from the acknowledgment of claims based on discovery and symbolic acts of possession to the requirement for actual occupation or possession.[30] Two examples will indicate how the views of jurists had developed by the 18th century. First Grotius who, in *Mare Liberum*, wrote:

> No one is sovereign of a thing which he himself has never possessed and which no one else has ever held in his name ... to discover a thing is not only to seize it with the eyes but to take real possession thereof ... The act of discovery is sufficient to give a clear title of sovereignty only when it is accompanied by actual possession.[31]

[24] *Ibid.* Vol. II *The Voyage of the Resolution and Adventure*, 1772-1775, p. 567.

[25] Note 23, *supra.*

[26] Keller, Lissitzyn and Mann, *op. cit. supra*, p. 148; Von der Heydte, "Discovery, Symbolic Annexation and Virtual Effectiveness in International Law" (1935) 29 *A.J.I.L.* 452-3; *Island of Palmas Case* 2 R.I.A.A. 846, see also Grotius, *Mare Liberum* (N.Y. 1916) p. 11 (II).

[27] See, generally, Keller, Lissitzyn & Mann, *op. cit. supra*; Von der Heydte, *loc. cit. supra.*

[28] Keller, Lissitzyn and Mann, *op. cit. supra*, pp. 148-149.

[29] See, *e.g.*, the claims of the British in North America described in Lindley, *op. cit.*, p. 130.

[30] See Von der Heydte, *op. cit. supra*, p. 457, *et seq.*

[31] *Mare Liberum, cit. supra*, note 6, pp. 11-12.

The second quotation is from Vattel who wrote in 1758, near to the time of Captain's Cook's voyages:

§ 207 All men have an equal right to things which have not yet come into the possession of anyone, and these things belong to the person who first takes possession. When, therefore, a Nation finds a country uninhabited and without an owner, it may lawfully take possession of it, and after it has given sufficient signs of its intention in this respect, it may not be deprived of it by another Nation. In this way navigators setting out upon voyages of discovery and bearing with them a commission from their sovereign, when coming across islands or other uninhabited lands, have taken possession of them in the name of their Nation; and this title has usually been respected, *provided actual possession has followed shortly after.*

§ 208 But it is questioned whether a Nation can thus appropriate, by the mere act of taking possession, lands which it does not really occupy, and which are more extensive than it can inhabit or cultivate. It is not difficult to decide that such a claim would be absolutely contrary to the natural law, and would conflict with the designs of nature, which destines the earth for the needs of all mankind, and only confers upon individual Nations the right to appropriate territory so far as they can make use of it, and not merely to hold it against others who may wish to profit by it. Hence the Law of Nations will only recognize the ownership and sovereignty of a Nation over unoccupied lands when the Nation is in actual occupation of them, when it forms a settlement upon them, or makes some actual use of them. In fact, when explorers have discovered uninhabited lands through which the explorers of other Nations had passed, leaving some sign of their having taken possession, they have no more troubled themselves over such empty forms than over the regulations of Popes, who divided a large part of the world between the crowns of Castile and Portugal.[32]

As far as State practice was concerned the earlier wide claims based on discovery were gradually abandoned.[33] In *Great Britain and the Law of Nations*, Smith wrote of British practice during a period stretching back to the late 18th century:

"During the period covered by the present work it may safely be said that the government of Great Britain has neither advanced any territorial claims of its own nor admitted any opposing claims on the mere fact of discovery unsupported by any acts of effective occupation and possession." [34]

Nevertheless, discovery was not altogether superseded, for in the extract from Vattel's *Law of Nations* quoted above there is support for a

[32] *Law of Nations, cit. supra*, I. XVIII, ss. 207-208, pp. 84-85 (italics added).

[33] Lindley, *op. cit.*, p. 133.

[34] Vol. II (1935) p. 1.

view which later was widely advocated, namely that symbolic annexation, or ceremonial occupation creates in the discovering State an inchoate title which must be completed by actual occupation within a reasonable time.[35] The symbolic act is regarded as evidence of both the *factum* and the *animus occupandi*. There are difficulties in applying the theory of inchoate title. The discovering State may have the best right to proceed to actual occupation, but if some acts of physical possession are required to complete the inchoate title, and if as has been recognised [36] the inchoate title so obtained can be negatived by even small evidence of effective occupation by another state, amounting itself to no more than inchoate title, then theory adds little to the doctrine of effective occupation unless the rules concerning, *e.g.*, the extent of territory in the case of overlapping claims, are to be construed more favourably to the discovering State. A further difficulty is that, if the discovering State must settle within a reasonable time, then in the case of discovery not followed up by possession there may be difficulties in deciding whether the inchoate title has lapsed. Attempts to suggest the fixing of a time limit have never received support.[37]

The inchoate title seems rather to fit into the pattern as part of the gradual change in practice and opinion over the centuries. While discarding discovery as a basis of title in favour of the more realistic doctrine of effective occupation, States nevertheless are still willing to ascribe some weight to the old practice provided it did not interfere or conflict with recognition of an established position of effective control. Even well into the 20th century States, including Australia were still willing to resort to symbolic acts, including flag raising and proclamations as a foundation or basis of title.[38] Such acts are still recognised

[53] *Supra*, note 32; see also Lindley, *op. cit.*, pp. 136-138; O'Connell, *op. cit.*, pp. 478-479; Von der Heydte, *loc. cit.*, at 461-462. *Island of Palmas* case, 2 R.I.A.A., at 846.

[36] *Island of Palmas* case, 2 R.I.A.A. at 846, 870.

[37] Fiore, *International Law Codified*, (transl. Borchard) (1918) s. 1068; In the *Island of Palmas* case, 2. R.I.A.A. at 846, Huber was apparently prepared to consider whether inchoate title from discovery in the early 16th century could still exist in 1898; see also Von der Heydte, *loc. cit.* at 462.

[38] See *e.g.*, Australia's activities in the Antarctic, A. C. Castles, "The International Status of the Australian Antarctic Territory", in *International Law in Australia*, ed. O'Connell (1965) p. 341, at. 347-349. See also Grenfell-Price, *The Winning of Australian Antarctic*, (1916) p. 23 describing the ceremony held by Mawson on January 13, 1930, at which a flag was raised and a Proclamation read on Proclamation Island, off Enderby Land.

both as evidence of the intention to acquire and as the beginning of the exercise of authority. The weight attached to an inchoate title may in the last resort depend on the acquiescence of lack of activity by other States.[39]

Against this background it seems that any inchoate title which Holland may have had either to Van Diemen's Land or to mainland Australia as a result of Tasman's discoveries had lapsed long before Cook's voyages. There was never any attempt to follow up the discoveries or to put forward any claim to territorial sovereignty.[40] Cook's act of taking possession of the East coast has, on the other hand, been considered as the legal basis of the British title to that area.[41] Before considering its validity as such, it should be recalled that Cook was careful to limit his claim to that territory of which he was the first discoverer.

The performance of symbolic acts of possession by Captain Cook could not form a valid basis for acquisition of sovereignty unless they were authorised by the British Government. The rule was recognised by Vattel [42] and has more recently been explained as follows: "The acquisition of sovereignty is a state act, and if the act of a discoverer is to have any validity in international law it must be endorsed by the state".[43] Cook had been authorised to take possession of certain territory in the course of his voyages. However, the authorisation was limited to the mythical Southern Continent and to islands not previously discovered by any Europeans. The Eastern Coast of Australia did not fall under either of these heads and, even if it had done so, as it was an inhabited territory the authorisation only extended to taking possession of "convenient situations" with the consent of the natives. (The same instruction was given to Tasman, *i.e.*, that native consent was required before taking possession). In these circumstances, it must

[39] *E.g., The Clipperton Island* case 1935, 2 R.I.A.A. 1105.

[40] Any objection by the Dutch to the settlement of Australia was, like that of the East India Company based on commercial grounds, O'Brien, *The Foundation of Australia 1786-1800* (1950) p. 128.

[41] *Halsbury's Laws of England*, Vol. 5 (3rd. ed. 1953) p. 502 states that Captain Cook annexed Australia under authority given by the Crown; In *Williams* v. *Attorney General* (1913) 16 C.L.R. 404, Isaacs, J. at 439 said that in 1786 "the whole of the lands of Australia were already in law the property of the King."

[42] S. 207, quoted *supra*, pp. 5-6 MS; see also *op. cit.* II s. 74, Lindley, *op. cit.* pp. 284-291.

[43] Waldock, "Disputed Sovereignty in the Falkland Island Dependencies" (1948) 25 *B.Y.I.L.* 311, 323; *contra* Keller, Lissitzyn & Mann, *op cit.* p. 151.

be concluded that there was no express prior authorisation. Even so, the purported annexation could have been adopted by some act of ratification; but no official recognition of New South Wales as British territory was forthcoming until 1786. To date British sovereignty over New South Wales from 1770 would therefore seem an exaggeration; nevertheless, so flexible are the rules concerning proof of effective occupation that there is little doubt that Cook's activities would be accepted as the earliest "evidences" of British activity in Australia, at least in regard to the East coast.

B. Occupation

(1) Early Settlement, 1788 - 1802

(a) Historical Outline. As a step towards the solution of the convict problem caused by the loss of the North American colonies an Act of 1784 gave the King-in-Council power to declare the places in or out of his dominions to which such offenders would be conveyed.[44] Despite unofficial recommendations and suggestions putting forward New South Wales as either a colony or a convict settlement [45] it was not until an expedition to Southern Africa had returned an unfavourable report, that it was officially decided in 1786 to fix upon Botany Bay as the place to which offenders might be conveyed under the 1784 Act.[46]

The Commissions appointing Captain Phillip as Governor, dated October 12, 1786,[47] and April 2, 1787 [48] defined his jurisdiction as

> "our territory called New South Wales extending from the Northern Cape or extremity of the coast called Cape York, in the latitude of 10°37′ South to the southern extremity of the said territory of New South Wales or South Cape, in the latitude of 43°39′ South, and of all the country inland westward as far as the one hundred and thirty-fifth degree of East Longitude, reckoning from the meridian of Greenwich, including all the islands adjacent in the Pacific Ocean, within the latitude aforesaid of 10°37′ North and 40°39′ South."

[44] 24 Geo. III c. 56, 1784.

[45] See *e.g.*, Matra's scheme, and Sir George Young's scheme, *Historical Records of NS.W.* (*H.R.N.S.W.*), I, 2, pp. 1 & 13 and C.O. 201/1.

[46] Lord Sydney to the Lords Commissioners of the Treasury, Aug. 18, 1786, *H.R.N.S.W.* I, 2, pp. 14-19; Orders-in-Council, Dec. 6, 1786, *H.R.N.S.W.* I, 2, p. 30

[47] *Historical Records of Australia* (*H.R.A.*) I, 1, p. 1.

[48] *H.R.A.* I, 1, p. 2. An Act of 1787, 27 Geo. III, c. 2 relating to criminal jurisdiction used the same description.

This comprises the eastern half of the continent, and is an area vast in dimensions when compared with Captain Cook's modest claim. It included Van Diemen's Land (Tasmania) which was not then known to be an island, as well as parts of the coastline both North and South not yet seen by any Englishman, or indeed by any European. There was doubt as to the full extent of jurisdiction under the phrase "all the islands adjacent in the Pacific Ocean" which will be referred to below. Presumably Van Diemen's Land (Tasmania) was regarded as being included within the description when it was later discovered to be an island.[49]

The first fleet, a party of 1030, landed at Fort Jackson on January 26, 1788, and on February 7 a ceremony was held at which the British flag was raised and Governor Phillip took formal possession of his jurisdiction.[50]

Shortly after his arrival Captain Phillip sent a party to occupy Norfolk Island in accordance with his Instructions which directed him to secure it against occupation by any other European State, the party arrived there on March 19, 1788, and effected immediate occupation.

In the case of the mainland the spread of settlement was slow, especially in the early years and was restricted to an area within 50 - 100 miles of Sydney. No other mainland settlement was made until 1824 except within that area. In the first fifteen years, however, advances were made in coastal exploration. In 1798 - 99 Bass and Flinders circumnavigated Van Diemen's Land for the first time. In 1801 on a voyage from London to Sydney Matthew Flinders established definitely that there was no gulf dividing New South Wales from the Western part of the Continent, known as New Holland. In 1802-03 he circumnavigated the whole continent charting parts of the coastline, particularly on the East and North coasts, not previously known.

(b) Legal Principles. The Orders-in-Council and the Governors Commission designating New South Wales as a convict settlement could not *per se* be effective to transfer any territorial sovereignty to Great Britain without occupation, at least in international law.[51] Despite the

[49] See E. Sweetman, *Australian Constitutional Development* (1925) pp. 320-1.

[50] His Instructions, April 25, 1786, *H.R.A.*, I, 1, 9, directed him to make a formal proclamation, and to read his Commissions, Instructions, etc.

[51] See Roberts-Wray, *Commonwealth and Colonial Law* (1966) pp. 99-100; It is the settlement, with authority, which brings the territory within the Sover-

fact that they came 16 years later they might be regarded as ratification of Captain Cook's discovery, were it not for the fact that they purported to annex an extent of territory far wider than that claimed by him. However, whether regarded as a ratification or as an original discovery these instruments were no more than evidence of *animus occupandi* until occupation took place. The effectiveness of settlement will be considered in detail after tracing its history.

(2) The Spread of Effective Occupation 1802 - 1851

(a) Historical Outline (i) At the turn of the century the French showed some interest in the exploration of Australia's coast. In 1800 an expedition led by Baudin in the *Géographe* left Le Havre for Australia. It was organised by the Institut de France, but there has been speculation as to whether there was not a political motive in the expedition.[52]

The French presence caused alarm to Governor King. As a result of a rumour which circulated in Sydney after the French expedition had stayed there, suggesting that it was their intention to settle in Storm Bay Passage in South East Tasmania, he wrote to Lord Hobart on November 23, 1802 to inform him of this and to announce his own intention to settle Tasmania.[53] At the same time the Governor sent a vessel to seek the French expedition. The Commander of this vessel had "dummy" instructions to go via King's Island to Storm Bay Passage, "the dominion of which, and all Van Diemen's Land being within the limits of His Majesty's territory of N. S. W.," to survey suitable sites for settlement in the Derwent and in Frederick Henry Bay, to hoist His Majesty's Colours every day on shore and to place a guard of two men at each place to turn up ground; there were also instructions that the King's Colours were to be kept flying to indicate the intended settlement to Commanders.[54] King later wrote to Nepean

eign's dominions; formal annexation may however constitute acquisition in remote unoccupied areas, *ibid.*, at pp. 107-108.

[52] See J. P. Faivre, *Expansion français dans le Pacifique 1800-1842* (Paris, 1953) Chapter IV, p. 153 *et seq.*; Scott, *Terre Napoleon, A History of French Explorations and Projects in Australia* (Methuen, 1910).

[53] *H.R.A.* I, 3, p. 737; the Instructions to the officer in command appear *ibid.* p. 738.

[54] *H.R.A.* I, 4, 259; the dummy instructions, dated Nov. 22, 1802, were *ibid.*, 248, and were apparently intended to deceive Baudin, see *H.R.A.* I, 4, p. 676, n. 98.

explaining that he had taken this action as he "considered it my duty to establish H.M.'s right to that island being within the limits of this territory..." [55] Baudin was able to satisfy the commanding officer and also King, that he had no instructions to settle Van Diemen's Land.[56] Despite this assurance King continued his persuasions to London in favour of a settlement in Bass Strait and there is little doubt that fear of French activity there was the chief though not the only motive, at a time when the war between the countries had been resumed.[57] This fear was not altogether unfounded, for a report advocating the invasion of Sydney was later submitted to the Governor of Mauritius by Péron,[58] one of the leaders of Baudin's expedition, but no move either to invade or to settle was ever taken.[59]

Settlement in Van Diemen's Land followed soon after the events described. Expeditions from Sydney in 1803 and London in 1804 settled on the Derwent and in 1804 another settlement was made on the North Coast in Port Dalrymple.

French activity in Australian waters at this time was not confined to the events described above; several French navigators, including Baudin in the *Géographe*, made a contribution to the exploration of the coast, especially in the Bass Strait area and in the South and West and they could rightly claim to have been the first discoverers (in the sense of visual perception) of several portions of the coast line.[60]

(ii) Between 1804 and 1824 the population in N.S.W. and Van Diemen's Land increased from 5,000 to over 30,000. The area of main land settlement was still centred around Sydney, but discovery of a route across the Blue Mountains in 1813 had opened up large areas for settlement and exploration which, by 1824 extended from Moreton Bay to Port Phillip and up to 200 miles inland. Coastal exploration

[55] *H.R.A.* I, 4, p. 247.

[56] *H.R.A.* I, 4, p. 151.

[57] Bass Strait was the direct line of communication between Sydney and London. The Governor had earlier wished to settle at Port Phillip to forestall any French settlement, *H.R.A.* I, 3, 490.

[58] Scott, *Life of Matthew Flinders* (1914) p. 436, contains a translation of this report dated December 11, 1802.

[59] In 1810 when Mauritius was under British blockade Napoleon instructed Governor Decaen to fit out a squadron and take Port Jackson (*Correspondence de Napoleon 1er* (1866) Vol. XX, No. 16, 544, June 9, 1810) but he could not carry out this order.

[60] See Sharp, *The Discovery of Australia* (1963) for a detailed account of the explorers who first sighted part of Australia's coastline.

was virtually completed by King's surveys in the North and West in 1817 and 1822.[61]

(iii) The period from 1824 to 1851 was one of fast expansion. The population jumped to 400,000 and the territory of N.S.W. was divided between four separate colonies.

In the North, two unsuccessful settlements were established at Fort Dundas (1824 - 1829), and Fort Wellington (1827 - 1829), and a third, military and trading post at Port Essington (1938 - 1849) of slightly longer duration. The Governor's Commission was extended to Long. 129°E in 1825 to include the Fort Dundas settlement.

In the East Moreton Bay was settled in 1825 first by Convicts and later by free settlers. A settlement was begun at Port Curtis in 1846.

The greatest activity was in the South. (a) Van Diemen's Land became a separate colony in 1825 with a population of over 5,000. (b) On the mainland, Port Phillip was officially opened to settlers in September 9, 1836; settlement was rapid and Victoria became a separate colony in 1851 with a population of over 70,000. (c) South Australia was settled as a free and separate colony in 1836 through Adelaide, and although progress was at first slow, the population was 63,700 in 1850. During the same period exploration of the interior had proceeded steadily; although the first South-North crossing of the Continent was not achieved until 1860 - 61. By 1851 virtually all of the present area of N.S.W. and Victoria and the Eastern portions of South Australia and Queensland had been investigated.[62]

The acquisition of Western Australia will be considered separately after the legal principles arising from the occupation of the East.

(b) Effective occupation – Legal principles. Whether or not Britain had an inchoate title to the Eastern part of Australia by right of discovery or as a result of the first settlement and proclamations in 1788 territorial sovereignty could only be completed by actual possession. It has been a difficult task for international law to define not only the type of acts which may constitute possession, but also the area over which such possession can be regarded as operating. Vattel's opinion already quoted above,[63] that "the law of nations will only recognise the ownership and sovereignty of a nation over unoccupied lands when the Nation is in actual occupation of them, when it forms a settlement

[62] See generally on exploration, Scott *Australian Discovery by Land* (1929).

[61] *Ibid.* pp. 278 *et seq.*

[63] *Supra,* note 32.

upon them or makes some actual use of them", although consistent with his view permitting States to occupy lands not used or needed by the native population,[64] would, in practice, often lead to a "vacuum" in sovereignty.

In the practical context of a dispute between two States over territory which may not have been settled by either in the terms outlined by Vattel, or which may not even be capable of such settlement, a different solution must be found. An arbitrator or court is in such circumstances concerned not so much with the "ideal" title, as with the best of two opposing claims. Each side may produce a mass of evidence going back over centuries, beginning with discoveries and symbolic acts and continuing through all the evidence of State activity.[65] It is in this context that modern jurisprudence[66] has developed a doctrine of effective occupation, which is sufficiently flexible to permit adaptation to the circumstances of the case. These principles have also been applied in cases where title has been claimed not on the ground of acquisition by occupation but on grounds such as prescription or historic consolidation,[67] and it has been observed in relation to cases involving effective occupation that tribunals do not always clearly state the ground on which the award is being made.[68]

The modern concept no longer depends either on the actual use of land or even on the power to exclude other States but is based on "the principle that continuous and peaceful display of the functions of State within a given region is a constituent element of territorial sovereignty."[69] As acquisition is a State act there must be an intention to acquire territorial sovereignty either express or implied from the unambiguous exercise of sovereign power. The acts relied on to establish effective occupation besides being peaceful and continuous must be acts explicable only on the basis of the exercise of sovereign power. The elements which make up the principle of effective occupation

[64] *Supra*, note 9.

[65] *E.g.* In the *Island of Palmas* case, note 26 *supra*, the evidence went back to discovery in the early 16th century.

[66] *E.g.*, the *Island of Palmas* case, 1928, 2. R.I.A.A. 831; The *Clipperton Island* case, 1931, 2. R.I.A.A. 1105; The *Legal Status of Eastern Greenland*, (1933) P.C.I.J. See A/B No. 53. Minquiers & Ecrehos case [1953] I.C.J. Reports 47.

[67] See Blum, *Historic Titles in International Law* (1965) Chapter IV; Jennings, *op. cit.* pp. 23-28.

[68] Jennings, *op. cit.*, p. 23; Blum, *op. cit.*, p. 3.

[69] *Island of Palmas* case, 2 R.I.A.A. at 840.

have been elaborated and considered at length.[70] Lindley described it as "an administration sufficient for the protection of life and property." [71] Here it need only be said that the circumstances of the territory in question – the number of its inhabitants, its suitability for habitation – all affect not only the type of State activity required or accepted as proof, but the degree of continuity and the time to complete effective occupation.[72] The acquiescence or absence of competing claims is also a factor affecting the weight accorded to acts of occupation.

The extent of territory acquired by acts of occupation has in the past been influenced by various geographical principles, *e.g.*, the "watershed," "hinterland," "contiguity" and "sector" principles, which have in some case been put forward as a sole ground of title. While now largely discounted as a source of title [73] these principles are still helpful in determining the extent of territory covered by the display of power. Thus it has been said that:

> „when there is some manifestation of the *animus occupandi* by a display of sovereignty, the continuity or contiguity of the outlying area serves to give actuality to the display . . . The proximity, by raising a presumption of an actual intention and ability to control the outlying areas, operates to give the claimant the benefit of the rule that an effective occupation need not make an impact in every nook and cranny of the territory." [74]

There is also support for the view that occupation may extend over a territory even when its physical features are not fully known, provided that sufficiently general knowledge exists of the area.[75] The official document of annexation will naturally carry weight as a statement of intention, though ultimately it is effective possession which is the criterion for determining the extent of territory acquired.[76]

Although the detailed principles concerning effective occupation

[70] See cases referred to *supra*, note 66; see also Blum, *op cit*.

[71] *Op. cit.*, p. 159.

[72] As to Antarctic regions see Waldock, "Disputed Sovereignty in the Falkland Islands Dependencies" (1948) 25 *B.Y.I.L.* 311; *International Law in Australia, cit. supra*, note 38.

[73] See *e.g. Island of Palmas* case 2 R.I.A.A. at 854-855; Waldock, *loc. cit.*, 341 *et seq.*; these doctrines are of more use in demarcation disputes when the problem is rather "to find for the first time a natural and convenient frontier," Macdonnell (1899) 1 *Jo. Soc. Comp. Leg.* 276, 286.

[74] Waldock, *loc. cit.* at 345.

[75] *The Legal Status of Eastern Greenland* case, 1934, P.C.I.J. See A/B No. 53 at 26, 50.

[76] Lindley, *op. cit.* pp. 271 and 283.

were developed in the 19th and 20th centuries they have been applied retrospectively to events contemporary with those here described,[77] and therefore must be taken into account. This is the more so as jurists had not by the end of the 18th century developed rules capable of satisfactory application. Vattel's doctrine requiring actual use of land which has already been referred to will serve as a comparison with the more recent theory.

The British *animus occupandi*, as evidenced by the Orders-in-Council of 1786 and the instructions to Governor Phillip, has already been referred to. Turning to the question of occupation it is apparent that the problem concerns not so much its effectiveness but the extent of territory over which it could operate. One can distinguish the case of Norfolk Island, where acquisition of sovereignty was immediately effected by the occupation in 1788 of a relatively small and uninhabited island.

On the mainland the factors to be taken into account were very different. There was on the one hand the purported annexation of a vast area, of which the coastline was only partly known and the interior not at all, inhabited by a native population which, although scattered and relatively unorganised, outnumbered the small band of settlers for many years; [78] all these factors weighed against effectiveness. On the other hand the difficulties in settling the tropical North and the lack of opposition from any other State would tend to give strength to any slight evidence of sovereignty if any such display could be established. However, beyond the areas of actual settlement and inland exploration there was scarcely any evidence of such activity, apart from the formal instruments of annexation and some coastal exploration; it was not until after the rapid expansion between 1824 and 1851 that a reasonably strong case of effective occupation could be made out beyond the South-East area.[79]

That the British position beyond the settled areas was regarded as weak is confirmed by the panic action of the N.S.W. Governor in 1802. His instructions to the party sent to "forestall" the French in Van Diemen's Land clearly recognise the value of physical presence and even use of the soil (in accordance with Vattel's principle) to reinforce

[77] See the cases referred to *supra*, note 66.

[78] The native population estimated to have been up to 300,000 in 1788 had been reduced by 1965 to 40,000, plus 60,000 of mixed blood.

[79] See above: Historical Outline.

the symbolic acts of possession, which together with Bass and Flinders' exploration and earlier visits were the only British activity in that area.

It does not necessarily follow from the lack of activity by Great Britain that any other State could have acquired territorial sovereignty over the unsettled parts of Australia by occupation. For whether one regards the title accruing to Great Britain as a result of the discoveries of Captain Cook and the symbolic annexation of the Eastern half of the continent together with actual settlement of part of this area, as inchoate or merely weak, the result in either case would be the same, *e.g.*, that no other State could establish sovereignty for itself by effective occupation without British acquiescence, either as a matter of international law [80] or as a matter of fact. Whether there would have been acquiescence to foreign intrusion becomes a political question, though all evidence suggests unwillingness to allow foreign intrusion. The whole argument is rendered academic when one considers that the chief obstacle to foreign settlement and the chief factor which kept Australia British was the superiority of British sea-power at the beginning of the 19th century, during and after the Napoleonic Wars.[81]

(3) The Occupation of Western Australia

Early navigators, including the Englishman William Dampier, reported New Holland (Western Australia) as a barren and desolate place. Although Vancouver may have made a formal claim to King George's Sound in 1791,[82] the first official move to exercise authority came in 1825, mainly as a result of activities of whalers on the South West Coast. Governor Darling was instructed to send a small garrison to King George Sound.[83] On November 24, 1826 he wrote to Earl Bathurst requesting that his Commission be amended to take in the whole territory of Australia: "If generally known that we had actually assumed the Sovereignty, and were proceeding to settle the Western

[80] See Blum, *op. cit. supra*, Chapter III "Acquiscence as the Juridical Basis of an Historic Title," *cf.* Vattel, *op. cit.*, II, ss. 86, 98 to the effect that a State may not appropriate more territory than it actually needs to use.

[81] *Cambridge History of the British Empire*, Vol. 7, pt, 1 (1933) p. 93. Scott, *Terre Napoleon* (1910) p. 266.

[82] Vancouver, *A Voyage of Discovery to the North Pacific Ocean and Round the World* Vol. 1 (London, 1798) p. 35, describing the symbolic acts of possession performed at King George the Third's Sound on September 29, 1791, in respect of the country seen "so far as we might explore its coasts."

[83] *H.R.A.* I, 12, p. 218, and also p. 194.

coast, it might possibly tend to prevent the interference of any foreign power and might set the matter at rest." [84] He instructed the commanding officer of the King George's Sound garrison, in any communication he might have with the French discovery ships, to avoid expressing any doubt as to the whole of New Holland being within his jurisdiction, and to signify that the whole of New Holland was subject to His Majesty and that he had orders for the settlement of the area.[85] The garrison arrived on December 25, 1826 and raised the British flag. No action was taken on the Governor's request as different plans with regard to Western Australia were put into operation not long after.

Captain Stirling who had visited Western Australia in the area of the Swan River in 1827, later submitted a report to Governor Darling, enclosing a document entitled *Narrative of Operations*: "I am therefore of the opinion that it ought to be immediately retained, for the French nation have a shadow of a right founded on discovery to a portion of that coast which cannot be too speedily extinguished by British occupation . . ." [85] The note to this part of the document refers to the surveys by the French vessels *Géographe* (after which the Bay is still named) and *Casuarina* in 1801 and 1803. On his return to London Stirling pressed the case for British settlement in Western Australia stressing its possible importance in trade with the East, and pointing out the possibility of foreign appropriation in the absence of British possession.[86] His argument proved persuasive, for on November 5, 1828, the Colonial Secretary, Sir George Murray, wrote to the Lords Commissioners of the Admiralty signifying His Majesty's pleasure that a ship of war be despatched:

> without the smallest loss of time, to the Western coast of New Holland, with directions, that he take formal possession of the western side of New Holland in His Majesty's name. It is desirable that the place on which he shall take possession be at or as near as possible Swan River, and that he maintain on that spot, an uninterrupted possession on behalf of His Majesty until arrival of further instructions.[87]

This instruction was forwarded to Captain Fremantle of the *Challenger*,[88] who proceeded to the Swan River and carried out his in-

[84] *H.R.A.* I, 12, p. 700.
[85] *H.R.A.* I, 2, p. 701. This is the first "official" claim to all Australia.
[86] *H.R.A.* III, 6, p. 551 at 578, April 18, 1827; see also *ibid.* note 120, p. 863.
[87] Letter of July 30, 1828 to Under Secretary Hay, *H.R.A.* III, 6, p. 585.
[88] *Diary and Letters of Admiral Sir C. H. Fremantle, G.C.B. relating to the Founding of the Colony of Western Australia,* 1829. Edited by Lord Cottesloe (1928) p. 15; for the acknowledgment, see *H.R.A.* III, 4, p. 613.

structions on May 2 1829 by taking "formal possession" of "the whole of the West coast of New Holland in the name of His Britannic Majesty"; the Union Jack was hoisted on the South head of the river.[89]

Stirling was appointed Lt. Governor on December 30, 1928 [90] and the first immigrants arrived in 1829 and 1830. An Act of 1829 authorised the Governor to make laws in His Majesty's settlement on the Western coast of New Holland, and define its boundaries.[91] Progress was slow and settlement was confined to the south-west corner. By 1849 when it became a convict settlement the population was only 5.000 but this increased to 15.000 by 1860. Exploration was also slower in the West than in the East and although substantially complete by the 1870's continued until the end of the century.

The foundation of the Colony of Western Australia demonstrates once again the importance attached in practice to the symbolic ceremony of annexation, accompanied by physical presence. On the question of occupation the acquisition of Western Australia followed a similar pattern to that of the rest of Australia. It was only with the gradual extension of settlement and exercise of authority that British sovereignty became perfected. Again, there was a complete absence of competition by other States.

II The Acquisition of New Zealand

A. Discovery and Symbolic Claim

Abel Tasman was the first European to sight New Zealand in December, 1642 but there is no record of a formal claim.

In 1769 - 70 Captain Cook circumnavigated and substantially charted the two islands. On November 15, 1769 he took formal possession at a flag raising ceremony at Mercury Bay on North Island.[93] A similar ceremony was held at Queen Charlotte's Sound on January 31, 1770 [94] this time the claim included lands adjacent. The same com-

[89] November 7, 1828, *Diary, cit. supra*, p. 16; instructions to Fremantle, *H.R.A.* III, 6, p. 613.

[90] *Diary*, pp. 23-24.

[91] *H.R.A.* III, 6, p. 600.

[92] 10 Geo IV, c. 22.

[93] Journals *cit. supra*, note pp. 203-204. Possession was taken of "the place."

[94] *Ibid.*, p. 243. In this case reference was made also to "adjacent lands."

ments apply to the symbolic claims made by Captain Cook in both places. His act was not expressly authorised except possibly in regard to the taking possession of "convenient stations" and was never ratified.

But Cook was not the only one to claim territories in New Zealand, for on July 12, 1772, a French party who had been under the command of Marion du Fresne, (earlier killed by the Maoris) buried a bottle on an island in the Bay of Islands containing an *Act de Prise de Possession* to the Territory of New Zealand, under the name of "France-Austral." [95] Whether or not this was an authorised act is not known, but the French took no further official steps in relation to New Zealand until the 1830's. Any claim to title arising from either discovery referred to must have long since lapsed. Nevertheless the British did rely on Cook's discovery in support of their later annexation.

B. Association with New South Wales 1788 - 1839

The Commissions of Governor Phillip and later Governors defined their area of jurisdiction as comprising adjacent islands in the Pacific, though the exact area comprised in this description was never determined.[96] The express reference to Norfolk Island in Phillip's instructions would be an argument against the inclusion in the jurisdiction of islands such as New Zealand which were even further from N.S.W.[97] Even if New Zealand had been included within the area described this alone would not have sufficed to convey territorial sovereignty to Great Britain in the absence of some acts of settlement or administration. However as a result of the settlement in New Zealand of traders, escaped convicts and sailors, the need arose for the exercise of some authority there, and in 1814 the Governor of N.S.W. appointed a magistrate to New Zealand.

[95] Kelly, *Marion Dufresne* at the Bay of Islands (1951) p. 82; a translation of this document appears at pp. 84-85 (Affaires Etrangères, Archives, New Zealand, 1772-1839, Miscellaneous Papers, T.I).

[96] This description has continued to cause uncertainty in municipal law, if not in international law, even in recent times, especially as regards certain islands off the coast of Queensland. See: Lumb, *The Maritime Boundaries and New South Wales* (1964); Cumbrae-Stewart, "Australian Boundaries," *University of Queensland Law Journal* 1, 6-7; O'Connell, "Australian Coastal Jurisdiction," in *International Law in Australia* (1965) pp. 246, 268.

[97] Ward, *British Policy in the South Pacific*, pp. 34-40.

The uncertainty which may have existed concerning the status of New Zealand was resolved by an Imperial Act of 1817 [98] concerning criminal jurisdiction. This Act provided for the exercise of jurisdiction over certain offences committed in New Zealand, Tahiti or other islands "not within His Majesty's dominions nor subject to any European state or power," as if such offences had been committed on the high seas. Later the Courts established in New South Wales were given jurisdiction over these offences [99] but from 1817 there was no exercise of jurisdiction within New Zealand, which had been put beyond the scope of British Territorial claims by the above Act.[100] In fact, a British resident was sent to New Zealand in 1833, accredited as to a foreign sovereign and with limited powers.[101]

(c) The Cession of Sovereignty and Occupation 1840

(1) Historical Outline

The circumstances which finally prompted Great Britain to take positive action in New Zealand was the incorporation in 1839 of the New Zealand Company, which had already made large purchases of Maori lands and was about to establish large scale settlement. The Colonial Office decided to acquire sovereignty in order to exercise authority over the settlement and the Company.[102] The status of New Zealand had been considered in a Colonial Office memorandum to the Foreign Office, drawn up by Sir James Stephen in 1839, which was the basis of the official view recognising the sovereignty of the native chiefs.[103] The question was relevant to the means by which acquisition by Great Britain could be achieved. It was acknowledged that despite the difficulties in obtaining the cession of sovereignty which resided in a "people composed of numerous dispersed and petty tribes, who pos-

[98] 57 Geo. 3, c. 53.

[99] *H.R.A.* I, 16, pp. 562-563.

[100] *Ibid.*, pp. 486.

[101] *H.R.A.* I, 16, pp. 562-3; Ward, *op. cit.*, p. 82. The British Resident, Busby, organised the native chiefs to declare New Zealand as an independent State to repel Frenchman de Thierry's projects; Ward, pp. 75-76.

[102] Ward, *op. cit.*, p. 110 *et seq.*

[103] *Correspondence Relating to New Zealand* 1840, Encl. in No. 38; Ward, *op. cit.*, p. 75 refers to other acts of formal recognition; see also Lindley, *op. cit.*, p. 41.

sess few political relations to each other and are incompetent to act, or even to deliberate, in concert," their free consent was essential.[104]

Letters Patent were issued on June 15, 1839 extending the limits of N.S.W. to include "any New Zealand territory which is or may be acquired by Her Majesty." [105] Hobson, who was to be Governor, arrived at the Bay of Islands early in 1840 and proclaimed his entry into duty. He was instructed to treat with the aborigines, to recognise Her Majesty's Sovereign authority over parts of the island they may be willing to place under Her Majesty's dominion and to assert sovereignty over the South Island if he found it uninhabited except but by a "very small number of persons in a savage state and incapable from their ignorance of entering intelligently into any treaty with the Crown" [106] . . . He had signed the Treaty of Waitangi with 80 chiefs in the area by February, 6 1840. The chief Article is as follows:

> I. The chiefs of the Confederation of the United Tribes of New Zealand, and the separate and independent chiefs who have not become members of the Confederation, cede to Her Majesty the Queen of England, absolutely and without reservation, all the rights and powers of sovereignty which the said Confederation or individual chiefs respectively exercise or possess, or may be supposed to exercise or possess over their territories as the sole sovereigns thereof.[107]

On May 21, 1840 British Sovereignty of the North Island was proclaimed on the ground of cession, but the process of obtaining signatories was not yet completed and continued until October 10. On May 21 sovereignty was also proclaimed over the South Island on the ground of discovery by Captain Cook though the report of Major Bunbury who had been sent to investigate the position there was not received until June 28; [108] treaties were also signed in the South Island, but fewer than in the North.

The settlement of New Zealand was rapid, a number of sites being occupied in 1840 and 1841, and on May 3, 1841 New Zealand was declared a separate colony.[109] Although it could be argued that, apart

[104] *Corr. rel. to N.Z.* 1840, Normally to Hobson (Instructions) Aug. 14, 1839 (Parl. Papers, XXXIII, 238); Ward, *op. cit.*, p. 76; Lindley, *op. cit.*, p. 41.

[105] C.O. 381/55.

[106] Note 104, *supra*; see also *Corr. rel. to N.Z.* 1940, Nos. 17 and 18; Lindley, *op. cit.*, p. 42.

[107] 6 Hertslet 579; G.B. Parl. Pap. 1840/311; C.O. 209/7; the text also appears in Ward, *op. cit.*, p. 111.

[108] See Ward, *op. cit.*, p. 77.

[109] Under an Act of 1840, 3 & 4 Vic. c. 62, Letters Patent were issued on Nov. 16, 1840 & declared in New Zealand on May 3, 1841.

from any question of cession or discovery, effective occupation was established immediately, nevertheless when the Nanto-Bordelaise Company, with official French government approval sent a colonising expedition to the South Island in 1839-40, immediate action was taken. Hobson, hearing of the French intention to settle at Banks Peninsula sent a vessel to Akaroa (on the Peninsula). The British flag was raised and a magistrate was left in residence to demonstrate the exercise of sovereignty. The French party had to accept British sovereignty, though official recognition did not come until 1844.[110]

(2) Legal Principles

The early jurists paid a great deal of attention to the question of whether territory inhabited by "backward" natives could be occupied as *terra nullius*. But although until the 19th century the views were against such occupation no clear principle was laid down as to how such territory could be acquired. Vattel, for example, denied the right of States to occupy territory actually in use by natives, though allowing their right to settle and establish colonies upon land "which the savages have not special need of and are making no present and continuous use of," [111] but he did not specifically state how this territory not used by the savages might be acquired, though approving in principle the practices of English settlers who bought such lands.[112] It must follow from the recognition of native ownership or even sovereignty in their territory by early writers that, short of conquest, some element of consent would be essential before a State could acquire sovereignty over such territory. Express judicial recognition has been given to the fact that the American colonies were obtained by cession or conquest.[113] Nevertheless, many modern writers who deny the capacity of uncivilised people in international law argue that purported treaties of cession entered into by such people cannot be recognised by the law of nations.[114] That this overlooks the consistent practice of States

[110] Ward, *op. cit.*, pp. 115-116; for French practice as regards New Zealand see also Harrop, *England and New Zealand* (1926) Ch. V, pp. 94-138.

[111] *Op. cit.* I, XVIII s. 209, p. 85; see also II, VII, s. 98, p. 143 permitting occupation of native lands in case of absolute need.

[112] *Op. cit.* I, XVII s. 209, p. 86; at II, VII, s. 97, p. 142 (note 9 *supra*) he suggests that States ought not to assume sovereignty without consent.

[113] *Johnson* v. *M'Intosh* (1823) 8 Wheaton, 543; See also Blackstone I, 106. 7 (L. 14-15) Kent, *Comm.* 3. 384.

[114] *Supra*, pp. 1-12 MS, Lindley, *op. cit.*, pp. 18 *et seq.*

in their dealings with native peoples has been demonstrated by Lindley,[115] who also considered State practice in order to discover what rules could be deduced as to the form and content of, and capacity of parties to, such agreements.[116] He has replied to the suggestion that they could not be regarded as rules of law as follows:

> It is difficult to see how, having regard to the universality of the practice of grounding a colonial protectorate upon an agreement with the local authority, and to the importance attached by the European Powers to these agreements in their relations *inter se*, the requirement for such an agreement can be regarded otherwise than as a rule of law.[117]

In the case of New Zealand there was an additional factor in that Great Britain recognised the sovereignty of the Maories both before the Treaty of Waitangi and in its terms. Nevertheless doubt is cast upon the status of this treaty in international law, mainly on the ground that the chiefs could have no sovereignty,[118] with the result that the acquisition of New Zealand is classed as discovery and occupation. It is not proposed to take up here this already protracted argument, except to point out that the cession as a source of title has been recognised not only by British courts [119] but by an international tribunal.[120] Though perhaps the question is still relevant in the municipal sphere,[121] in international law, the fact that the provisions of the

[115] *Op. cit.*, pp. 24-44; see also O'Connell, *op. cit.*, pp. 468-470. Among examples which can be referred to are the *Delagoa Bay Arbitration* (1875) Moore I.A. 4984 in which both England and Portugal relied on cessions by Native Chiefs, and in *re Southern Rhodesia* (1918) A.C., at 214, where native sovereignty was recognised.

[116] *Ibid.*, pp. 167-177.

[117] *Ibid.*, p. 176.

[118] *E.g.*, Rutherford, *The Treaty of Waitangi and the Acquisition of British Sovereignty in New Zealand, 1840* (1949); Robson, *New Zealand, The Development of its Laws and Constitution* (1954); Foden, *Constitutional Development of New Zealand in the First Decade* 1839-1849 (1938); see also *R* v. *Symonds* 1847 NZ P.C.C. 1840-1932; *Wi Parata* v. *Bishop of Wellington* (1877) 3 N.Z. Jur. R. (N.S.) SC. 70. *Halsbury, supra* note 41, states that Crown authority had been asserted long before 1840.

[119] *E.g., Hoani Te Heuheu Tukino* v. *Aotea District Maori Land Board* [1941] A.C. 308, 324 (P.C.); the recognition of ownership in Article II of the Treaty was however held subject to legislative enactments.

[120] K. J. Keith "International Law and New Zealand Municipal Law," *The A. G. Davis Essays in Law*, p. 130, at 137 has drawn attention to the *American and British Claims Arbitration* (agreement of 1910) 6 R.I.A.A. 166, 541, 543, in which the Treaty of Waitangi was acknowledged as a cession of sovereignty.

[121] See authorities cited *supra*, note 118; *cf. Re the Ninety Mile Beach* [1963] N.Z.L.R. 78, and Roberts-Wray, *op. cit.*, p. 630.

treaty which recognised Maori ownership of land could not be enforced unless incorporated by legislation does not mean that the treaty could not be regarded as a source of title.[122] In any event, whatever deficiencies there were in the treaty. British sovereignty was asserted almost immediately by effective occupation.

One further point remains to be mentioned, concerning the apparent retraction of recognition of sovereignty in regard to the South Island, despite the fact that recognition had not earlier been limited to the North. Hobson did not wait for a report on the capability of the South Islanders, but went ahead on the basis of Cook's discovery. Such a declaration is surprising in view of the lapse of time and the Act of 1817 disavowing the British title, and provoked the following comment from the Colonial Office [123]

> „It seems to me to prove, if proof were wanting, how much wiser was the course taken of negotiating for a cession of the sovereignty than would have been the course of relying on the proceedings of Captain Cook or the language of Vattel in opposition to our own statute book."

Nevertheless in view of the actual occupation which completed British Sovereignty, the considerations of policy which resulted in Hobson's declaration need not be considered.[124]

Comparisons and Conclusions

Discovery and Symbolic Act.

The Eastern coast of Australia and most of the coast line of New Zealand were discovered by Captain Cook. The extent of territory covered by his symbolic annexations is doubtful and is certainly less than was ultimately acquired by Great Britain in each case. His authority to make the annexations is also uncertain. Nevertheless it seems that he acted in the belief that he was entitled to claim for the British Crown all territories of which he was the first discoverer, while refraining from claiming territories known to have been visited be-

[122] Subsequent efforts to have this recognition of sovereignty and native ownership withdrawn were unsuccessful, see Lindley, *op. cit.*, pp. 344-346; *In re Southern Rhodesia* [1919] A.C. 211.

[123] A. J. Harrop, *England and New Zealand* (1926). The comment was made by Mr. Stephen on Hobson's despatch which reached the Colonial Office on July 9, 1840. The reference is to the statutes referred to *supra*, n. 98.

[124] Ward, *op. cit.*, p. 77.

fore.[125] Whatever the weight attached to these annexations as a source of title they must in the case of Australia be regarded as the first evidence of British activity. The status of New Zealand's acquisition is so uncertain as between occupation and cession, that discovery might also be accorded weight were it not for the express denial of territorial sovereignty in the 1817 Act.

Throughout the history of acquisition of territory in both Australia and New Zealand reliance was placed at every stage on the symbolic act of possession – the formal reading of a proclamation usually coupled with a flag raising ceremony. Such ceremonies were also held in 1883 and 1884 when South Eastern New Guinea was annexed, first by Queensland and later by the British Government,[126] by the Australian expedition to the Antarctic in 1930 [127] and in the case of Heard and McDonald Islands on several occasions and notably in 1947.[128] So flexible is the doctrine of effective occupation that far from supplanting symbolic annexation it has adopted it both as unambiguous and public demonstration of intention and as evidence of State activity. The value attached to such acts depend on a multitude of other factors, including the existence of opposing claims. In the examples given where intrusion by other States was feared, physical presence in addition to formal proclamation was stipulated (*e.g.* Van Diemen's Land, 1803, Western Australia, 1829 and Akaroa 1840). This practice is recognition that a State cannot preserve territory for itself by discovery or proclamation, unsupported by actual occupation, against encroachment by other States.

Occupation

Comparing Australia and New Zealand from the point of view of occupation the obvious difference is that whereas in Australia effective occupation was established gradually over many years, in New Zealand it was operative almost from the beginning. The rules concerning effectiveness are so geared to the comparison of titles set up in opposition rather than to the establishment of an absolute title by occu-

[125] *Supra*, note 23.

[126] The first proclamation was disowned by Great Britain as being without authority: see Lindley, *op. cit.*, p. 114; see also Legge *Australian Colonial Policy* (1956) Ch. II, pp. 7, 22 *et seq.*

[127] *Supra*, note 38.

[128] See A. C. Castles, "International Law and Australia's Overseas Territories" in *International Law in Australia*, p. 292, 307 *et seq.*; see also (1953) 1 *Sydney Law Review* 374.

pation that it is not possible in the case of Australia to determine when the process was completed.

Cession

The most important difference between Australia and New Zealand is that in the case of the former beyond a general Instruction to Captain Phillip to "conciliate their affections," agreement by the natives, either formally or informally expressed, was never thought necessary; Australia has always been regarded as a case of occupation.[129] In New Zealand on the other hand the procedure of acquisition was governed by the prior recognition of native sovereignty. It was thought necessary to get formal consent through a treaty of cession. The status of this treaty has continued to be the subject of controversy and it has never been certain in municipal law whether New Zealand is a case of occupation or cession. In international law, it can be argued that it was a case of necessity in New Zealand to secure consent before peaceful occupation, whereas in Australia it was neither necessary nor possible. This argument however only serves to illustrate Lindley's view that State practice distinguished between politically organised and unorganised societies.[130]

The denial of native sovereignty and consequently of capacity to enter into international treaties results in the relegation of native cessions to the status of factors to be considered in determining occupation in cases of disputed sovereignty.[131]

Occupation or Cession

After his examination of theory and State practice Lindley suggested that

> "the rule regarding appropriable territory can now be stated as follows . . . If the territory is uninhabited, or is inhabited only by a number of individuals who do not form a political society, then the acquisition may be made by Occupation. If the inhabitants exhibit collective political activity which, although of a crude and rudimentary form, possesses the elements of permanence, the acquisition can only be made by way of Cession or Conquest or Prescription." [132]

The British practice in the case of both Australia and New Zealand

[129] *Cooper* v. *Stuart* (1889) 14 A.C. 286, 291.

[130] *Op. cit. supra*, p. 45; see also In re *Southern Rhodesia* (1919) A.C. 211, 233-234.

[131] *Island of Palmas* case, 2 R.I.A.A., at 858.

[132] *Op cit.*, p. 45.

was in accordance with these principles; and though there was no similar case in Australia, the New Zealand procedure was consistent with British practice in other territories throughout the 19th century.

Nevertheless the rules concerning occupation of *territorium nullius* seem inept to deal with the assertion of sovereignty over a backward people without any regard to their interests. Even as late as 1888 the Institut de Droit International could not decide whether to include inhabited territory in a definition of territorium nullius.[133]

Nor do the principles of cession seem appropriate to deal with a situation where one of the parties, through ignorance, lack of understanding or weaker bargaining position surrenders its sovereignty and its rights to deal with land unless some restraint or obligation is imposed upon the State appropriating the territory. Yet one has only to consider the Berlin African Conference of 1884-5 to realise that in the 19th century States were more concerned with their rights and duties *inter se* than with any obligations or restraints in their dealings with native peoples. Even Lindley acknowledged that "The members of the International Family will not dispute the validity of the acquisition by one of them of territory in respect of which none of the others has a valid prior claim, and this recognition does not depend upon the method by which the acquisition has been made." [134]

In reality each State acted according to the needs of the case. In Australia it was not necessary to conquer or to obtain a cession, whereas in New Zealand the Maoris were willing to cede sovereignty, but when it became expedient to assert sovereignty over the South Island, formalities were dispensed with.

The theorists of the 19th century tried to define these actions according to the rigid classification of acquisition rather than building upon the structure of State practice some principles for the protection of native peoples. It was not until the 20th century that Lindley and others sought to find such principles.[135] One must prefer the robust view of Fauchille:

> „Les puissances civilisées n'ont pas plus de droit de s'emparer des territoires des sauvages, que ceux-ci n'ont le droit d'occuper les continents européens." [136]

[133] *Ibid.*, pp. 16-17, quoting IX Ann. 173 and 247.
[134] *Ibid.*, p. 45.
[135] *E.g.*, Snow, *The Question of Aborigines in the Law and Practice of Nations* (Washington, 1919).
[136] *Op. cit. supra* note 5, s. 547, p. 699.

PROF. GEORG SCHWARZENBERGER

Professor of International Law in the University of London
Director, London Institute of World Affairs

Breisach Revisited
The Hagenbach Trial of 1474

The trial in 1474 of Peter von Hagenbach deserves to be considered as a forerunner of contemporary international war crimes trials.[1] It is all the more relevant because the oral proceeding at this trial centred on one of the most controversial issues of post-1945 war crimes trials: the defence of superior orders.

I. THE HISTORICAL BACKGROUND

Duke Charles of Burgundy had raised his country to the zenith of power it was to attain in the fierce struggles between the rising territorial sovereigns for supremacy inside their territories and expansion at one another's expense. His friends called him Charles the Bold. His enemies decried him as Charles the Terrible, a title for which his massacres of the inhabitants of Nesle in 1472 had fully qualified him.

In 1469, financial difficulties had forced the Archduke of Austria to pledge to Charles his possessions on the Upper Rhine, including the fortified town of Breisach. Charles installed Peter von Hagenbach as his Governor or Landvogt.

So long as Charles held the pledged territories, he was entitled under the agreement to exercise there territorial jurisdiction, subject, however, to leaving unimpaired the ancient liberties of the pledged towns and their inhabitants. Actually, Charles had no intention of ever returning these places to the Archduke of Austria and set out on a determined policy of incorporating them into his Burgundian empire.

[1] The object of this paper is to reconsider the subject in the light of comments received since the publication of an earlier contribution to *The Manchester Guardian*, September 28, 1946.

On war crimes in general, see the writer's *The Law of Armed Conflict* (Vol. II of *International Law as Applied by International Courts and Tribunals*) 1968, p. 467 *et seq.* and the bibliographies to Chs. 40-44.

In trying to reduce the citizens of Breisach to a state of submission, Hagenbach merely carried out his master's instructions. The brutality with which he and his henchmen acted was his personal contribution to Burgundian policy. His regime of arbitrariness and terror extended to murder, rape, illegal taxation and wanton confiscation of private property, and the victim of his depredations included inhabitants of neighbouring territories as well as Swiss merchants on their way to and from the Frankfurt fair.

Charles' hardly concealed ambition – his quest to transform Burgundy into a Kingdom and use it as a spring-board to gain the Imperial Crown – was enough to make for him powerful enemies. Yet, the outrages of Hagenbach, remarkable even by the standards of the late fifteenth century, greatly contributed to forging what, until then, had been considered impossible, that is, alliances against Burgundy by all her neighbours: Austria, Berne, France, and the towns and knights of the Upper Rhine, all formerly at loggerheads with one another.

To strengthen their case against Charles, the Allies enabled the Archduke of Austria to offer repayment of the full debt. On flimsy pretexts, Charles refused to accept payment. A revolt by Hagenbach's German mercenaries at Breisach and the citizens of that town enabled the Allies to seize Hagenbach and put him on trial even before their war with Burgundy in 1476, in which Charles was defeated and killed in the battle of Nancy (1477).[2]

II. Organisation of the Tribunal

The Archduke of Austria, in whose territory Hagenbach had been captured, ordered his trial. Whereas an ordinary trial would have taken place in a local court, the Allies agreed on an *ad hoc* tribunal, consisting of twenty-eight judges from the Allied towns. Eight of these were nominated by Breisach, and two by each of the other allied Alsatian and Upper Rhenanian towns, Berne, a member of the Swiss

[2] See Ph. Melanchton, *Chronica Carionis* (1588), pp. 1037-1042; *Johannis Knebel Capellani ecclesiae Basiliensis diarium*, September 1473 - January, 1476 (*Basler Chroniken*, Vol. II - 1880 - ed. by W. Vischer and H. Boos), p. 1 *et seq.*; A. C. de Barante, *Histoire des Ducs de Bourgogne de la Maison de Valois*, 1364-1477 (1839), Vol. 9, pp. 289 and 405 *et seq.*, and Vol. 10, p. 1 *et seq.*; J. F. Kirk, *History of Charles the Bold*, Vol. II (1863), p. 378 *et seq.*; H. Brauer-Gramm, *Der Landvogt Peter von Hagenbach* (1957 – with helpful historical bibliography), and J. Calmette, *The Golden Age of Burgundy* (1962), p. 170 *et seq.*

Confederation, and Solothurn, allied with Berne. As Breisach's sovereign, Austria provided the presiding judge.[3]

It is debatable whether, in form, the tribunal can be described as an international tribunal. The question turns on the date when the Swiss Confederation had effectively seceded from the Holy Roman Empire.

The Holy Roman Empire did not formally recognise the secession of the Swiss Confederation until the Peace Treaty of Westphalia (1648).[4] In fact, as early as the seventies and eightees of the fifteenth century, the process of Swiss emancipation from the Empire was rapidly advancing. To select as the decisive date the Peace Treaty of Basle of 1499, with which the recognition of the *de facto* independence of the Swiss Confederation is usually linked would appear to overformalise this particular event.[5]

Moreover, by the time of the Breisach Trial, the Holy Roman Empire had degenerated to such an extent that relations between its members were conducted on a footing hard to distinguish from international relations. In this state of disintegration, alliances, counter-alliances, treaties of subsidy, policies of neutrality and balance of power were more significant than the Emperor, the Diet or the Reichskammergericht.[6] Thus, in the relations between these units, which, *de facto*, were largely independent, law fulfilled functions more com-

[3] See further Knebel, *loc. cit.* in note 2 above, p. 85, and Barante *loc. cit.* in note 2 above, Vol. 10, p. 13 *et seq*.

On doubts regarding the participation in the trial of the Swiss Confederates and sixteen knights, see Knebel, p. 85, note 4. See also Brauer-Gramm, *loc. cit.* in note 2 above, p. 309 *et seq*.

[4] Para. 61 of the Peace Treaty of Münster between the Emperor and France (*e.g.*, in E. Hövel (ed.), *Pax Optima Rerum* (1948), p. 27). See also the bibliography *ibid.*, pp. 254-255, and further F. Dickmann, *Der Westfälische Frieden* (1959), p. 432 *et seq.*, and 573.

[5] See further Kirk, *loc. cit.* in note 2 above, Vol. II, p. 243 *et seq.* and 387; J. B. Moore, *A Digest of International Law*, Vol. I (1906), p. 72; L. C. Green, 4 *M.L.R.* (1948), pp. 493-494, and the present writer, 71 *L.Q.R.* (1955), p. 425 *et seq.*; Brauer-Gramm, *loc. cit.* in note 2 above, pp. 269 and 273; E. Reibstein, *Völkerrecht*, Vol. I (1958), p. 202; Dickmann, *loc. cit.* in note 4 above, pp. 38-39, and D. Schindler, *Schweiz* in Strupp-Schlochauer, *Wörterbuch des Völkerrechts*, Vol. 3 (1962), p. 225

[6] See, for instance, S. Pufendorf, *Gründlicher Bericht von dem Zustande des H. R. Reichs Deutscher Nation* (1715); R. Huch, *Römisches Reich Deutscher Nation* (1934), p. 355 *et seq.*, and Brauer-Gramm, *loc. cit.* in note 2 above, pp. 154, 241, 262, 307 and 323, and, on the alliance of 1474 between the Swiss Confederates and the *Niedere Vereinigung*, *Basler Chroniken*, Vol. 5, (ed. A. Bernouilli - 1895), p. 503.

parable and akin to those of international law than municipal law. Similar to the relations between the Italian City-States while these still belonged to the Roman Empire of the German Nation,[7] the relations between Burgundy and its enemies fall into a category of quasi-international law. Its essential characteristic is a state of *de facto* equality on which entities conduct their mutual relations as if they were subjects of international law.

III. The Law Applied by the Tribunal

In the preliminary inquisitorial proceedings, Hagenbach was subjected to severe torture. In view of the obviousness of his crimes, this was utterly pointless and produced predestined confessions and their equally automatic withdrawal in the oral proceedings.

At the public trial, a representative of the Archduke of Austria acted as the plaintiff. Both sides were represented by their spokesmen who, as it happened, were both from Basle.

In the submission of Heinrich Iselin, the Plaintiff's spokesman, the Defendant had "trampled under foot the laws of God and man."[8] More particularly, Hagenbach was charged with murder, rape, perjury and other *malefacta*, including orders to the non-German mercenaries he had brought to Breisach, to kill the men in the houses where they were quartered so that the woman and children would be completely at their mercy.[9]

Hans Irmy, who conducted Hagenbach's case, relied primarily on the defence of superior orders: "Sir Peter von Hagenbach does not recognise any other judge and master but the Duke of Burgundy from whom he had received his commission and his orders. He had no right

[7] See, for instance, A. P. Sereni, *The Italian Conception of International Law* (1943), p. 3 *et seq.* (useful bibliography).

[8] De Barante, *loc. cit.* in note 2 above, Vol. 10, p. 15.

In Knebel's view, the explanation of the huge attendance of spectators at the trial was, "*quia omnis homo optavit mortem illius tyranni, traditoris, sodomite et obpressoris tam virginum quam mulierum, qui non satis erat ullum malum quod animo cogitare potuit*" (*loc. cit.* in note 2 above, p. 84).

See also Brauer-Gramm, *loc. cit.* in note 2 above, pp. 235 and 282-284.

[9] Knebel, *loc. cit.* in note 2 above, p. 86 *et seq.*; de Barante, *loc. cit.* in note 2 above, Vol. 10, p. 15; H. Heimpel, Vol. 55 (New Series) *Zeitschrift für Geschichte des Oberrheins* (1942), p. 321 *et seq.* (especially valuable on the procedural aspects of the trial and the irrelevance, in relation to the actual charges, of the tortures applied) and *Stengel Festschrift* (1952), p. 443 *et seq.*, and R. K. Woetzel, *The Nuremberg Trials in International Law* (1962), p. 19 *et seq.*

to question the orders which he was charged to carry out, and it was his duty to obey. Is it not known that soldiers owe absolute obedience to their superiors? Does anyone believe that the Duke's *Landvogt* could have remonstrated with his master or have refused to carry out the Duke's orders? Had not the Duke by his presence subsequently confirmed and ratified all that had been done in his name." [10]

In his own address to the Tribunal, Hagenbach took the same line and asked for an adjournment to obtain the necessary confirmation from his master.

In an interlocutory judgment, the Tribunal refused this request on the grounds that to accept the defence put forward by, and on behalf of, Hagenbach would be contrary to the law of God, and that his crimes were established beyond doubt. The Tribunal found the accused guilty and condemned him to death.[11] The executioner of Colmar was selected from among eight competitors. Prior to the execution, Hagenbach was deprived of his knighthood as one who had committed all the crimes it had been his duty as a knight to prevent. Finally, the Marshal of the Tribunal gave his order to the executioner with the words: "Let justice be done." [12]

Hagenbach's crimes had been committed before the outbreak of open war between Burgundy and her enemies. Thus, in a strict sense, they were not war crimes. At that time, the borderline between peace and war was, however, even more fluid than in the centuries to come.[13] Although the occupation of the pledged territories by Burgundy rested on a consensual basis, these territories remained foreign territories. In any case, the administration of these territories, and Breisach in particular, in open breach of the treaty obligations undertaken by Charles of Burgundy made this occupation more akin to a wartime

[10] De Barante, *loc. cit.* in note 2 above, Vol. 10, p. 16.

According to Knebel, *loc. cit.* in note 2 above, p. 89, Irmy "*dixit, quod ea, que dominus Petrus de Hagenbach fecisset, non sua voluntate, sed de mandate domini nostri imperatoris et sui graciosi domini ducis Burgundiae fecisset.*" See also *ibid.*, pp. 87 and 91, and Heimpel, *loc. cit.* in note 9 above (1942), pp. 354-356.

For more charitable views on Hagenbach, see Kirk, *loc. cit.* in note 2 above, Vol. II, p. 409 *et seq.*, and Brauer-Gramm, *loc. cit.* in note 2 above, p. 308 *et seq.*

[11] De Barante, *loc. cit.* in note 2 above, Vol. 10, p. 17 *et seq.*

[12] De Barante, *ibid.*, p. 19.

[13] On the factual aspects, see, for instance, Brauer-Gramm, *loc. cit.* in note 2 above, pp. 60-61, 82, 181 and 229.

than a peacetime occupation.[14] Thus, broadly, these crimes fall into the category of what, since 1945, would be termed crimes against humanity, rather than war crimes in the strict sense of the term.

[14] See, *e.g.*, Knebel, *loc. cit.* in note 2 above, pp. 47, 49, 59, 77 and 78; de Barante, *loc. cit.* in note 2 above, Vol. 9, p. 405 *et seq.*, and Vol. 10, p. 1 *et seq.*

DR. D. LUMB

University of Queensland

Legality and Legitimacy: The Limits of the Duty of Obedience to the State

The relationship between ruler and ruled, state and citizen, is a question which has dominated the speculation of political philosophers for centuries. Its significance, however, extends beyond the realm of political philosophy. It is a matter which now falls within the domain of international law.

The positivist tradition which tends to see international law in terms of a relationship between States can only with some difficulty be accommodated with a recognition of norms which prescribe limitations on the exercise of sovereign authority. In recent legal thought a "built-in" limitation has been recognised as a part of the definition of sovereign authority – a recognition which is in some part due to the criticisms of the natural lawyers who have pointed to the inadequacies of the older positivist tradition. Indeed it is to the natural law tradition to which recourse must be had in explaining the post-war developments affirming the sanctity of the rights of individuals. In particular the Nuremberg Trials stand out as having provided the impetus to the achievements of the past two decades in this regard.

In times of crisis when the positive legal order as such provides insufficient protection for the basic rights of the governed, criteria of legal validity are sought in a higher set of principles – principles which in some way or other also form part of the fabric of the legal order although not incorporated in that order in written form. It is at this time that the older tradition of natural law is invoked to provide answers which the instruments of *lex posita* are not equipped to provide.[1]

As I have stated, the Nuremberg Trials stand out as a milestone in the history of the struggle for the international recognition of human

[1] See Silving, "In Re Eichmann: Dilemma of Law and Morality" (1961) 55 *A.J.I.L.* 307 at pp. 355-358; *cf.*, Skhlar, "Legalism" (1964) at pp. 151 *et seq.*

rights. The rights were affirmed at the same time as penalties were imposed on those leaders and other functionaries in the Nazi state for breaching them.

It is proposed in this essay to examine certain concepts of natural law in the writings of two leading schoolmen [1a] Aquinas and Suarez which seem to be of fundamental importance in the development of the idea of human rights which control the exercise of sovereign authority and then to see in what way the Nuremberg Trials have affirmed such supra-positive norms.

I. The Relationship between Lex Naturalis and Ius Gentium

One of the major issues which recurs in the works of the medieval scholars is this. Is there a basic human nature which affords a certain standard for human action or is there an everchanging human nature prescribing different standards of action for different historical epochs? The answer to this question is to be found in the analysis of the concept of the *ius gentium*.

The Augustinian school, which found favour with Duns Scotus and William of Occam, had propounded a theory which seemed to take away the very foundation of the natural law as a continuing body of rules. This school inclined to the view that human nature could be considered both in its *status innocentiae* and in its fallen state: the *lex naturalis* endured in the former state, the *ius gentium* in the latter. Such an interpretation, of course, presents a definite picture of mankind: once upon a time a perfect idyllic state existed where freedom abounded, where there was no coercion and where men *shared* the fruits of the earth. Such a state had been radically affected through

[1a] The schoolmen were the medieval philosophers and theologians of the period between the eleventh and sixteenth centuries who speculated on the nature of man and society as well as on "things divine." Aquinas of course is the leading exponent of this tradition of thought which has affinity with the realism of Aristotle. Suarez is associated with the second flowering of scholasticism in Spain in the sixteenth century. While coordinating their philosophical conclusions within the framework of their Christian theology they nevertheless recognized the autonomy of the secular order. It is true that in one sense of the term the word "tradition" may not entirely encompass the divergences in thinking of Aquinas and, for example, Duns Scotus but a broader use of the term would enable us to use it to describe the thought of Aquinas adapted and modified as it was by Suarez and others.

man turning to evil. Bound now by positive institutions, his liberty is often denied him and the fruits of the earth have been divided.[2]

Aquinas approaches the question in a different manner. He distinguishes between a preceptive form of natural law and a permissive form. Natural law prescribes that one must perform or abstain from performing certain actions, but it also permits or recognizes as valid certain other things which benefit mankind.[3] Suarez mentions a third category: where the natural law merely favours a certain state of affairs.[4]

The question remains: what is the relationship between the *ius gentium* and natural law? If natural law permits common ownership, while the institution of private property has been introduced by the *ius gentium*, can it be said that the natural law is changed or is in conflict with the *ius gentium*? The answer to this question depends on the status which one attributes to the *ius gentium*.

Aquinas' treatment of the *ius gentium* is not at all satisfactory. He wavers between the opinion which regards the *ius gentium* as those precepts which are common to man alone, and the opinion which associates the *ius gentium* with the natural law as a collection of remote conclusions dependent on an existing *status quo*.[5] In the *Summa Theologica* article 4 of Q.95, Pt. 1-11, he compares the various ways in which positive law is derived from the law and distinguishes the *ius gentium (conclusio)* from the *ius civile (determinatio)*:

> to the law of nations belong those things which are derived from the law of nature, as conclusions from premises, such as just buyings and sellings, and the like, without which men cannot live together, and these are part of the law of nature, since man is a social animal. But those things which are derived from the law of nature by way of particular determination, belong to the civil law, according as each state decides what is best for itself.

However, in another place he switches to a definition, according to which the *ius gentium* is equated with that part of the natural law which is common to man only, although at the same time he asserts that the *ius gentium* is grounded on some type of utility.[6] In these two

[2] Villey, *Leçons D'Histoire De La Philosophie De Droit* 142-43 (1957).

[3] *Summa Theologica*, I-II, p. 94, art. 5, ad 3.

[4] *De Legibus* Bk. 2, ch. 14, s. 6. He speaks of a state of affairs which has its foundation in *conditione naturali*, for example, that a son should inherit from a father who dies intestate, and the practice of giving credence to two witnesses.

[5] Senn, *De La Justice et Du Droit* 58 (1927).

[6] S-T, II-II, q. 57, art. 3.

articles at least three meanings are given to the concept: 1) that it is the social part of the natural law, 2) that it is the natural law in so far as that is common to man alone, 3) that is consists of rules based on utility.

To the reader, it may seem as if there are a number of distinctions which do not give any precise standard by which he may judge the *ius gentium*. Let us try to see why Aquinas emphasizes the features mentioned above. In the first place, it seems, he was drawing attention to the development of social institutions which enabled men to live harmoniously together. At the same time he was troubled by the "naturalistic" view (which was closely associated with a picture of an original state of innocence) according to which a body, not so much of rules, but of rights, existed at some time or other, but had given way to the harsh realities of social intercourse and even conflict when there was a need for the reconciliation and limitation of these rights. Finally in attributing to the *ius gentium* the status of rather remote conclusions he was drawing attention to the simplicity of the original *status naturae* as compared with the complicated system of rules to which social intercourse had given rise.

It is only when we turn to the discussion of the *ius gentium* in the *De Legibus* of Suarez that we find a sustained attempt to get rid of these ambiguities and to give an autonomous status to the *ius gentium*. Suarez blatantly refuses to accept the notion, implicit in certain parts of Aquinas' discussion of a dualistic natural law. We cannot, he says, conceive of man outside of social intercourse. Laws and rules, rights *and* duties, are therefore necessary to enable him to live in peace and justice with his neighbour.[7] There was no need to set up a secondary natural law to deal with the "social" question and consequently no need to consider the *ius gentium* to be the result of a complicated deductive process. What was important was to consider man and society as they presented themselves to the observer.[8]

In saying this, Suarez was emphasizing two very important features. He was aware that society had the capacity to develop and had developed, and he recognized the importance of various institutions based on a certain utility which facilitated the intercourse of the members of

[7] See *De Legibus*, 2, 17, 9.

[8] *Ibid.* For a discussion of Suarez's treatment of *ius gentium* see Barcia Trelles, "Les Théologiens Espagnoles du XVI siècle et L'École Moderne du Droit International," *Academie De Droit International, Recueil Des Cours*, Vol. I, p. 441-71 (1933).

any society. Such institutions, however, did not have an absolute character; their status and existence was the outcome of social recognition rather than of the demands of nature.[9] Once established, they did have a certain degree of continuity. They were distinguished from what was the subject-matter of civil law on the ground that they were not instituted by one nation but by most nations by mutual imitation.[10]

Among the examples which Suarez gives to demonstrate the existence of the *ius gentium* are institutions which pertain to the law of the state (such as prescription) and institutions which pertain to intercourse between nations, the *ius inter gentes* (such as the right to wage a just war).[11] Aquinas had paid attention only to the former type and had little conception of a *ius inter gentes* because he was thinking in terms of a *civitas maxima* – the Holy Roman Empire. By the seventeenth century the Empire was no longer the universal institution it had been. The era of the national state had arrived. Suarez is one of the first to recognize this second type of *ius gentium* and even to attribute to it a closer relationship with natural law than the former type.

> Communities have need of some system of law whereby they may be directed and properly ordered with regard to this kind of intercourse and association ... For just as in one state or province law is introduced by custom, so among the human race as a whole it was possible for laws to be introduced by the habitual conduct of nations. This was more feasible because the matters found within the law in question are few, very closely related to natural law and most easily deduced therefrom in a manner so advantageous and so in harmony with nature itself that while this derivation may not be self-evident, that is, not essentially and absolutely required for moral rectitude, it is nevertheless quite in accord with nature, and universally acceptable for its own sake.[12]

On the other hand, the first type of *ius gentium* embodied precepts which did not have for their immediate end the harmonious fellowship of nations but were directed to the internal organization of a state. Nevertheless, says Suarez:

> they are of such a nature that, in the possession of similar usages or laws, almost all nations agree with one another, or at least they resemble one

[9] *De Legibus* 2, 19, 2.
[10] *Ibid.* at s. 6.
[11] *Id.* at s. 8.
[12] *Id.* at s. 9. Barcia Trelles, *op. cit.*, at 462-69.

another, at times in a general manner, and at times specifically, so to speak.[13]

It is clear that this type of *ius gentium* is in no way founded upon something which has always existed. It is the product of historical development and must be seen in this light. And yet Suarez asserts that, once these customs are established, natural law would seem to incline to their recognition as benefiting the existing state of mankind. But this does not imply any permanence, for circumstances might change and a new rule develop. Nor does this imply moral rectitude in the precepts of the *ius gentium*.[14] The one qualification is that the *ius inter gentes* is more permanent in that it requires the consent of nearly all nations before it can be changed.[15]

Suarez's approach would seem to obviate the problem which disturbed the minds of earlier writers, namely, the growth and development of society. By rejecting the distinction between a primary and a secondary natural law, an individual and a social natural law, a natural law based on inclination and a natural law based on intricate deduction, he paved the way for an approach to the natural law and the *ius gentium* which preserves their autonomous characteristics. Based on custom and utility, the *ius gentium* has no longer an absolute character; it is the product of historical development, even though it is true to say that looked at from the point of view of its usefulness to a present state of society it is approved by the natural law.

There remains one further issue to discuss. Suarez does speak of natural law as being changed by the *ius gentium* in so far as the *ius gentium* introduces a change in the subject matter of the natural law.[16]

The context of this assertion is his discussion of common ownership and liberty. Aquinas had offered the opinion that slavery (and private property) was a beneficent institution which had a semi-permanent status. In one article, for example, he had said:

> Considered absolutely, the fact that this particular man should be a slave rather than another man, is based, not on natural reason, but on some

[13] *De Legibus* 2, 19, 10. Contract, for example, in its general aspect, is an institution which is found in the legal systems of most nations, but it differs in so far as its forms or detail is concerned within these nations.

[14] *De Legibus* 2, 20, 7. Suarez mentions as an example of a common custom the toleration of prostitutes. *Ibid.*

[15] *Id.* at s. 8. The institution of just war may give way to a compulsory system of arbitration. See Barcia Trelles, *op. cit.*, at 470-71.

[16] *De Legibus* 2, 14, 12.

resultant utility, in that it is useful to this man to be ruled by a wiser man, and the latter to be helped by the former ... Wherefore, slavery, which belongs to the right of nations, is natural in the second way, but not in the first.[17]

Suarez, of course, draws the line between what is useful and what is natural. Accordingly, it might have been expected that he would explain slavery on the ground that it was merely a useful custom which need not necessarily be justified by recourse to the reason which Aquinas attributes to it. However, he seems to approach the problem in a different way.

It will be recalled that Suarez mentioned a permissive or concessive form of the natural law. Common ownership and liberty he says, must be understood as part of the natural law in this way:

With respect to these things, the natural law lays down no precept enjoining that they should remain in this state, rather does it leave the matter to the management of men, such management to accord with the demands of reason.

It is thus permissible, he says, for men to introduce rules and institutions of their own making to regulate the exercise of those things which natural law permits.[18]

It seems to us that Suarez is here making a distinction between natural law and natural rights.[19] Indeed in the very opening of his discussion of the *ius gentium* he notes a distinction between *ius utile* and *ius legale*. The former he points out has to do with a faculty or right of doing something.[20] It is not until he faces the liberty and common ownership questions that he reverts to this distinction. The natural law of dominion, he says, has conferred on man the power over his liberty, but in so far as man thereby has a claim to the enjoyment of something, nothing is said of the conditions under which the right may be exercised.[21] The natural law of dominion is different from preceptive natural law, continues Suarez, in that "it consists of a certain fact,

[17] S-T, II-II, q. 57, art. 3, ad 2.

[18] *De Legibus* 2, 14, 6.

[19] See Rommen, *The Natural Law in the Renaissance Period*, 24 Notre Dame Lawyer, 460, 483-89 (1948-49). Gierke, *Political Theories of the Middle Ages* 81-82 (1938).

[20] *De Legibus* 2, 17, 2. "Jus enim interdum significat moralem facultatem ad rem aliquam, vel in re, sive sit verum dominium, sive aliqua participatio ejus, quod est proprium objectum justitiae." *Ibid.*

[21] Suarez uses the word *ius* here interchangeably with *facultas* and *actio*.

that is, a certain condition or habitual relation of things." [22] Such a condition may change, as distinct from the precepts of the nature which may never change. Natural law protected common ownership while property was held in common. When property was divided the *ius naturale utile* was to that extent modified.[23] As far as slavery was concerned, this was not even an institution of the *ius gentium*: it was merely a part of positive penal law. Consequently, liberty was still positively part of the natural law.[24]

The fundamental position is that the *ius gentium* may detract from the plenitude resident in natural rights. Perhaps we could say that Suarez was on the brink of recognizing the whole question of natural rights and their dependence on an ordered system of relationships (e.g. restriction of liberty of one in the interest of all). This would lead to the question of natural rights and positive rights.

However, he speaks of natural rights only in the context of liberty and property.[25] Could it not be said that natural rights are also existent as far as the other precepts of the natural law are concerned? If natural law forbids murder, ought not we to recognize a right to life? In one part of his work, Suarez admits that prescription and concession are related. But he does not carry this thought to completion. If indeed we assert that other precepts of the natural law are connected with rights, it would seem that such rights also would be subject to limitation.

It seems that even if we do admit the full category of natural rights, the problem of "change" or of circumscription can be viewed in the same way as we viewed preceptive natural law – on the collision of duties pattern. In many cases there will be no question of the non-recognition of these rights. The right to life invariably subsists. In a few cases one or other of these rights may not be applicable in the circumstances. The felon is deprived of his liberty, because the community has the right to be protected from his actions. In such cases, a judgment has to be made as to which right is to be accorded superiority. It is precisely this judgment which is within the province of *ius gentium* and is ultimately positive law to make.

[22] *De Legibus*, 2, 14, 16, 17 and 18.

[23] I.e. when the right of private property came into existence.

[24] *De Legibus* 2, 18, 9. It is clear that Suarez is adverse to attributing to slavery the status of a universal custom.

[25] However Suarez hints at the "right to life." "Nam etiam natura dedit homini vitam quoad ejus ac pessessionem." *De Legibus* 2, 14, 18.

The duty of obeying positive law

In so far as the natural law and the *ius gentium* constituted the framework within which the civil legislator operated, it will now be appropriate to examine in some detail the relationship between enacted law and this body of higher law, and in particular the nature of the duty cast upon the citizen when confronted with an iniquitous law.

The following passage indicates the general scholastic view that the obligation to obey the law was to be derived more from the subject matter of the law than from the sanction attached to it.

> ... The notion of law contains two things, first that it is a rule of human acts; secondly that it has coercive power. Therefore a man may be subject to the law in two ways. First, as the regulated is subject to the regulator and in this way whoever is subject to a power is subject to the law framed by that power ... Secondly, a man is said to be subject to a law as the coerced is subject to the coercer. In this way the virtuous and the righteous are not subject to the law, but only the wicked. Because coercion is contrary to the will; the will of the good is in harmony with the law ...[26]

In this passage Aquinas points out that only those who are unwilling to obey the rule of law are subject to the penalty which the rule imposes. Those who are willing to obey it and do in fact obey it are not subject to the penalty.

On the other hand, it could be argued, that even if we accept this distinction, there still does not seem to be any reason for saying that one is *morally* bound by the law, for a person may submit to such a rule without considering that he is under any moral obligation to obey it. Suarez does examine this objection. In his view it is necessary to distinguish an immediate from a mediate effect of law; the prescription or prohibition of an action on the one hand and on the other hand the good which is achieved through such prescription or prohibition.[27]

The important thing is that these two effects, in Suarez's mind, are not separated from one another: execution of the rule is bound up with good action. It is for this reason that Suarez considers that the

[26] S-T, I-II, 96, 5.

[27] *De Legibus*, 3, 15, 14. He points out that even a permissive rule of law is associated with obligation. It binds not, of course, the person in whom the permission is vested, but other persons both private and official to recognize the exercise of the permitted right. On this matter see J. Dabin, *General Theory of Law* (Twentieth Century Legal Philosophy Series, Vol. IV) 273.

sanction which accompanies the rule is, on its own, an insufficient moral reason for obedience:

Coercion without the power of binding in conscience either is morally impossible, seeing that its justification is based on fault, or certainly is insufficient because in many important cases it would not adequately promote the ends of society.[28]

In this passage, Suarez makes two important points. First of all he considers that the sanction is an insufficient moral justification of obedience. A penalty, he says, ought not to be imposed on a person unless he is in fault. Clearly when one is judging fault (*culpa*) the standards embodied in the legal rule itself which imposes liability in this or that case do not determine the issue, for one must have recourse to a standard by which the legal rule itself may be judged. Therefore, it can be asserted that something over and above the penalty must be present before obedience to a rule of positive law can be morally justified.[29]

The second reason to which Suarez has recourse is a *factual* one, or perhaps we can say a *sociological* one. In many cases, he points out, the fear of a penalty will not by itself secure obedience. Perhaps he was thinking of cases where the potential lawbreaker may commit the illegal act without fear of detection, and of cases where, because of the weakness of the law-enforcing agency, rules may be broken with impunity.

One could say that mere fear alone, while having an auxiliary effect in compelling obedience, is merely the negative facet of the whole problem of "law-abidingness." A subject's motive in obeying a rule of law may be compounded of a mixture of self-regarding and altruistic motives, in which fear may play a great part.[30] If however we seek a moral justification for obedience, we must look to the normal good-intentioned citizen. What ought to attract him to obedience is the

[28] *De Legibus*, 3, 21, 8. Of course, authority without power is ineffectual so far as political government is concerned.

[29] See A. P. D'Entrèves, "The Case for Natural Law Re-examined" (1956) 1 *Natural Law Forum* 5, at 27. And see H. Rommen, *The Natural Law* (4th printing, 1955) 200-201: "Compulsion is an element of wrong rather than of right."

[30] For a discussion of the motives for obedience see J. Bryce, 2 *Studies in History and Jurisprudence* (1901). Ch. 9, and Appendix. Bryce, however, does not satisfactorily distinguish between motive and justification. See also A. L. Goodhart *English Law and the Moral Code* (1953) 18-28.

value of the rule itself and its place in the legal system of his country.[31]

But there is some difficulty in this position in relation to all rules of positive law. Suarez in certain places is inclined to entertain the idea of a mere *culpa civilis* with respect to rules of positive law the subject-matter of which is contingent and related to temporary needs of the community. In such cases the obligation of the citizen will be merely to submit to the penalty which attaches to such a rule as distinct from obeying the rule itself.[32] As against this it could be said that it will be very difficult to draw the line between the minor type of rule and that which has more permanent value. The minor type of rule, when viewed as a rule functioning in relation to the legal system as a whole, assumes an importance which does not exist if it is evaluated in isolation from the system.[33]

Finally is must be pointed out that, although the schoolmen regarded obedience to positive law as morally necessary, they did not think that obedience must be accompanied by a perfect moral disposition in the subject. The obligation was not one of obedience *ex mero motu*.[34] The citizen fulfils his obligation even though he grudgingly obeys a law which he finds to be contrary to his personal interests; although, of course, this attitude of mind is less laudable than that of the public-minded citizen who accepts the law on its merits.

* * *

We have considered the nature of the duty of obedience to positive law: it is now necessary to examine the limits of this duty of obedience. The schoolmen are agreed that, subject to an important exception to be referred to, the citizen is under no duty to obey an unjust law.

[31] It is interesting to note that the word "sanction" has more than one meaning. It is often used to indicate the penalty which is attached to a rule and which compels obedience. But it can also mean that the rule itself is good or in accordance with some higher standard. See Miriam T. Rooney, *Law, Lawlessness and Sanction* (1937) 12, and F. Brentano, *On the Knowledge of Right and Wrong* (1902) 5: "Sanction signifies making fast. Now a law may be fixed in a double sense: It may be fixed in the sense of becoming law, as when a proposed law receives its ratification on the part of the highest legislative authority; secondly, in the sense of being rendered more effectual by attaching to it positive punishments, perhaps also rewards."

[32] *De Legibus*, 3, 22, 10 and 5, 4, 2-13.

[33] For a recent discussion of the concept of a "purely penal law" see Bayne, *Conscience Obligation and the Law* (1966).

[34] *De Legibus*, 3, 29, 1-12.

Human law has the nature of law in so far as it partakes of right reason; and it is clear that, in this respect, it is derived from the eternal law. But in so far as it deviates from reason, it is called an unjust law, and has the nature not of law, but of violence.[35]

However, the unjust law has this similarity to just laws; it issues from the body which has legislative authority in the community and it is the intention of that body to bind the members of that community.[36]

The schoolmen distinguish two types of unjust laws. The first type is that which violates a precept of the natural law; the second is that which is not directed to the common good, which is beyond the legislative competence of the legislator, or which imposes an unfair burden on the citizen.[37] The words "intrinsic" and "instrumental" may be used to distinguish these forms of injustice in positive law.[38] A rule which is contrary to a precept of the natural law as such must not be obeyed under any circumstances.[39] As for the second type of unjust law it does not bind in conscience unless obedience would cause scandal or disturbance "for which cause a man should yield his right." [40]

Let us examine these forms of injustice in greater detail. As Suarez points out, the first type of injustice exists where the very content of the rule of positive law is unjust. The example given is a rule of positive law prescribing idolatry – a rule which imposes a duty on the citizens to worship false gods.[41] Equally, however, a law contravening other fundamental human values such as life, liberty or property would fall within this category of injustice. In so far as the natural law requires that these values be recognized by the lawgiver, a rule of posi-

[35] *S-T*, I-II, 93, 3 ad 2. See also *De Legibus*, 1, 9, 11. A rule of positive law may, however, justly permit something which is prohibited by the natural law, e.g. prostitution; *S-T*, I-II, 93, 3 ad 3; *De Legibus*, 1, 9, 6. But it cannot prohibit what is ordained, or ordain what is prohibited, by the natural law.

[36] *S-T*, I-II, 92, 1 ad 4; 3 ad 2.

[37] *S-T*, I-II, 96, 4. *De Legibus*, 1, 9, 13.

[38] *De Legibus*, 1, 9, *passim*.

[39] *S-T*, I-II, 96, 4. *De Legibus*, 1, 9, 11. It would seem that the unjust law would comprise any rule or order emanating from a state official, not merely the rule which emanates from the legislature.

[40] *S-T*, I-II, 96, 4. *De Legibus*, 1, 9, 20. It must be pointed out that the intrinsically unjust law does not bind either in conscience or *in foro externo*, i.e. it has no legal validity. However, the instrumentally unjust law may be obligatory *in foro externo* although not in conscience.

[41] *S-T*, I-II, 96,4.

tive law denying or disregarding such values cannot bind. Of course, the natural law does not prescribe that life, liberty, property and other human values be recognized as inherent in individuals under all circumstances. The precepts of the natural law are endowed with a certain "openness." The rights of the individual are subject to curtailment by the laws of the State where a just cause exists.[42] The existence and application of such laws does not, of course, infringe the natural law; on the contrary they are required by it where the appropriate circumstances exist.

The second type of unjust law mentioned by the schoolmen is of an instrumental nature. While the content of the rule of positive law may in itself be just, its form or manner of operation may create injustice. This may happen in one of three ways. The law may not be directed to the common good: it may be framed in such a way as to impose an unjust burden on a certain section of the community; or it may be framed in such a way as to confer an unjust benefit on members of that community. Such a law leads to instrumental injustice. However, as Suarez points out,[43] many laws actually have the effect of imposing burdens on some sections of the community which are not imposed on others.[44] This, he says, is justifiable when it is required by the common good:

> It frequently happens that what is expedient for the whole community will be harmful to this or that individual, but, since the common good is to be preferred to the private good whenever the two cannot exist simultaneously, therefore, laws are made in absolute form for the sake of the common good, and take no account of individual cases.[45]

But even in such a case the harm to private individuals should not be multiplied so as to outweigh the advantages accruing to the community as a whole and exceptions should be included if necessary so that the law can be administered as far as possible in a just manner.[46] Moreover, in deciding whether to enact legislation of a remedial nature, the legislator must decide whether the removal of one evil may lead to greater evils. "A given useful result must be attained in such a

[42] *E.g.*, for action amounting to criminal conduct.
[43] *De Legibus*, 1, 9, 13.
[44] *E.g.*, a taxation law.
[45] *Ibid.*, 1, 7, 14.
[46] *Ibid.*, 1, 7, 14.

fashion as not to impede thereby the attainment of a result still more useful." [47]

Secondly, a law may infringe the canons of distributive justice by imposing burdens or conferring benefits on citizens without regard to the individual capacities of the citizens.[48] This second type of injustice is complementary to the first type. The common good often demands a disproportion in the burdens which are imposed on various groups within the community. In Suarez's opinion, distributive justice is bound up with practicality. Positive law should ordain what is readily attainable by members of the society as a whole and should not prescribe what is difficult or impossible of performance by the ordinary citizen. Therefore, the legislator should keep in mind the customs of the community – the natural aptitudes and attitudes of the members who make up the community – in passing laws.[49]

Thirdly, an injustice may occur when the "legislator" acts outside his authority in making a law.[50] Suarez points out that in so far as the power of making laws is vested in the body (monarch or popular assembly) holding supreme power in the country, a rule which is made otherwise than in accordance with the expressed will of this body cannot bind. The head of the household for example cannot bind the members of his household in respect of matters which fall within legislative authority. An inferior official within the State who acts outside his jurisdiction cannot bind the citizen, nor can a foreign ruler oblige the citizens of a country over which he does not possess legislative authority.[51] In all such cases the rule which issues is contrary to commutative justice and is a form of instrumental injustice.

The crucial difference between intrinsically and instrumentally unjust laws lies in this fact: that, while an intrinsically unjust law cannot bind the citizen who is under a duty to disobey it in all cases, the instrumentally unjust law will bind if injury would be done to peace and order within the community through disobedience.[52] In other words, in the case of instrumental injustice, the citizen merely has a limited *right* to disobey, which must be forfeited where the consequences of

[47] *Ibid.*, 1, 7, 15.
[48] *Ibid.*, 1, 9, 16.
[49] *Ibid.*, 1, 9, 17-19.
[50] *Ibid.*, 1, 8, passim.
[51] *Ibid.*, 1, 8, 8-9.
[52] This seems to be an application of the doctrine that where two evils will result from an act, the lesser evil is to be preferred.

disobedience would adversely affect the standard of law-abidingness in the community. In many legal systems the injustice in the rules of positive law will be found to be of this second type. The citizen aggrieved by one or other of the variety of rules which impose unfair burdens or are directed to the good of only one section of the community, might be inclined to disobey such a rule. On reflection, however, he will put himself in the place of his fellow citizens and will recognize the disastrous effects to social stability if others acted in the way in which he felt inclined.

In the case both of intrinsic and instrumental injustice, the right of disobedience only exists where the law is manifestly unjust. The presumption is always in favour of the validity of a law made by a duly constituted authority:

> ... partly because the legislator is in possession of a superior right, partly also because he is directed by superior counsel and may be moved by general reasons hidden from his subjects, and partly because, if this presumption in his favour did not exist, the subjects would assume an excessive privilege to disregard the laws ... since the latter can hardly be so just as that it is impossible for them to be treated as doubtful by some individuals, apparently for plausible reasons.[53]

The anarchist then has no standing in the thought of the schoolmen.

Finally, we may refer to the types of disobedience which, in the schoolmen's opinion, would be justifiable in reaction to an unjust law. Disobedience may take the form of passive disobedience (nonviolent disobedience), active disobedience (disobedience accompanied by force) or, in extreme cases, insurrection (revolt against the legislative authority). Both passive and active disobedience would be justifiable in cases of intrinsically unjust laws but only passive disobedience would be justifiable in the case of instrumentally unjust laws. The reason for this distinction lies in the fact that in those cases in which violence is used against an instrumentally unjust law, greater evil and harm would be done to the community as compared with the benefit to the individual concerned.[54] Insurrection, on the other hand, is only justifiable where the legislator has behaved in a tyrannical manner, that is to say, where he has enacted a number of intrinsically unjust laws. In such a case, the legal system as a whole has become corrupt and it is the right of the community to rise up against the upholders of

[53] *De Legibus*, 1, 9, 11.
[54] See L. Duguit, 3 *Traité de droit constitutionnel* (1930) 790 *et seq.*

the system. The proviso is that such a right ought not to be exercised where a greater evil would result from the revolt than from the continuance of the tyrannical system.[55]

II. The Nuremberg Trials and Iniquitous Laws

At the Nuremberg War Crimes Trials, the theoretical principles outlined above became a concrete reality. Both the International Military Tribunal and the various tribunals which conducted the Nuremberg Subsequent Proceedings developed the concept of the crime against humanity and in doing so laid down the limits of obedience of the subject to the State in terms of obedience to a higher law which had been incorporated into the positive international legal order.[56]

In the trial of the major war criminals before the I.M.T., the accused were charged with the commission of war crimes and crimes against humanity.[57] The Tribunal stated that war crimes had been committed on a vast scale never before seen in the history of war.

> There can be no doubt that the majority of them arose from the Nazi conception of "total war," with which the aggressive wars were waged. For in this conception of "total war," the moral ideas underlying the conventions which seek to make war more humane are no longer regarded as having force or validity. Everything is made subordinate to the overmastering dictates of war. Rules, regulations, assurances and treaties, all alike, are of no moment; and so, freed from the restraining influence of international law, the aggressive war is conducted by the Nazi leaders in the most barbaric way. Accordingly, war crimes were committed when and whenever the Fuehrer and his close associates thought them to be advantageous.[58]

The slave labour policy – the persecution of racial groups – the confiscation of property on a gigantic scale – all these acts characterized the occupation policies of the Nazis.[59]

Some doubt has arisen as to the actual scope of the crime against

[55] *S-T*, I-II, 42, 2 ad 3.

[56] See generally Woetzel, *The Nuremberg Trials in International Law*; *cf.*, Skhlar, *Legalism*, pp. 151 *et seq.*

[57] See Garcia-Mora, *Crimes against Humanity and the Principles of Non-Extradition of Political Offenders*. 62 Michigan Law Review (1964) 927 at pp. 928-34.

[58] *Nazi Conspiracy and Aggression - Opinion and Judgment of the International Military Tribunal* (Washington, 1947) pp. 56-7. (Hereinafter cited as *Judgment*).

[59] The evidence relating to Nazi atrocities is found in *Judgment*, 57-82.

humanity, which is defined in Article 6 (c) of the Charter. It appears to contain certain novel principles. They are found in the phrases:

(a) before or during the war,
(b) against any civilian population,
(c) whether or not in violation of the domestic law of the country where perpetrated.

The first principle is revolutionary, for it signifies that international law provides sanctions against individuals in time of peace not only in time of war. The existence of this principle in the I.M.T. Charter taken in conjunction with the third principle would seem to indicate that international law can override the sovereignty of the state to which the perpetrator of the crime owes allegiance. Of course, there existed the practical limitation that the acts constituting the crime against humanity must be connected in some way with a crime within the jurisdiction of the Tribunal (either a crime against peace or a war crime).[60]

The use of the words "against any civilian population" implies that protection is extended not only to civilians of occupied territories but also to subjects whose own state violates international law. Belligerent occupation (an essential condition to the commission of a war crime) is not necessary. The use of the word "population" seems to imply participation in a programme directed against groups and not isolated acts against individuals.[61]

Unfortunately, the International Military Tribunal did not enter into a detailed examination of the crime against humanity.

It made the following observation:

> With regard to crimes against humanity, there is no doubt whatever that political opponents were murdered in Germany before the war, and that many of them were kept in concentration camps in circumstances of great horror and cruelty. The policy of terror was certainly carried out on a vast scale, and in many cases was organized and systematic. The policy of persecution, repression, and murder of civilians in Germany before the war of 1939, who were likely to be hostile to the Government, was most ruthlessly carried out. The persecution of Jews during the same period is established beyond all doubt. To constitute crimes against humanity, the acts relied on before the outbreak of the war must have been in execution of, or in connection with, a crime within the jurisdiction of the Tribunal.

[60] See *History of the United Nations War Crimes Commission and the Development of the Laws of War* (Ed. Wright, London, 1948) hereinafter cited as *History*.

[61] *Ibid.*

The Tribunal is of the opinion that revolting and horrible as many of these crimes were, it has not been satisfactorily proved that they were done in execution of, or in connection with, any such crime. The Tribunal therefore cannot make a general declaration that the acts before 1939 were crimes against humanity within the meaning of the Charter, but from the beginning of the war in 1939 war crimes were committed on a vast scale which were also crimes against humanity; and insofar as the inhumane acts charged in the indictment, and committed after the beginning of the war, did not constitute war crimes, they were all committed in execution of, or in connection with, the aggressive war, and therefore constituted crimes against humanity.[62]

The most significant part of this statement is that where the Court refused to make a general declaration as to crimes against humanity. Several writers, misunderstanding this statement, have written as though no act committed before the outbreak of war could be a crime against humanity. Leventhal thinks that the Tribunal was reluctant to give a broad application to crimes against humanity because of the novelty of the offence: for this reason it dealt with them as analogous to recognized offences against international law.[63] But an examination of the convictions of Streicher and Seyss-Inquart shows that the convictions were based primarily on acts committed before 1939. Streicher as Editor of "Der Sturmer" had in the immediate pre-war years incited the German people to the heights of intolerance with his antisemitic articles. It was due to his ideological warfare that the Nazi persecution of the Jews was intensified. Frequent references are made in the Judgment to his responsibility for acts of violence against the Jews, especially the demolition of the Nuremberg synagogue in 1938.[64]

Seyss-Inquart had been a high Nazi official in Austria between May 1937 and September 1939 when he was appointed Chief of Civil Administration of South Poland. The Tribunal noted that he had cooperated with the S.D. in the deportation of Jews to the east as well as allowing the Gestapo to dispose of political opponents to the Nazi regime in Austria.[65] These acts were carried out in execution of a crime against peace, namely the annexation of Austria, and therefore fell within the scope of Article 6 (c).[66]

Dr. Schwelb considers that the I.M.T. took jurisdiction over certain

[62] *Judgment*, 84.
[63] "The Nuremberg Verdict," 60 *Harvard Law Review* 857, 886 (1946-7).
[64] *Judgment*, 129.
[65] *Judgment*, 154.
[66] *History*, 201.

activities occurring before 1939.[67] His conclusions are as follows:

(a) The I.M.T. stressed the notion that the crime must be in execution of a crime within the jurisdiction of the Tribunal. Consequently it made no general declaration with respect to pre-1939 acts. But with respect to individual accused, it was not prevented from treating acts committed before 1939 as crimes against humanity.[68]

(b) The Tribunal treated the crime against humanity as a kind of subsidiary provision to be applied whenever any particular act was not specifically regulated by the Hague Regulations. It was a type of *clausula generalis,* the purpose of which was to make sure that inhumane acts violating general principles of the laws of all civilized nations committed in connection with war would not go unpunished.[69]

(c) The Nuremberg Trial did not signify the recognition of the crime against humanity applicable in war and peace, irrespective of the nationality of the individual victim.[70]

(d) The Nuremberg Trial did not sweep away the sovereignty of the German State. The one state sovereignty involved, that of the German Reich, had disappeared with the disappearance of Germany as a sovereign state. The laws and customs of war were not a restriction on state sovereignty – they merely regulated the relationship between a state and persons who were not subject to its sovereignty.[71]

Agreement can be expressed with the first conclusion but not with the other conclusions. Concerning conclusion (b), it is clear that in its discussion of the evidence, the Tribunal was aware of the massive proportions of the offences committed against the people of the occupied countries. They were acts of a more universal and sinister character, and more dehumanizing, than the simple acts mentioned in the Hague Regulations. Streicher, for example, was not charged with having committed specific acts of murder or robbery, but with the instigation of radical persecution. This was the crime against humanity par excellence – the doctrine of racial supremacy was oriented towards the annihilation of ethnic groups.[72] In this respect, the crime

[67] "Crimes against Humanity," 23 *British Year Book of International Law,* (1946) 178.

[68] *Ibid.*, 205.

[69] Schwelb, *op. cit.*, 206.

[70] *Ibid.*

[71] *Ibid.*, 207.

[72] See Radin, *International Crimes,* 32 Iowa Law Review (1946) 33, 48. He considers that the ideological crimes of the Nazi philosophers (such as Rosenberg) were more serious than the acts of "trigger-men" such as Kaltenbrunner.

against humanity was not treated as a subsidiary crime.[73]

Conclusions (c) and (d) may be taken together. Their essence is that German sovereignty remained unimpaired in the light of the crime against humanity. The crime against humanity was declared to extend to "any civilian population" and to apply "wether or not in violation of the domestic law" of the country to which the accused owed allegiance. As was pointed out above, in the case of Streicher the Tribunal seems to have found the latter guilty of crimes against humanity committed against German nationals before 1939. The authorization of German law proved to be incapable of operating as a defence to a contravention of international law. The only practical limitation was that the crime must be in execution of or in connection with a crime within the jurisdiction of the Tribunal (a crime against peace or a war crime).[74]

So far as the Nuremberg Subsequent Proceedings are concerned, an important discussion of the limits of obedience to sovereign power is to be found in the *Justice Case*.[75]

The *Justice Trial* opened at Nuremberg in February 1947 and concluded in December of that year. Principal accused were Schlegelberger, Under Secretary in the Ministry for Justice, Klemm, State Secretary in the Ministry, Lautz, Chief Public Prosecutor of the Reich, Cuhorst, Chief Justice of the Special Court at Stuttgart, and Rothaugh, Chief Justice of the Special Court at Nuremberg.

The essence of the prosecution's charge was that the accused had participated in acts which constituted judicial murder and that, having destroyed law and justice in Germany, they utilized "the emptied forms of legal process for persecution, enslavement and extermination on a vast scale." [76] This took the form of participation in the enactment and enforcement of certain statutes, decrees and orders which were criminal both in inception and execution, and of active assistance to the S.S., Gestapo, S.D., and criminal police.[77]

The evidence before the Tribunal showed that the Ministry of

[73] See *Judgment*, 66-7.

[74] The discussion will be resumed when certain cases decided under Control Council Law 10 have been discussed.

[75] A report of the case is to be found in Vol. 6, *Law Reports of Trials of War Criminals* - Selected and prepared by the United Nations War Crimes Commission (London, 1948) pp. 1-110 (hereinafter cited T.W.C.).

[76] Taylor, Final Report to the Secretary of the Army on the War Crimes Trials held under Control Council Law No. 10 at 69.

[77] 6 *T.W.C.*, 2-3.

Justice and the courts were equipped for terroristic functions in support of the Nazi regime. Since 1933, the judicial system had deteriorated. Two main processes were evident. Firstly, the power of life and death was more broadly vested in the courts; secondly, the penal laws were extended in such indefinite terms as to vest in the courts the widest discretion as to the choice of law and the construction of that law. Statutes dealing with criminal matters were especially vicious. Many of these established crimes by analogy, or allowed the court to decide the case in accordance with the sound sentiment of the people.[78]

Two basic rules governed the conduct of the Ministry of Justice. First of all, there was the absolute power of Hitler to enact, enforce and adjudicate law. The second was the incontestability of such law. In German legal theory, Hitler was supreme legislator, supreme judge. The device of issuing "Judge's Letters" widely used by Thierack, the Minister for Justice, was an effective means of enforcing compliance with the will of Hitler.[79] Perhaps the most significant activity of the Ministry was its participation in the *Nacht und Nebel* Plan by which persons accused of committing acts endangering the security of German occupation forces were transported to Germany to be secretly tried there.

The Court examined the development of the concept of the crime against humanity.[80] It referred to text books on international law, *inter alia*, Hyde, to prove that "the family of nations is not unconcerned with the life and experience of the private individual in his relationships with the state of which he is a national."[81] Evidence of this concern had been apparent since the First World War with the ratification of treaties protecting racial and religious minorities.

In the view of the Tribunal, Control Council Law 10 (c) should be construed to exclude isolated acts. There must be

> proof of conscious participation in systematic governmentally organised or approved procedures, amounting to atrocities and offences of that kind specified in the act and committed against populations or amounting to persecutions on political, racial, or religious grounds.[82]

Offences before 1939 were of international concern. Whether or not

[78] 6 *T.W.C.*, 6.
[79] *Ibid.*, 8.
[80] *Ibid.*, 45 *et seq.*
[81] *Ibid.*, 45.
[82] *Ibid.*, 47.

they were technical violations of the laws of war, they fell within the scope of the crime against humanity.[83]

Reference was made to the great number of documents which established the "Draconic" character of the Nazi criminal laws, and which showed that the death penalty had been imposed by courts in thousands of cases – in cases of offences against the war economy, offences committed under the *Nacht und Nebel* plan, offences committed by Poles and Jews, and offences amounting to "high treason." It was stated that in times of a national emergency the death penalty might be justifiable in the cases of crimes against the war economy.[84] However, cases where the death penalty was clearly not justifiable were those of alleged treason,[85] *Nacht und Nebel* offences,[86] and offences against the racial laws.[87]

Lemkin has summarised the Nazi interference with local law in the occupied countries. He points out that in pursuance of the "New European Order" it became necessary to deprive local courts of jurisdiction over many matters. General criminal law (based on analogy) was introduced into the occupied areas in complete disregard of Article 43 of the Hague Regulations.[88] In some instances, the occupant had declared that the authorities should not be bound by law and that certain matters should be accomplished without recourse to legal criteria.[89] The introduction of German Law into these countries could not be justified on the ground of military necessity, because the integration of the occupied countries into the "new order" was clearly a political objective and had no relation to the needs of the army of occupation. The law itself was devoid of moral content – it was based on discrimination and not on equality.

> This new conception of criminal law was a definite encroachment upon the rights of the individual citizen because it subjected him to the arbitrary opinion of the judge as to what constituted an offence. It destroyed the feeling of legal security and created an atmosphere of terrorism.[90]

One commentator has pointed out that the qualification contained

[83] *Ibid.*, 47.
[84] *Ibid.*, 51.
[85] *Ibid.*, 52-3.
[86] *Ibid.*, 53-62.
[87] *Ibid.*, 62-4.
[88] *Axis Rule in Occupied Europe*, Ch. 3, pp. 25 *et seq.*
[89] Lemkin, *op. cit.*, 30.
[90] 6 *T.W.C.*, 7, n. 1.

in Article 43 of the Hague Regulations – the qualification of military necessity – was meant to require genuine military necessity, not mere expediency.[91] The Nazi attitude was one directly opposed to this generally accepted doctrine of military necessity. It was based on the German doctrine of necessity (Kriegraison) "whose logic conduces inevitably to the abrogation of all restraints upon belligerent activity." [92]

To the extent that a defendant was shorn of the safeguards generally required by all civilized systems, a violation of Article 43 occurred. Examples of such violations would be the denial to the accused of the opportunity of pleading not guilty, of introducting evidence on his own behalf, or the imposition of excessive penalties.[93]

There is some doubt as to whether the denial of a fair trial itself is a crime against humanity. From various parts of the judgment in the *Justice Trial* one might conclude that the denial of a fair trial is itself such a crime. For example, it was said that certain cases tried by Rothaug "lacked the essential elements of legality." [94] Yet the Tribunal seemed to lay more stress on the "acts of murder, torture and illegal imprisonment and other inhumane acts," which resulted from the degradation of the judicial system.

The great contribution of the judgment in the *Justice Trial* to international jurisprudence is its recognition of the guilt of members of the legal profession for war crimes and crimes against humanity. It is not only the "triggermen" who are guilty of these crimes.

> The person who persuades another to commit murder, the person who furnishes the lethal weapon for the purpose of its commission, and the person who pulls the trigger are alle principals or accessories to the crime.[95]

The Nazi system demanded a response from every profession. The disgraceful conduct of the Judges, the Prosecutors and the Ministry of Justice was caused by their refusal to recognize the value concept of law, by their readiness to assist a political programme based on mere expediency. This was the outcome of the *German positivist tradition.*

[91] Freeman, "War Crimes by Enemy Nationals Administering Justice in Occupied Territories," 41 *A.J.I.L.* (1947) 579, 581.

[92] *Ibid.*, 584.

[93] Freeman, *op. cit.*, 609.

[94] 6 *T.W.C.*, 102.

[95] 6 *T.W.C.*, 62.

... The Nazis, faithful to the German positivist tradition, "legalized" arbitrariness by disguising their acts of political expediency as formal law . . .[96]

Yet this did not erase their guilt under international law. The very essence of their crime was that the Nazi body of law constituted a violation of international law and that participation in the enactment and enforcement of this law amounted to complicity in the crime.

The defence of superior orders

A major defence raised at the Nuremberg Trials was that the accused had acted in obedience to orders emanating from superior authority and that therefore compliance with such orders exculpated them from guilt.[97]

Article 8 of the Charter of the I.M.T. was as follows:

> The fact that the defendant acted pursuant to order of his Government or of a superior shall not free him from responsibility, but may be considered in mitigation of punishment if the tribunal determines that justice so requires.[98]

In its judgment, the International Military Tribunal pointed out that the law of nations had never recognized this defence:

> That a soldier was ordered to kill or torture in violation of the international law of war was never recognized as a defence to such acts of brutality, though, as the Charter here provides, the order may be urged in mitigation of the punishment.[99]

The true test was whether "moral choice was in fact possible." [100] Duress became the determining element. No reference was made to the question of knowledge.

On the other hand, cases decided under Control Council Law 10 would seem to confirm the conclusions reached by Lauterpacht that the defence of superior orders as such was not recognized by international law; either lack of knowledge of the illegality of the order, or coercion forcing the accused to commit the act, had to be proved.

The tribunal in the *High Command Trial* considered that the rejec-

[96] Loewenstein, "Law and the Legislative Process in Occupied Germany," 57 *Yale Law Journal* (1947-8) 724, 734.

[97] See generally Dinstein, *The Defence of "Obedience to Superior Orders" in International Law* (1965).

[98] Control Council Law 10 contained a similar provision.

[99] *Judgment*, 53.

[100] *Ibid.*, 54.

tion of the plea of superior orders followed of necessity from the fact that the acts charged in the indictment were criminal under international law. It was evident that the admission of the plea would subvert the very basis of international common law; for the excuse offered by a commander that he had acted under the authority of the national government would mean the rejection of a higher law binding individuals to the observance of an international code of conduct.[101] For the accused to escape responsibility, it had to be shown that there existed such circumstances that a reasonable man would apprehend that he was in such imminent physical peril as to deprive him of freedom to choose the right and refrain from the wrong.[102] Moreover, there was no obligation on the part of the private soldier to make a careful examination of the rules of international law. Quite clearly, he was not expected to have a collection of text-books to which resort could be made in cases of doubt.[103]

In this case, many of the accused were field commanders who had transmitted orders from the Chiefs of Staff to their corps commanders. The same general principles regarding knowledge were applicable to their case.

To establish the guilt of a field commander, it had to be shown that he had passed on an order that was criminal on its face, or that it was known by him to have been criminal.[104] A higher obligation rested on the shoulders of the higher officers whose knowledge of international law was presumed to be more comprehensive – for example, Lehmann, the Judge Advocate General, was found guilty for his participation in the drafting and composition of many orders which were handed down to field commanders.[105]

In the *Hostages Trial*, the tribunal confined itself to a discussion of the *mens rea* issue. Evidently, it was not prepared to accept the plea of duress as an excuse for the execution of thousands of hostages:

It is true that the ... rule compels a commander to make a choice between possible punishment by his lawless government for the disobedience of the illegal order of his superior officer, or that of lawful punishment for the crime under the law of nations. To choose the former in the hope that

[101] 12 *T.W.C.*, 72.
[102] *Ibid.*
[103] *Ibid.*, 73.
[104] *Ibid.*, 74.
[105] *Ibid.*, 117-8.

victory will cleanse the act of its criminal characteristics manifests only weakness of character and adds nothing to the defence.[106]

The tribunal was aware of the onerous nature of the obligation placed on the shoulders of the soldier; but the duty of obedience to international law was supreme.

In the *Milch Trial*, the tribunal stressed the obligation of the higher officers of the realm to choose whether they should obey the orders which a dictator might issue. It could not be said at the beginning – the Führer's decisions are final; we will have no voice in them; it is not for us to reason why. The defendant had argued that, once the Nazi Regime had become entrenched, he could not extricate himself and had to stay to the bitter end. But the tribunal made a categorical reply to this – the choice was between obedience to Hitler and therefore international criminal activity, and obedience to right and justice.[107]

No reference was made to the plea of duress, and the assumption is that, in the case of the leading military officials of the realm, duress can rarely, if ever, be advanced as an excuse for the commission of acts criminal under international law. While the International Military Tribunal paid lip-service to duress and moral choice, not one of the defendants in that trial was acquitted on the ground of duress. In the majority of cases, then, the plea of superior orders is reduced to a plea of lack of *mens rea*, and the question of responsibility is determined according to ordinary principles.

Closely allied with the plea of superior orders is the plea of necessity raised by the defendants in the industrialist cases. This plea is one in which the defendant offers as an excuse for his actions the circumstance that he was forced to comply with certain directives of the government, which involved serious breaches of international law, such as the use of forced labour and concentration camp inmates in factories.

At the outset, we may make a general observation that the position of a businessman is quite different from that of an ordinary soldier. As everyone knows, the soldier lives under an iron discipline – the consequences of disobeying orders are exceedingly harsh. No such discpiline exists in the case of businessmen.

The Flick, Farben and Krupp Tribunals, while accepting the plea of

[106] 8 *T.W.C.*, 51.
[107] 7 *T.W.C.*, 40-2.

necessity in general as a valid defence, differed in respect of the application of the plea. In the *Flick Trial*, the court accepted Wharton's definition of necessity:

Necessity is a defence when it is shown that the act charged was done to avoid an evil both serious and irreparable; that there was no other adequate means of escape; and that the remedy was not disproportionate to the evil.[108]

In the opinion of the Tribunal, the defence was available to certain defendants:

The defendants lived within the Reich. The Reich, through its hordes of enforcement officials and secret police, was always present, ready to go into instant action and to mete out savage and immediate punishment against anyone doing anything that could be construed as obstructing or hindering the carrying out of Governmental regulations or decrees.[109]

But proof that the defendants had voluntarily participated in the slave labour programme would negative the defence. In the case of two of the defendants (Flick and Weiss) proof was adduced to show that they had taken the intiative in certain transactions and, to that extent, they were deprived of the defence.[110]

In the *Farben Trial*, approval was given to this statement of the law. The Tribunal found that the plea of necessity could be validly raised by civilian defendants. The test to be applied was whether moral choice was possible.[111] The majority of the defendants were acquitted on this ground. However, Judge Herbert dissented vigourously. In his opinion, the evidence established that Farben officials had as a matter of policy co-operated in the slave-labour programme.

... Despite the existence of a reign of terror in the Reich, I am nevertheless convinced that compulsion to the degree of depriving the defendants of moral choice did not in fact operate as the conclusive cause of the defendants' actions, because their will coincided with the governmental solution of the situation, and the labour was accepted out of desire to, and the only means of, maintaining war production.[112]

In the *Krupp Trial*, the Tribunal, while recognising the defence, refused to allow its application to the facts of the case. In discussing the elements of the defence, it pointed out that there had to be an

[108] 9 *T.W.C.*, 19.
[109] 9 *T.W.C.*, 20.
[110] *Ibid.*, 20-1.
[111] 10 *T.W.C.*, 57.
[112] *Ibid.*, 62.

actual *bona fide* belief in danger to a particular individual – subjective, not objective, criteria were applicable.[113] Compulsion must operate upon the will of the defendant to the extent that he is thereby compelled to do what otherwise he would not have done. If the will of the accused coincided with that of the regime, the defence was not available. Evidence showed that the officials of Krupp had voluntarily participated in the slave-labour programme.[114] In any case, no irreparable evil threatened the accused. The worst fate that could have befallen them would have been the loss of their properties and positions.[115] The assumption here is that the possibility of such losses can never justify the commission of acts contrary to international law.

One might question the silence of the Flick and Farben Tribunals on this point. It is hard to see how a programme of slavery involving suffering for thousands of people and directly contrary to international law could be justified on the grounds of necessity, merely because these firms would disappear as commercial entities if their directors had been virtuous and brave enough to oppose the Nazi slave labour programme.

The cases which have been discussed support the view that international law does not recognize the plea of superior orders as a general defence. The plea has been approached from the standpoint of the general principles of criminal law, the defences of which are available to those who are charged with crimes against the law of nations. On the one hand, knowledge is required of the criminality of the order. In this respect, the ordinary soldier is under no obligation to examine minutely every order which he receives: there is, to some extent, a presumption of legality. However, if he executes an order which contravenes recognized moral standards, he incurs criminal liability.[116] On the other hand, duress will influence liability. In this respect, the Krupp Tribunal's enunciation of the elements of duress seems to be the most acceptable.

Reference may be made to the argument often raised by defence counsel in the trials to the effect that disobedience of orders would entail instant punishment, most probably death or the concentration camp. There is sufficient evidence to show that many of the higher

[113] *Ibid.*, 143.
[114] *Ibid.*, 149.
[115] *Ibid.*, 149-150.
[116] Keenan and Brown *Crimes Against International Law* (1950) 132-6.

officers openly sabotaged Hitler's orders:

Malgré l'absolutisme d'Hitler, il y a eu, sous son regne, des infractions à la discipline commune, des demissions retentissantes que n'a suivi aucune sanction. En 1941, un Brauchitsch, un von Leeb ont pu marquer leur intention de saboter les instructions du Fuhrer sur le traitement des commissaires sovietiques.[117]

It is clair that the elements of duress were absent in the majority of cases involving commanders and higher officials of the regime: the evil sought to be averted was seldom irreparable, while there were adequate means available for avoiding the execution of the order. Gilbert mentions a case in which a German captain received an order from a higher officer to the effect that he should "get rid of" seventy prisoners of war. He refused to obey this order whereupon the commanding general came down and gave the order. The captain still refused to obey it and instructed his lieutenant as follows:

I hereby order you to evacuate these prisoners to Corps, and authorise you to use your weapons if anybody tries to stop you, and I hold you personally responsible to me for their safe arrival.[118]

The prisoners were evacuated. Nothing happened to the captain.[119] If an inferior officer could brazenly refuse to carry out orders in this way, how much easier must it have been for men such as Keitel, Jodl and Milch to avoid execution of illegal orders, if not by direct refusal, then by skilful evasion.

These were the men in the inner councils, the men who planned as well as carried out; of all people the ones who might have advised, restrained, halted Hitler instead of encouraging him in his satanic courses.[120]

The most important development in the Trials was the recognition of the liability of businessmen, although it might be thought that the plea of duress was given too much latitude in the *Flick* and *Farben Trials.*[121] There are some writers who are sceptical of the existence of a principle which imposes mandatory social responsibilities on those

[117] Donnédieu de Vabres, "Le Proces de Nuremberg Devant les Principes Modernes du Droit Pénal International," *Recueil des Cours* Vol. 1, 1947, 481 at 572.

[118] *Nuremberg Diary*, (1948) 142-3.

[119] *Ibid.*

[120] *Closing Speeches of the Chief Prosecutors*, 59.

[121] See Zeck, "Nuremberg: Proceedings Subsequent to Goering and Others," 26th *Nth. Carolina Law Review*, (1947-8) 350, 388.

enjoying "private power positions." [122] Yet one cannot escape the fact that there was voluntary participation on the part of these civilians in the slave labour programme of the Nazis, which gave rise to ordinary criminal liability.[123]

It is said that the principles enunciated in the trials confront the individual with an impossible choice between obedience to "duty" and obedience to conscience – a premium is placed on cowardice and escapism in the proper carrying out of orders.[124] Criticism such as this fails to grasp the essence of the Nuremberg Trials. It was the emphasis on duty towards the international order not on service compliance with arbitrary orders of the national leaders – which characterised the trials. The cowardice prescribed was that of the official who sheltered behind the orders of a regime, whose foundations signified a disregard for the values of the international community.

CONCLUSION

A philosophical tradition operates in every legal system or positive legal order. The doctrine of *natural law* based as it is on a recognition of a higher law has in the past been accepted as a criterion for determining the ultimate validity of a positive legal order and affording a basis for resistance to such an order which violates the fundamental principles of humanity. The Nuremberg Trials stand out in this respect as a positive affirmation of the limits of state from within the international legal order.

The development of the concept of the crime against humanity and the rejection of the defence of superior orders are in effect grounded on the basic elements of the scholastic legal tradition – a definition of *lex* or "willed" law in terms of its subordination to a common law of mankind, the *ius gentium*. Thus the crime against humanity is essentially a concept which involves reference to the common dictates of humanity extending beyond a particular national framework, while the rejection of the defence of superior orders is itself derived from a recognition of the doctrine that the holders of power must justify the

[122] See Kronstein, Book Review, 53 *Columbia Law Review*, (1953) 139, 144.
[123] Reply by Taylor to Kronstein, *ibid.* 197, 208.
[124] Hankey, *Politics, Trials and Errors*, 59. Maugham, *United Nations Organisation and War Crimes*, 48.

exercise of their authority by reference to those same dictates of humanity.

The developments which the Trials set in train, or at least contributed to, are still continuing. The Genocide Convention, the Declaration of Human Rights and now the draft Covenants on Civil and Political Rights have been the result of the demand for enshrinement of basic human rights in fundamental documents which will be binding on those who wield sovereign power. In this respect the Human Rights Year may be characterized as a further positive achievement within the international legal order.

J. E. S. Fawcett

Fellow of All Souls College, Oxford

Natural Sanctions in International Law

I

To ask what are the sanctions of international law is to ask why any rule of international law is observed. The Austinian definition of a sanction, as an enforcement of obedience, may then be too narrow, if it means compulsion by some external authority. A milder and, it is believed, a not less effective criterion is proposed here, that an international sanction is whatever causes a rule or prescription of international conduct to be observed, rather than infringed or disregarded; the use or demonstration of force in some form is not then excluded, but is seen as only one of several possible causes of observance.

The difference intended here between rule and prescription is between what is and what is not law: so a "rule" is to be understood as a rule of international law, and a "prescription" as a moral, political or other form of non-legal directive to States. Correlative in part to such rules and prescriptions are international obligations, so that the statement that "State X was internationally obliged to do this" is normally equivalent to the statement that "there was a rule of international law or an international prescription that this be done," though it is only in the first case that the State could be said to be under an international legal obligation. But there are other senses of obligation, which deserve attention. There may be an obligation to take a certain course, because physically there is no alternative; or because the possible alternatives are for some overriding reasons unacceptable, which may have to be implied or imagined, as in "they were obliged to surrender" or "Austria was obliged to accept the Anschluss with Germany"; or again because the course is the only way in which one or more desired objects of social or economic policy can be obtained. Among international obligations the first of these three senses can at least for present purposes be ignored, but all three may in some circumstances merge into one another: for example, when a State finds itself obliged to make a drawing from the International Monetary Fund to correct a grave imbalance of payments it might, and probably would in different contexts, be said that there was financially no alternative, and that any alternative was politically unacceptable, and that it was the only way to achieve economic stability. Where a State is obliged to take a particular course to avoid greater evils or to achieve a desired good, its obligation may be described for present purposes as pragmatic.

But the conceptual differences that have been noted must not be allowed to obscure the fact that obligations, which depend on rule or on prescription or are pragmatic, are not mutually exclusive: a particular rule may embody a prescription, and pragmatic obligations may be transformed into a rule! Their close connection in fact is demonstrated in such disparate fields as the protection of human rights and the uses of outer space, and examples may be taken from the first.

The proposition

> No one shall be subject to torture, or to cruel, inhuman or degrading treatment or punishment

appears, on the distinction made above, as a prescription in the Universal Declaration of Human Rights, Article 5, and as a rule in the European Convention on Human Rights, Article 3, and the UN Civil and Political Rights Covenant, Article 7. Again

> All peoples have the right of self-determination

is to be found in General Assembly Resolution 1514 - XV paragraph 2 and in Article 1 (1) of both the UN Covenants. A parallel is to be found in the adoption, without a word changed, of parts of the General Assembly Resolution 1962 - XVIII on the uses of outer space, in the Outer Space Treaty (1967).

It is plain that formally at least a proposition in the treaty or covenant imparts a promise and a legal obligation, while in a United Nations declaration or resolution, it is a declaration of principle or intent, without legal commitment, a prescription not a rule; though even this seemingly obvious distinction might not be entirely easy to maintain for the right of self-determination.

But the question for our present purpose is what is the difference between treaty and resolution in degree of obligation? It may be replied that this is a false question, because the declaration or resolution does not involve an obligation at all. But this will not do for two reasons: first, the prohibition of torture and inhuman treatment is a matter of obligation for States, whether it is embodied in a treaty or declaration or in neither; indeed, the fact, that the European Convention declares that in no circumstances whatsoever may there be derogation from it, suggests that it may be one of the few *fundamental* rights. Secondly, if it is said that nevertheless, where the proposition in a treaty or resolution is not declaratory of an existing rule, a treaty serves to convert a prescription from a moral into a legal obligation, the question of the difference in degree of obligation remains. This is the kernel of the problem of the sanctions of international law.

The assumption is often tacitly made that an international obligation, which is qualified as legal, requires by that bare fact alone a greater force. The obligation to observe the law is so well secured, it is said, in municipal law by adequate machinery that a legal obligation is of a higher degree than any other kind of obligation. But the analogy is misleading, and since there are other misleading analogies from municipal law, which bear on the problem of the sanctions of international law, they will now be considered together.

II.

Unless the differences between the origins and functions of municipal and international law are observed, false analogies on sanctions are likely to be drawn.

Measures of enforcement of municipal law normally include such legal sanctions as fines, imprisonment, or awards of damages, imposed through the machinery of courts, bailiffs, prisons and police; and may abnormally be extended to the use of teargas and weapons by the police, capital punishment, or military operations. International law also contains legal sanctions and provides for the use of force, but it would be a mistake to make such measures, or their lack of use, the sole criterion of the degree of observance of international law for several reasons. First, even the normal legal sanctions just described are in the daily life of a whole community only exceptional causes of law observance; and, while fear or anticipation of sanctions are obviously efficient and commoner causes, that efficiency will vary with the degree of certainty and thoroughness of the application of sanctions. In and between communities the variation is wide, as where the great majority of housebreakers are not even traced, or tax evasion is a common and accepted practice, or there can be unlimited detention without trial. It is possible then to exaggerate the difference between municipal law and international law in respect of their observance. In any case, it would be wrong to conclude in either system that, because there is from time to time failure of enforcement, there is no enforceability.

Secondly, while it is conceptually very convenient to treat a State, being a subject of international law, on the same general lines as an individual, subject of a system of municipal law, it must be seen that this is in part a metaphorical usage and that the fundamental differences must not be overlooked when it comes to sanctions. A State has no will and does not act or make decisions. It is rather an amalgam of conflicting forces and interests, working through a multiplicity of human and collegial agents. The act or decision, which can be internationally attributed to a State, is determined by the resolution of the conflict through its political and social mechanisms, and whether the act or decision is or is not conformable with rules of international law will depend on which forces or interests have prevailed. That there will be a collision of forces and interests in the making of the decision can be assumed from the fact that when a State acts on the international plane, it is seldom a trivial matter, if only for the multiplier effect, political or economic, which every governmental act has. It is upon these collective forces and interests, rather than as in municipal law upon the minds and wills of individuals, that the sanctions of international law have to operate.

It is true that the distinction made here between a State and an individual does not extend to all subjects of municipal law systems, in particular corporations. But far from invalidating the distinction, the form and activities of large corporations serve to underline it; for it is precisely because they may assume some of the characteristics of the State, already described, and become as it were a State-within-the-State, that the instruments of municipal law may be no less extended in controlling them than are those of international law in governing the relations of States themselves. Indeed, where a great corporation has wide international ramifications, it may well have more power, and more individuals dependent upon it, and command more resources, than many States. Shell or General Motors could make a very passable showing as members of the United Nations.

A third and perhaps the most important reason for applying municipal law analogies with caution in the field of sanctions is that the rules of international law, whether customary or conventional, are rooted in the consent of States, and are largely expressions of what over a long experience has been found to be workable in their multifarious relations.

The factor of consent is to be found of course also in the creation of municipal law, but in a more attenuated form, which the number of members of even the smallest communities makes necessary; and it has long been accepted that a law passed in a legislature, after a minority has voted against it on its merits, is still law binding even those members of the community, who find it objectionable. Rousseau rationalised this by offering the social contract as a form of association "par laquelle chacun s'unissant à tous, n'obéisse pourtant qu'à lui-même, et reste aussi libre qu'auparavant" but "met en commun sa personne et toute sa puissance sous la suprême direction de la volonté générale." Here it may be remarked how novel and striking a development is the use of the majority principle, still far from universal, in collective decisions of States. In 1919 Lord Robert Cecil, contemplating the establishment of the League Council, could say that it was inconceivable that any assembly of States could take decisions by majority vote, an observation on which those might reflect who rail against the veto principle in the Security Council.

The second factor differentiates international law from municipal law rather more sharply than the first. The British approach to law-making is perhaps unique among systems of municipal law in leaving important areas of the constitution, criminal procedure, and industrial relations, to be covered by "working" arrangements [1] rather than by legislation. Many customary rules of international law can be seen as "working arrangements," and they may come to be crystallised in a codifying treaty. But they are not the less effective as rules.

These two factors, original consent and practicability, operate together to make the rules of international law less dependent upon legal sanctions than municipal law; for often the reason for the rule is a natural sanction.

[1] *E.g.*, The constitutional "conventions," and the Judges' Rules.

III.

The ground of natural sanctions is international order, and empirical factors in the rule, which cause its observance. International order here means that minimum of coexistence, recognition of common interests, and co-operation – the *causa coeundi* of Cicero – without which there could be no international relations.

The empirical factors are the reason for the rule; among them are the geographical distribution of States, their physical environment, their resources and relationships of power, and social and economic forces working in them.

Natural sanctions, which induce the observance of rules of international law are the need for predictability and reciprocity, the recognition of common interests, and moral compulsions.

An important function of any system of law is to make more predictable the behaviour of its subjects in the fields of action which it covers, and so to give some assurance to each of the treatment he may expect from others. The need for predictability is expressed in a number of ways in international law: for example, the rule *pacta sunt servanda,* the obligation to consult, the principle of reciprocity. *Pacta sunt servanda,* if treated as a rule of positive law, is a mere tautology; but as a principle of natural law it underlies the whole of international order. The obligation to consult may not on the face of it appear to be a very substantial obligation. But how widely and thoroughly it is relied on and performed is demonstrated by the protests made when it is disregarded. The give-and-take called for by the principle of reciprocity is an essential part of predictability, and these principles have much to do with the relative solidity of international rules in such diverse fields as diplomatic immunities, extradition, tariffs, and currency.

The recognition of common interests has played a growing part in the making and observance of international rules: for example, in the use and conservation of natural resources, the raising and protection of international labour standards, mutual defence arrangements, international commodity agreements, and the support of international monetary reserves. Two points may be noticed here. First, in these and similar fields the pragmatic considerations, described earlier, are strong: State X becomes a party to an oil pollution convention, or to a multilateral defence agreement, or undertakes as an IMF member to maintain parity rates for its currency, because its Government finds that there is a compelling national interest in the common benefits these arrangements offer; this compelling national interest is a natural sanction inducing observance of the rules involved. Second, these are also fields in which natural sanctions work upon domestic forces and interests, which were earlier described as composing the State. Consider the parts played by the oil companies in the establishment of certain international rules governing the discharge of oil at sea, and by the central banks in contractual arrangements to support monetary reserves, and the long and continuing influence of the trades unions on the adoption and enforcement of international labour conventions. The inadequacy of ITU regulations on the allocation of radio wavelengths is an example of a failure to reconcile conflicting domestic interests.

Moral compulsions are not the least natural sanctions for being put last, for they explain and underpin many international rules. They are among the sanctions which do most work domestically in the State, in Parliaments, non-governmental organisations, and in the people at large, as is shown by the political momentum which the protection of human rights has developed since 1948. It is worthy of note here that the first use of mandatory economic sanctions has been essentially for the protection of civil and political rights.

IV.

What these brief reflections have tried to show is that what international law can and does do, and what it cannot do, may be better understood if the part played in it by natural sanctions as distinct from its legal sanctions, and the use of coercion or force, is stressed. But it is not intended in any way to belittle its legal sanctions, such as non-recognition, penal legislation, or compulsory arbitral or judicial settlement of disputes; or to suggest that natural sanctions are comprehensive. The efficacy of natural sanctions in international law can in any even only be as wide as man's comprehension of his environment, and of the right solutions of his social and economic problems, where those solutions must be international.

DR. IAN BROWNLIE
Fellow of Wadham College, Oxford

An Essay in the History of the Principle of Self-Determination

The significance of the principle of self-determination has long been undersetimated, or suppressed, in the Anglo-Saxon Countries in spite of the repeated appearance of communities deriving from native political struggle from the American War of Independence until the present day, and the homage paid to the principle in the form of federal constitutions and other structures providing autonomy. The object of this essay is to present, in a provisional way, the main elements in the history of the principle of self-determination, taking the United Nations Conference on International Organisation as a convenient terminal. It is true that it is not easy to give precise definition to the principle of self-determination but it appears to have a core of reasonable certainty. This core consists in the right of a community which has a distinct character to have this character reflected in the institutions of government under which it lives. The concept of distinct character depends on a number of criteria which may appear in combination. Race (or nationality) is one of the more important of the relevant criteria but the concept of race can only be expressed scientifically in terms of more specific features, in which matters of culture, language, religion and group psychology predominate. The physical indicia of race and nationality may evidence the cultural distinctiveness of a group but they certainly do not inevitably condition it. Indeed, if the purely ethnic criteria are applied exclusively many long existing national identities would be negated on academic grounds as, for example, the United States and Canada.

The institution of the option appears during the sixteenth century religious struggles in Europe and was to some extent a corollary of the principle on which territorial and religious questions were settled in the Peace of Westphalia. It is of course the case that the option of nationality and the plebiscite are institutions associated with the more recent history of the principle of nationalities; but it does not follow that there is any ideological relation flowing from a similarity of mechanics between the early and later examples. Nevertheless there is some significance in the persistence of the *ius emigrandi* and other forms of option in some of the important treaties of the seventeenth and eighteenth centuries.

The writer is not competent to refer to developments in other philosophies, but as a matter of progenitive political influence, both simple, and indirect in the form of counter-products and contradictory derivatives such as marxism, it is Western philosophy that is most relevant to the enquiry. It is Western philosophy which is found in alliance with the most successfully expanding commercial and political structure in the period between 1700 and 1945. The ideological roots of self-determination are to be found in at least three distinct but related concepts which can be traced in the history of Western philosophy. The first is that of equality between men, an idea which persisted in *natural law* doctrines in contradiction to the facts of systems based on feudalism or slavery. The second is that man, as a rational being, has the possibility of choice even although the possibilities may be limited, for the believer, by Divine providence, and, for the determinist, by environment and social conditioning. The most influential vehicle of economic determinism has been marxism, but marxism has always accepted and propagated the idea of change through organised struggle. Moreover, marxism has not been based on a simple economic determinism but allows that the economic base can be infected, and changed, by elements in the ideological superstructure. The third concept is that of social contract and this has proved the most dynamic in the present connection.

As early as Aquinas debate had begun on the proper relation of the ruler and his subjects and, as feudalism weakened, attempts to explain the foundations of Civil Society became more persistent. It could be said either that status became less significant or, preferably, that status tended to become a function of the principle of equality. A diversity of publicists including Thomas Hobbes and Hugo Grotius propounded ideas of social contract which revolved around the assumption that the authority of the monarch was conditional and consequently that he owed duties toward his subjects. Among the more influential proponents of the social contract and related concepts were John Locke, Tom Paine and Jean-Jacques Rousseau. The doctrine was by no means monolithic but the general conception, which was hostile to absolute monarchy, was the equality of citizens and the existence of a status under the law valid as against the ruler whose authority derived from the consent of the people. Such ideas were current political coin in the course of the eighteenth century and the doctrine of the Rights of Man received some practical application. The American Revolution of 1763 embodied the ideas of Locke. The Declaration of Independence sums it all up:

> We hold these truths to be self-evident, that all men are created equal, that they are endowed by their Creator with certain inalienable rights, that among these are life, liberty and the pursuit of happiness. That to secure these rights Governments are instituted among men deriving their just powers from the consent of the governed; that whenever any form of Government becomes destructive of these ends, it is the right of the people to alter or abolish it and institute new Government.

Thus the corollary of the rights of the individual in society is the right of communities to make choices of identity and form of government. The American Revolution proclaimed this not in explicit terms but, perhaps more effectively, by example. The French Revolution moved from similar principles of equality and government by consent of the people but in this case the principle of national liberation was expressly formulated and propagated. The decree of the Constituent Assembly in May 1790 declared that humanity formed a single community and, further, "que dans cette grande société générale les peuples et les États considerées comme individus jouissent des mêmes droits naturels et sont soumis aux mêmes règles de justice que les individus des sociétés partielles et secondaires..." Henceforth "les droits des peuples" were established on the agenda of political life in Europe and elsewhere. The subsequent overlaying of revolutionary principles in French politics did not in practice hinder the spread of ideas which had an innate attraction.

The nineteenth century in Europe at least is commonly seen as a period of stability. In terms of the principle of nationalities some changes were made in implementation of the principle but more important was the groundwork which was done and which was to lead to the changes in the map of Europe of 1919 - 1920. The early precedent was the emancipation of Latin America from Spanish control. In this case the intellectual inspiration was the French revolution. In Europe nationalism sapped the foundations of existing political power in Poland, Finland, Austria - Hungary and the Balkans, finding adherents in the middle class and also in socialist movements. The powers in the Concert of Europe fostered the principle of self-determination to an extent by supporting its operation in an opportunist context: thus its aim was principally the Turkish Empire. In the Treaty of Paris in 1856 it was provided that the Principalities of Wallachia and Moldavia were to be newly organised, taking into account the wishes of the populations. In 1848 the French Ministry of Foreign Affairs affirmed the principle of nationality in a circular to diplomatic agents and its sponsors included Thiers, Guizot and Napoleon III. By the last decades before the outbreak of the World War the principle was to be found in a great variety of political contexts. Thus there was an Italian doctrine of nationalities which was behind the movement for reunification. In Italian legal doctrine its exponents included Pasquale Stanislao Mancini (1817 - 1889), who expounded his views in an inaugural lecture in 1851, and Guido Fusinato (1860 - 1913). In 1913 Stalin wrote a tract entitled "Marxism and the National Question" in which there is some thoughtful discussion of the "nation" as a phenomenon and reference is made to some of the contemporary literature. In the words of Stalin:

> The right of self-determination means that a nation may arrange its life in the way it wishes. It has the right to arrange its life on the basis of autonomy. It has the right to enter into federal relations with other nations. It has the right to complete secession. Nations are sovereign, and all nations are equal (Chapter II).

"The Right of Nations to Self-Determination" was the subject of an article written by Lenin in 1914 and, indeed, for some time international socialist programmes had recognised the right: witness the resolution of the International Socialist Labour and Trade Union Congress, held in London, July 27 to August 1, 1896.

The influence, in terms of preparation for future political events, of the principle of nationalities was extensive by 1914, but its reflection in the literature of international law was very imperfect. Anglo-Saxon and French writers were often either hostile or indifferent. Funck-Brentano and Sorel, *Précis du droit des gens* (1877), are sceptical though not dogmatic in opposition. Hall's *International Law* (first edition, 1880) avoids discussion of the relation of nations or peoples to States. The first edition of volume one of Oppenheim's *International Law* (1905), at pp. 73-74, states that there are five morals to be deduced from the history of the Law of Nations and:

The third moral is that the principle of nationality is of such force that it is fruitless to try to stop its victory.

The principle is not, however, employed as *lex lata* in the substance of the book. The well known Italian writer Pasquale Fiore, in a treatise published in 1879, expressed the opinion that the subjects of the law were States, not nations. However, a number of writers were concerned to relate the nation and the State and frequently established the relation, by means of the concept of citizenship, in a fashion which was not specifically inimical to self-determination. Historically this approach could be, and was, justified by pointing to multi-national states which had resulted from voluntary association. Vattel in 1758 had promoted the legal and political concept of citizenship and distinguished the nation and the State (*Le Droit, des Gens,* I, Chapters XVI - XIX and see especially chapter XVI, para 195). Klüber, Wheaton, Halleck and others follow this general line. At the same time the framework of citizenship could provide a formal basis for denying self-determination to minorities. In the later nineteenth century the whole position was affected by the contradiction between the partial acceptance of self-determination in European and Balkan affairs by States which were building colonial empires. The latter process rested in part on expedients involving the partial or total denial of the independent personality of polities in Asia and Africa, and especially the use of the protectorate system, and in part on forcible annexation.

In 1914 or in 1919 when the machinery of peace settlement was at work, it would have been difficult to conclude that as a matter of positive law States accepted the principle of self-determination. Nevertheless in the peace settlement the principle was to have a dispositive and normative effect greater than that of many long accepted rules of law. In 1916 President Wilson stated that "Self-determination is not a mere phrase. It is an imperative principle of action, which statesmen will henceforth ignore at their peril," and it featured extensively in the Fourteen Points. In the deliberations of the Allied Supreme Council in Paris in 1919 and 1920 the lineaments of the territorial settlement for Europe were agreed upon. In spite of certain compromises and the inherent difficulty of drawing lines through areas of mixed population, the resulting settlement was to a great extent on national lines and has for the most part survived in the incomplete settlement after the Second World War. The extent to which the principle of self-determination intruded into the discussions of the Allied Supreme Council can be gauged by a study of the records published in the first series of *Documents on British Foreign Policy 1919 - 1939* (edited by Woodward and Butler). Where necessary implementation of the principle was aided by use of plebiscites under international supervision. The delegates in Paris were lobbied by representatives from Arab communities, such as Hejaz, and from Bessarabia, the Caucasus and many other areas of Europe, all praying in aid the principle of self-determination. In Eastern Europe the diplomacy of the new Soviet State in the years 1918 to 1924 produced a pattern of treaties concerned with territorial problems in which the substance of the principle of self-determination was to be found. A considerable number of Soviet treaties provided for option of citizenship. Treaties with Afghanistan and Turkey among others recited and applied the principle of self-determination in their provisions. Soviet proposals to Rumania in respect of Bessarabia and to Poland in respect to Western Byelorussia and Western Ukraine at this period were based on the right of self-determination.

The diplomacy of the years 1918 to 1924 in Europe evidenced the dynamism of the principle of self-determination and yet there was a distinct reluctance on the part of many states to accept the principle as prescriptive for future conduct. The Covenant of the League of Nations is the best evidence of this. The articles are primarily concerned with the peaceful relations of the status quo although treaty revision is provided for in the neglected Article 19 on ill-defined conditions. In Article 22 the Mandate system is set out and the content of this system perfectly reflects the ambivalence of attitude: it was not a mere exercise in cynism and yet the League practice in the matter was unlikely to present any real threat to colonialism at large or to the dominant interests of Mandatory powers. Another factor in the situation was the domesticity of some attachments to self-determination. Italian doctrine on the principle of nationalities was specific to reunification in the nineteenth century and was not intended or permitted to obstruct Italian colonial aspirations in Africa. Similarly Latin American doctrine in the period after independence failed to give any firm place to self-determination and in the settlement of frontier disputes uti-possidetis and the interpretation of existing boundary treaties were the predominant issues. The Final Acts of

Inter-American conferences of the period 1925 to 1939 and related treaties make no reference to self-determination except obliquely in the form of a concern for non-intervention affecting existing parcels of sovereignty. There was however, a residual and rather local form of anti-colonialism which found expression in the Final Act of the Meeting of Ministers of Foreign Affairs at Habana in July 1940. This contains the "Act of Habana concerning the Provisional Administration of European Colonies and Possessions in the Americas" in which a "declaration" occurs which refers to "the desires of the inhabitants of the said islands or regions" and under which appropriate arrangements may be made "in accordance with the principle reaffirmed by this declaration that peoples of this continent have the right freely to determine their own destinies . . ."

In general it is true to say that the principle of self-determination marked time in the period 1920 to 1940 except in so far as developments in the law relating to the use of threat of force were an important adjunct to self-determination. At the same time the extensive use of the principle in European affairs in the peace settlement of 1919 and 1920 had an important estoppel effect and nationalist movements received a large impetus in the Arab world and in colonial Asia; but this cumulative pressure had no immediate counterpart on the legal plane. It is true, however, that a rather desultory form of self-determination occurred as the "older" (white) Dominions of the British Empire were accepted on the plane of international law in the period 1919 to 1939, and Ireland contracted out more or less on its own terms in 1922. The Irish Constitution of 1937 provides in Article I:

> The Irish nation hereby affirms its inalienable, indefeasible, and sovereign right to choose its own form of Government, to determine its relations with other nations, and to develop its life, political, economic and cultural in accordance with its own genius and traditions.

Association on the principle of consent was expressed in some cases in terms of a federal principle, as in the Constitution of the U.S.S.R. in the editions of 1924 and 1936.

The corollary of the principle of nationalities after the Peace Treaties of 1919 and 1920 was the existence of non-national citizens and a too great association of nationality and citizenship. The concept of the "minority," endowed with a special legal status in order to maintain an equality of individual status in the State, was an implicit acceptance of the exclusiveness and aggressive nationalism which was the expression of self-determination in European conditions. The arrangements of 1919 had been drawn quite finely on national lines and the exceptions were consequently the more prominent. German and Hungarian revisionism employed co-national minorities as agents in political operations, and Hitler was able to obtain a measure of acceptance for his policies from some states until March 1939 because of his reliance on self-determination as against Czechoslovakia and Poland.

The next stage in the inquiry is the period from 1941 onwards when the Allies in the Second World War engaged in the formulation of war aims. Two of the principles proclaimed in the Atlantic Charter of 14 August 1941 were as follows:

First, their countries seek no aggrandisement, territorial or other;
Second; they desire to see no territorial changes that do not accord with the freely expressed wishes of the peoples concerned; . . .

On January 1, 1942, twenty-six Allied nations joined in a formal "Declaration by United Nations," subscribing to the principles of the Atlantic Charter, and twenty-one States adhered in subsequent years of the war. In 1942 a resolution of the Third Meeting of Ministers of Foreign Affairs of the American Republics declared their support for and adherence to the principles of the Atlantic Charter. There was thus for the first time a wide multilateral acceptance of the principle of self-determination. However, the old ambivalence persisted. Thus Churchill and a current of American opinion represented by Cordell Hull were hostile to an application of the Atlantic Charter which would involve not only the occupied countries of Europe but also the colonial empires of Britain, France, Belgium, and the Netherlands. Thus the Dumbarton Oaks Proposals, the first blueprint for a new international order, contained no reference to self-determination and no provision for a trusteeship system. The comments of governments on the Dumbarton Oaks Proposals prior to the San Francisco Conference included a considerable number of comments and amendments relating to the position of dependent peoples and to self-determination and making express reference to the principles of the Atlantic Charter. The Latin American States were prominent in this respect. Moreover, the United Kingdom and the United States made draft proposals on trusteeship, whilst Australia produced a new draft chapter on "Dependent Peoples." The outcome, indicated below, was a victory for the *principle* of self-determination. However, chapters XI,

XII and XIII of the Charter, which were concerned with specific obligations and implementation, retained a measure of the ambivalence inherent in League thinking on the matter: and at San Francisco the colonial powers made efforts to keep these chapters on a voluntary and permissive basis.

The fact remains that amendments were proposed jointly by the United States, U.S.S.R., United Kingdom and China on 5 May 1945 which introduced the provisions now embodied as Article 1, paragraph 2, and Article 55 of the Charter. Both amendments referred to relations among nations "based on respect for the principle of equal rights and self-determination of peoples." The amendments were instigated by the U.S.S.R. In discussions of the Trusteeship system self-determination played a somewhat oblique role although Article 76 (b) does include a reference to "the freely expressed wishes of the people concerned": but the arrangements were to be based on the free conclusion of agreements. The Trusteeship system was voluntary and related to temporary political factors. The general issue of non-self-governing peoples was dealt with sparsely in the Declaration Regarding Non-Self-Governing Territories in Chapter XI of the Charter, and these provisions contain no reference to self-determination. However, the pass had been sold in relation to those other parts of the Charter referred to above and United Nations practice was to give the weak provisions of Article 73 an infusion of the principle of self-determination as a part of the overall "law of the Charter." In the actual application of the Charter the text of Chapter XI would be given much less of a subordinate status in relation to the Trusteeship Chapters than was originally intended. Once the Charter was in force it was to be increasingly difficult to deny the legal content of the principle of self-determination. The more realistic lawyers in the West have more recently ceased to consign the principle to the realm of politics and have begun to examine its precise legal ramifications. An empirical indication of the change in Western literature is the almost complete absence of reference to self-determination, in Hackworth's *Digest*, published 1940 to 1943, compared with Whiteman's *Digest*, Volume V. pp. 38-87 (1965).

Principal Sources

I. Asamoah, Obed Y., *The Legal Significance of the Declarations of the General Assembly of the United Nations.* The Hague 1966.
Kelsen, Hans, *The Law of the United Nations,* London 1951.
Kunz, J. L., 31 Hague *Recueil* (1930, I), pp. 111-172: "L'option de nationalité."
Nys, Ernest, *Le Droit international,* I, 1904.
Russell, Ruth B, and Muther, Jeanette E., *A History of the United Nations Charter,* Washington 1958.
Scelle, Georges, *Précis du droit des gens,* 1932, II, pp. 257-295.
Sereni, A. P., *The Italian Conception of International Law,* New York 1943.
Starushenko, G., *The Principle of National Self-Determination in Soviet Foreign Policy,* Moscow, n.d. (Trans. from Russian ed.).
Stoerk, Felix, *Option und Plebiscit bei Eroberungen und Gebietscessionen.* Leipzig 1879.
Triska and Slusser, *The Theory, Law and Policy of Soviet Treaties,* Stanford 1962.
Wambaugh, Sarah, *A Monograph on Plebiscites,* Washington 1920.
Whiteman, Majorie M., *Digest of International Law,* Dept. of State Public, U.S.G. P.O. 1963.
II. *Documents on British Foreign Policy 1919 - 1939,* Ed. by E. L. Woodward and Rohan Butler H.M.S.O. 1947. United Nations Conference on International Organisation, San Francisco, 1945, 15 Volumes.

R. Purves
Wadham College, Oxford

Prolegomena to Utopian International Projects

The intention of this short paper is to provide a review of some of the most important schemes for international organisations which have emerged from the history of western societies prior to the establishment of the League of Nations. It is not intended as a detailed examination: it is only an introduction to demonstrate that schemes for international projects have been proposed – often in considerable detail – at stages earlier in history than one may at first imagine.

The ancient autonomous Greek city-states developed between themselves a remarkably refined system of law and custom to regulate their commercial and diplomatic relationships. This system belongs quite properly to the realm of *international* law in that these city-states retained their independence of spirit and proud autonomy, even to the exclusion of the union or federation of Hellas which might have been suggested by the common language and religion.[1]

It was, however, the common religion which provided such continuous unifying influence as could be found in ancient Greece. Indeed, the oldest hellenic international organisation was probably the Amphictyonic League (or Council), the antiquity of which is indicated by its being organised on a tribal, rather than a State, basis.[2] The twelve independent tribes sent representatives twice a year to the Council which met in autumn at the temple of Demeter at Anthela and in spring at the temple of Apollo at Delphi. These representatives were divided into two classes: – *Hieromnemones* and *Pylagorae*, the

[1] Elizabeth York, *Leagues of Nations: Ancient, Mediaeval and Modern*. London 1919. *Vide* p. 8 ff.

[2] There were numerous "amphictyonies" in ancient Greece, all having a religious basis: the one here referred to is the most important because of its association with and supervision over Delphi, the religious centre of ancient Greece.

(Greek *amphictiones* = "dwellers around").

latter class consisting for the most part of orators and statesmen who were elected half-yearly. Each tribe had two votes, all of equal value, and chose their *Hieromnemones* by election or by lot before delegating them, together with twice their number of *Pylagorae* to attend the Council. There appears to have been a secretariat and a General Assembly of all others who happened to be present at the gathering.

The equality of voting, whether it be viewed as a strength or a weakness of the constitution, appeared increasingly anomolous as certain city-states became relatively more powerful and influential. Attempts were made to redistribute the votes more realistically, but these motions were defeated, as, for example, when the Spartan delegates proposed after the Battle of Plataea that those States which had not fought against Persia be disenfranchised.[3] The defeat of this motion, because of its political implications, is indicative of the fact that the League was considered as essentially a religious institution, and not a vehicle for either nationalistic or political manipulation. In this respect, the Oath of the League is significant for its religious basis: the members swore that they "would destroy no city of the Amphictyons, nor cut off their streams, in war or peace, and if any should do so they would march against him and destroy his cities, and should any pillage the property of the god, or be privy to or plan anything against what was in the temple at Delphi, they would take vengeance on him with hand and foot and voice, and all their might..." [4] The aims of the League are clear: to protect the holy places and to lessen the brutality of war,[5] and in accordance with the provisions of the Oath "sacred wars" were waged in 595, 355, 340, and 280 B.C. because of acts of sacrilege. The good offices of the League were available for arbitration of disputes between cities – an accommodation used mostly by the weak states; the strong states, observes Holm, "always resorted to the arbitrement of war." [6]

[3] *Vide* Plutarch *Life of Themistocles*.

[4] *Vide* E. York, *op cit.* Ch. 1.

[5] Curtius, *History of Greece*, Vol. 1, p. 116, remarks: "These are the first attempts at procuring admission for the principles of humanity in a land filled with border feuds..."

Encyclopaedie Britannica 1967 Edition (hereinafter referred to as *Britannica*) on the subject of Amphictyons, notes concerning the Oath that "in this regulation can be seen one of the origins of Greek inter-state law."

[6] Adolf Holm, *History of Greece*, Vol. 1, p. 229.

Britannica endorses this allusion to the weakness of the League:

"The judgments of the council were sometimes considered unfair and were

In any event, issues such a obligatory arbitration, Hellenic national unity, or even the conducting of a common foreign policy, were quite outside the concept of this League and it remained more of an ecclesiastical synod than a federal parliament. Its political influence was enlarged in 346 B.C. by Philip of Macedon, and later by Alexander the Great, and Augustus Caesar eventually attended to a redistribution of votes: but for all this, the League did not lend itself to transformation into a political mechanism and it eventually submerged under an imposed Roman administration, leaving as a legacy the concept which it had fostered of a national identity for the Hellenes and a model for the much later international project of Henry IV of France.

Ancient Greece provides examples of numerous political "international" or "inter-state" organisations, two of which merit a brief examination, not because they were in any sense "universal" in the modern use of the term, but because they did evolve some interesting machinery for international co-operation.[7]

The first such organisation was the Delian League comprised of various maritime city-states including the Hellenic cities in Asia Minor, the Aegean islands, the Cyclades, Euboea, and others on the shores of Thrace and the Propontis. The chief city, however, was Athens, and although the League was formed as a defensive alliance against the common threat of Persia, Athens found it useful to transform it in due course into an Athenian empire. Initially it was agreed that the member states would contribute either money or ships towards the maintenance of a common fleet, and that the Council of the League would meet at Delos where the temple of Apollo was used as the treasury. Eventually, and unhappily, the Athenians moved the treasury to Athens, compelled tribute and military assistance from the other member states (which became, in fact, subjects to Athens), and deprived these states of their autonomy.

The other organisation – the Achaean League – also was formed as a defence alliance against some common enemy. Based on the city of Achaia in the Gulf of Corinth, it had existed in a nebulous form for

successfully defied by the states affected. The inability of the council to enforce its resolutions was chiefly due to its composition: the majority of the communities represented were even in combination no match for individual cities like Athens, Sparta or Thebes; the support of the great powers was necessary if more than moral influence was to be employed."

[7] *Vide* J. A. O. Larson, *Greek Federal States - Their Institutions and History*, Clarendon Press, Oxford, 1968.

some time, until the threat of Macedonian invasion after the death of Alexander the Great and the growing power of Rome to the West produced a lively interest among most of the Peloponnesian cities in using the League structure as a defence organisation. Apparently, the aim of the League was a union on a federal basis of the whole of the Peloponnesus and, ultimately, of all Hellas, and membership grew from the original twelve cities to about seventy, including Sparta and Corinth. The important feature of this League is the federal structure with city autonomy for domestic matters and a central Assembly for foreign affairs. Each city had an equal vote, and a President – "strategus" – was elected annually, as was his Cabinet of ten. There was also a Council of 120 which prepared the agenda for the Assembly, a Senate, a Federal Law Court, and a small standing army and navy. Whilst the League could compel unwilling cities to join, it could not compel defaulting cities to pay contributions to the central funds: this critical financial weakness, and the League's late emergence as a political force, meant that it was in no position effectively to withstand the unified pressure from Rome.

The *Pax Romana* removed both the need and the opportunity for European international organisations on a co-operative basis between States, and out of the fall and disintegration of the Roman Empire emerged as cohesive forces only the thin and often faltering power of the Church and the Holy Roman Emperor, sometimes working together but more often providing rallying points for opposition to each other. The political struggles which convulsed Italy during the thirteenth century are reflected in the life and works of Dante, and some see in his *De Monarchia* an allegorical scheme for a central unified state or, at least, for a central council of rulers and a common court.[8]

Indeed, the Middle Ages saw the advent of many movements aimed at the Christian solution of conflicts by peaceful means.[9] The *Brothers of Peace* spread throughout France, and in Italy a dominican convened a solemn assembly of all the towns of Lombardy and an act of general pacification was passed. The Dominicans, the Franciscans, and even some heretical sects, pursued courses of pacificism, as did many prominent individuals, especially with the spread of humanism at the

[8] *Vide* E. York, *op cit.*, Chapter II, where this interpretation is adopted. Also F. H. Hinsley, *Power and the Pursuit of Peace*, Cambridge 1963, Chapter 1.

[9] *Vide* E. Nys, *Les Origines du Droit International*, 1894, Chapter XVIII, "Les Irenistes," p. 388 ff.

end of the fifteenth century. The pacifist content of humanism is evident in the writings of men such as Grocyn, Linacre, Colet, Latimer, Thomas More, Erasmus, Vivès, Postel and Thomas Campanella.

However, we have already overlooked a name too often ignored – that of George Podebradsky, King of Bohemia,[10] who produced a practicable and well-detailed scheme for an international organisation for the preservation of peace in Europe as early as 1464. This scheme has been termed by Zourek [11] "le premier projet diplomatique tendant à l'organisation de la paix et de la sécurité à l'échelle européenne," but it is remarkable also for its realism as much as for its anticipation of later projects of this century. It failed to be implemented because it was too advanced for its time and because it would have tended to diminish papal authority. In fact, Bohemia and its King were considered heretical after the Hussite reformation, and the project of George Podebradsky was sabotaged by clerics from the moment it was first presented to Louis XI of France by the Bohemian envoys, Kostka and Marini, in June 1464, despite the ostensible purpose of the scheme being the defence of Europe against the aggressive Turk. The Project (unio, liga generalis, concordia universalis) prohibited recourse to arms in settlement of disputes and provided for obligatory arbitration by an international court. The League's members were to use all means to settle disputes amicably between members, even in cases of clear aggression, and were to unite to obtain a settlement by arms only after all other methods had failed. Disturbers of the peace (violatores pacis generalis) and those that aided them were to be punished, and provisions were made for financial aid for the victims of aggression. Financial contributions were realistically provided for, with a special fund to fight the Turks. The organisation itself was endowed with its own *persona*, and the supreme organ was to consist of delegates from

[10] *Vide* generally, for an illuminating examination of this and other projects, F. H. Hinsley, *op. cit.* Chapter I. Also *Britannica* under "Podebrady" and Zourek, "Le Projet du Roi Tchèque George de Podiebrad" in *Annuaire Français de Droit International*, 1964.

The King's name appears variously in Czech as *Pirí z Podebrad* (*Britannica*), or *Jirí Podebradsky* (Zourek). *Britannica* uses the anglicized form *George of Podebrady*, noting that he was born in the town of Podebrady in 1420.

[11] Jaroslav Zourek, *op. cit.*

Vide Hinsley, *op cit.* Chapter 1: remarks that Podiebrady's project was probably aimed not so much at the establishment of peace in Europe as at obtaining the protection of Germany, France and Venice against the threat of the Emperor and the Pope.

all countries in a permanent congress (congregatio), with provisions for admission of new members. There was to be a Court of Justice (parlamentum seu consistorium) consisting of one judge and a number of assessors who would be responsible for administering not only the existing law but also, if necessary, such new law taken *ex gremio natura* as new conditions may require. Space does not permit here a more detailed examination of this advanced and interesting project, and we must pass to the next project for an international organisation within the European framework, but this time occasioned not by the incursions of the Turks but rather by the threat posed by the growth of the House of Austria to the other European powers, and in particular, France. This project is the Grand Design attributed to Henry IV of France, and modelled on the Amphictyonic League of Ancient Greece.

There is considerable doubt as to whether the scheme originated in the mind of Henry IV or in that of his chief minister, Maximilien de Béthune, Duc de Sully. Henry IV did have a reputation as a successful international arbitrator, and the little evidence there is of a treaty of alliance between France, England, and the United Provinces of the Low Countries of 1596 [12] suggests that something similar to the Grand Design was not entirely foreign to the king's mind. In any event, whatever scheme he had in mind ended with his untimely assassination in 1610, and we must rely for details of the Grand Design on Sully's *Mémoires des sages et royales oeconomies d'estat, domestiques, politiques et militaires de Henry le Grand*, which were commenced shortly after the king's death and which eventually appeared in the eighteenth century transformed into the *Mémoires de Sully*. From these *Mémoires*, it appears that the immediate object of the project was to check the House of Spain in Europe and to preserve the balance of power, and ultimately, to expel the Turks. This "république monarchie très chrétienne" was to be composed of fifteen states of three kinds, each state to send commissioners or delegates to a General Council which was continually assembled to deal with issues and to hear appeals from the six Minor Councils. There was provision for a combined army and navy, and finance was to be obtained by a special tax levied by all members.

In that the Grand Design was more in nature of an anti-Habs-

[12] *Vide* E. York, *op cit.*, pp. 89-90. Also Péréfixe, *Life of Henry IV*. An analysis of both the history and the content of Sully's *Mémoires* is to be found in Hinsley, *op. cit.*

burg alliance, it was less universal, less advanced, as well as less refined than the earlier project of George Podebradsky – but they both shared the common fate in that neither was implemented. Rivalries, disputes and bitter wars continued to convulse Europe, providing impetus for pacifist movements and material for further projects of international control.

Grotius (1583 - 1645) outlined the history of arbitration in his monumental *De Iure Belli ac Pacis* and demonstrated it as a means of settlement of disputes,[13] and in this he was manifestly inspired by the project of Eméric Crusé who had published in 1623 his *Nouveau Cynée ou discours d'État représentant les occasions et moyens d'establir une paix générالle et la liberté du commerce par tout le monde.* This book contained a proposal for a scheme of international consultation and arbitration on a truly universal – not merely European – scale. It was suggested that Venice might be a central place "où tous les souverains auraient perpétuellement leurs ambassadeurs, afin que les différends qui pourraient subvenir fussent vuidez par le jugement de toute l'assemblée . . . Que si quelqu'un contrevenait à l'arret d'une si notable compagnie, il encourrait la disgrâce de tous les autres princes qui auraient bien le moyen de le faire venir à la raison."

In 1660 the Landgrave Ernest von Hesse-Rheinfels proposed yet another project to facilitate peaceful consideration of disputes – a court for the community of sovereigns – in his *Der so wahrhafte als ganz aufrichtliche und discret gesinnte Katholik.* Later, in 1693, William Penn, famous Quaker and colonial proprietor, suggested a European Parliament in his *Essay towards the Present and Future Peace of Europe.* "The sovereign princes of Europe," proposed Penn, "would agree to meet by their stated deputies in a general diet, estates, or parliament, and there establish rules of justice for sovereign princes to observe one of another, and thus to meet yearly, or once in two or three years at farthest, or as they shall see cause, and to be styled the Sovereign or Imperial Diet, Parliament or State of Europe; before which sovereign assembly should be brought all differences depending between one sovereign and another that cannot be made up by private embassies before the sessions begin; and that if any of the sovereignties that constitute the imperial states shall refuse to submit their claim or pretensions to them, or to abide or perform the judgment thereof, and seek their remedy by arms, or delay their compliance beyond the

[13] Hugo Grotius, *De Iure Belli ac Pacis*, 1625, Bk II, Ch. xxiii, Sec. viii.

time prefixed in their resolutions, all the other sovereignties, united as one strength, shall compel the submission and performance of the sentence, with damages to the suffering party, and charges to the sovereignties that obliged their submission." In 1710, a fellow Quaker, one John Bellers of Gloucester, published a plan which was inspired both by the Grand Design of Henry IV and by Penn's *Essay* and which proposed an annual European "Congress, Senate, Diet or Parliament." Europe itself was to be divided into a hundred Provinces, each to send one member to the Parliament and to supply equal quantities of men, money, or ships for an international force.

During the 1713 Treaty of Utrecht, one of the French secretaries, Charles-Irénée Castel de Saint-Pierre, published anonymously his Project for *Perpetual Peace*, upon which he had been working since 1711. It was here suggested that there be a *Corps Européen*, with a law court, a Senate of representatives and a central City of Peace (Utrecht). Saint-Pierre worked out the scheme in very considerable detail, but its basis was the renunciation of war and the acceptance of compulsory arbitration by all states. "The Sovereign who shall take up Arms before the Union has declared War, or who shall refuse to Execute a Regulation of the Society, or a Judgment of the Senate, shall be declared an Enemy to the Society and it shall make War upon him ..." War was not absolutely outlawed – but it was lawful only with the approval or sanction of the Union for the checking of aggression. The author of *Paix Perpetuelle* was yet a realist – attached to the work was a note bearing the words: – "C'est un projet, y lit-on, dont peut-être ni vous ni moi ne verrons jamais un fruit; mais par reconnaissances de ce que nous avons reçu de bien de nos ancêtres, ne devons-nous pas tâcher d'en procurer encore plus grands à notre postérité?" Frederick the Great was also a realist: he wrote to Voltaire about the project: – "The thing is very practicable; it only needs, in order to succeed, the consent of Europe and several similar bagatelles."

Jean-Jacques Rousseau made the very pertinent observation about Saint-Pierre's project that it was doomed to failure because it required a fear of a common enemy to make nations consent to such a scheme. Here there was no Persia, as for the Greeks, no Turks, as for Podebradsky, no House of Austria, as for Henry IV, to compel cohesion and co-operation: public interest and love of peace alone would not do this. Nevertheless, Rousseau proposed his own Federation of

Europe [14] – a perpetual irrevocable alliance with a permanent Diet of Congress to settle disputes by arbitration or judicial pronouncement. There were the usual provisions for voting and contributions, concerted action against a declared enemy, guarantees of frontiers, and a list of members, all from Europe – but including Russia. Rousseau insisted that it was practicable, but must have been resigned to the fact that it would never be implemented any more than was Saint-Pierre's project, and for the very same reasons.

Kant's political thoughts are contained principally in the four essays, *The Principle of Progress, The Principles of Political Right, The Natural Principle of the Political Order,* and *Perpetual Peace.* In these essays, Kant expounded his contention that the one possible system for the world was one of International Law acknowledged and obeyed by every State, a system which was eventually imperative in that it was the Divine intention that Mankind should ultimately become united in a world-state. There would eventually and inevitably evolve a world-society founded on Right (i.e., the Law of Nature or the Law of God) and enjoined by Reason. In *Perpetual Peace,* Kant set out certain Preliminary and Definitive Articles, which stipulated representative government for each State, that no independent State was to be acquired through inheritance, purchase, exchange or donation, that standing armies were to be abolished, that no State was to interfere with the constitution or government of another, that wars were to be limited, that the Law of Nations should be founded on a Federation of Free States, and that the rights of men as citizens of the world should be limited only by conditions of universal hospitality.

Kant had quite definite reservations about Utilitarianism, but that did not prevent its founder, Jeremy Bentham, from contributing his own Essay on international organisations which differed from Kant's project, as one may expect, in being more positivist and somewhat less certain of Divine Purpose. Bentham had already recommended a code of international law, and in his *Fragment of an Essay on the Principles of International Law,* written about 1789, he also proposed a European Tribunal and stated that the two necessary conditions for the prevention of war were the reduction of the armed forces in Europe and the emancipation of the colonies. Bentham sets out four-

[14] J. J. Rousseau, *A Lasting Peace through the Federation of Europe,* first published in Amsterdam in 1761 and in Geneva in 1782. *Vide* also Hinsley, *op. cit.,* Chapter 3.

teen pacific Propositions, relating, *inter alia*, to the establishment of an international court of arbitration with a Congress or Diet consisting of deputies from each State empowered to enforce the decrees of the Court.

In 1814 the Comte de Saint-Simon published his *De la Réorganisation de la Société Européenne* which recommended a political Union of Europe, a Parliament of two chambers with a King, and that all Sovereigns behave like Good Christians. It was to be Czar Alexander I who was to transform this recommendation of Christian conduct into a Document of State when he flourished his Holy Alliance for the attention and amusement of the diplomats assembled at the Vienna Congress in 1815. This Holy Alliance – not to be confused with the Quadruple Alliance – was eventually signed by all the European sovereigns with the exception of the Pope, the British Regent and, not surprisingly, the Sultan of Turkey. The Holy Alliance offered little practical guidance, but simply stipulated that the sovereigns were to take "as their sole guide" for conduct "the precepts of the Holy Religion." These precepts could have provided a licence for fanaticism, as they had done in the past, and naturally precluded universal participation; while even in Europe they were amenable to manipulation and interpretation sufficiently to justify an almost unlimited range of political behaviour. Nevertheless, when the first Hague Conference was summoned in 1899, Czar Nicholas II referred back to the Holy Alliance as an inspiration for international co-operation.

Fifteen years later the First World War convulsed Europe. But this and the subsequent history are outside the scope of this short survey. Yet the mind could speculate on how much of the misery and destruction of that War could have been avoided if there had existed, if only in a skeleton form, any one of the schemes for international discussion and arbitration proposed by Podebradsky, Henry IV, Saint-Pierre, Penn, Rousseau, Kant or Bentham.[15] In the institution of the League of Nations on a universal scale one may see that some lessons had been learnt, and in its failure that even more remained to be

[15] For further international projects, *vide* J. Ter Meulen, *Der Gedanke der Internationalen Organisation in Seiner Entwicklung*, Martinus Nijhoff, The Hague, 1917.

For a general assessment of the contribution of these projects to modern international organisations, *vide* Hinsley, *op. cit.*, and R. Yorke Hedges, *International Organisation*, London 1935, especially Chapter V "The Evolution of International Government."

learnt. Perhaps one of the most important lessons is that *idealism* is not enough. Indeed, it may not even be essential, and in the ultimate analysis, because of the dogmatic enthusiasm and the obscuring of practical issues which flow as sinister undercurrents beneath the surface of idealism, it may even prove disastrous to the implementation of a workable international project.

PROF. ALFRED P. RUBIN
University of Oregon

The Use of Piracy in Malayan Waters

I. DEFINING PIRACY

The concept of "piracy" meaning acts of depredation on the high seas not licensed by a political power with which normal intercourse was at least from time to time maintained is to be found in ancient writings known to Medieval and Renaissance Europe.[1] It is not clear that all, or, indeed, any such acts were considered violations of law in the ancient world,[2] although, of course, punitive or suppressive expeditions were sent against freebooters from time to time.

In 1179 the Third Lateran Council condemned "piracy" when its victims were Christian.[3] Mutual promises to deal harshly with "pirates" appeared in the capitulations of the thirteenth century between Italian trading states and Moslem powers in the Near East.[4] In the *Intercursus Magnus* of 1496 between England and Burgundy it was provided that the goods of "pirates" were to be liable to seizure for use in compensating their victims but not other sanctions against the "pirates" were mentioned.[5] The French-Ottoman capitulations of 1535 included provision for stringent measures to be taken against "pirates." [6] In none of these documents is "piracy" defined.

[1] See, e.g., Thucydides, *The Peloponnesian War* (Jowett transl.), Bk. I Chs. 5, 8; Suetonius, *Lives of the Twelve Caesars* (Gavorse transl.) (Modern Library ed.), p. 4; Plutarch, *Lives of the Famous Greeks and Romans* (Dryden transl.) (Modern Library), p. 855. The first printed edition of Plutarch's Lives appeared in 1517. *Id.*, p. xxiii.

[2] Arthur Nussbaum, *A Concise History of the Law of Nations* (revised ed., New York, 1954), p. 9.

[3] *Id.*, p. 31.

[4] *Id.*, p. 56.

[5] G. Butler and S. Maccoby, *The Development of International Law* (London, 1928), pp. 213-214.

[6] Nussbaum, *loc. cit.*, p. 68.

In England there apparently was a common law crime of "piracy." Personal jurisdiction over the one accused of the crime appears to have vested as the result of capture or arrest regardless of the "nationality" (to use an inappropriate modern term) of the accused or his victim.[7] Jurisdiction to try cases of "piracy" was formally put into the Admiralty courts of England during the reign of Henry the Eighth by a statute which has been cited as the origin of British assertions of jurisdiction over "piracy." [8] However, since the statute does not mention "piracy" or clearly define a unique concept which can be called "piracy" to any purpose, it is difficult to attribute that effect to it. The statute merely places in Admiralty courts:

> treasons, felonies, robberies, murders, and confederacies hereafter to be committed in or upon the sea, or in any other ... place where the admiral or admirals have or pretend to have power, authority or jurisdiction ...

An interesting case of 1604 holds, in effect, that there is no English common law crime of piracy on the high seas, but perhaps it would be well to read this case with the constitutional struggles of early 17th century England in mind.[9]

Alberico Gentili, writing in 1588, denied that the Frenchmen captured by Spain after the expulsion of Dom Antonio from Portugal in 1580 were properly treated as pirates because it was clear from their having received written authority from the King of France that "it was that King whom they served, not Antonio." [10] Gentili obviously felt that this connection with a state authority should have been sufficient to remove them from the international law category of "pirates," although he appears to have agreed with the Spanish contention that those who served Dom Antonio, the unsuccessful contender to the Portuguese throne, without the express authority of a recognized sovereign deserved the label "pirates" and its legal results. Thus Gentili used the label "piracy" to deny the benefits of a status of belligerency to unsuccessful rebels, even when acting under a colorable dynastic claim of right. The benefits of a status of belligerency were

[7] W. S. Holdsworth, *A History of English Law* (London, 1922-1928), Vol. I, pp. 550, 553 note 6 *et seq*. The practice is the subject of some comment by Cockburn, C. J., in R .v. Keyn ("The Franconia") (1876) 2 Ex. Div. 163-167.

[8] S. Morrison, ed., *A Collection of Piracy Laws of Various Countries*, Research in International Law of Harvard Law School, Part V, 26 American Journal of International Law (Supp.) (1932), p. 910. The Statute is 28 Hen. VIII c. 15 (1536).

[9] Anon. (1604), Moore K. B. 756; 72 E. R. 886.

[10] Gentili, *De Iure Belli* (Rolfe transl.) ed. of 1589 (Oxford, 1933), p. 26.

believed by Gentili to go only to those "who have officially declared war upon us or upon whom we have officially declared war," but he did not define the body able to make such an "official" declaration.[11] "Pirates" were those against whom no official declaration of war had been made but with whom warlike acts may nonetheless be exchanged.[12] But this reason is circular since it defines "pirates" by saying what can legally be done to "pirates" but does not offer a clue as to when and against whom the label itself may be properly attached. A further clue to Gentili's thought may be found in his observation that:

> Piracy is contrary to the law of nations and the league of human society. Therefore war should be made against pirates by all men . . .[13]

Again, the assertion falls short of defining "piracy." It is interesting to note, however, the assertion that "human society" (not restricted to "civilized" or "European" or "Christian" society, but including all nations) is in league, i.e., that there is a political order which unites the entire world and that it is possible for some men to place themselves outside of this order, by doing which they become "pirates." As noted above, in Gentili's view the method by which people placed themselves in the legal position of "pirates" was by performing acts of war without an "official" declaration. But even if that is a correct reading of Gentili's formulations there are difficulties, for it would seem perfectly possible for a state to enter into hostilities with another without any declarations and without losing its right to be dealt with as a member of the international community and without having its commissioners treated as "pirates." In actual practice, in 1628 an English Order in Council forbade privateers molesting the Barbary corsairs because of an English unwillingness to go to war with Algiers; the corsairs were not felt to be properly classifiable as "pirates" despite their performing acts of depredation on the high seas against English merchants in the absence of any declaration of war.[14]

[11] *Id.*, p. 15.

[12] *Id.*

[13] *Id.*, p. 124.

[14] R. G. Marsden, ed., *Documents Relating to Law and Custom of the Sea* (London, 1915), Vol. I, p. 407; C. Bynkershoek, *Questionum Juris Publici* (Frank transl.) ed. of 1737 (Oxford, 1930), pp. 98-99. Evidence which strongly supports the view that the Barbary corsairs of the early seventeenth century could not logically have been considered violating the international law of the time because their activities in the Mediterranean Sea did not differ in substance

In 1604 Grotius attempted to bring the concept of piracy into play to justify Dutch use of force against the Portuguese in Eastern seas.[15]

> ... [I]t was ... through a common maritime right possessed by other free nations also, that the Roman people were authorized to distribute fleets ... to punish pirates captured at sea,[16]

he wrote. But Grotius did not attempt to define "piracy" at all except to observe that

> ... the name of "pirate" [may be] ... appropriately bestowed upon men who blockade the seas and impede the progress of international commerce.[17]

This class of men is so broad that it could be and was used by Grotius to include as pirates "the Portuguese" in general. It is in any case not a complete definition but only one class of men who might be considered to deserve the legal results attaching to the many acts which Grotius apparently felt could be denominated "piracy." It was never generally accepted, as other states of Europe, including England, later asserted the right to exclusive control of large areas of the seas.[18]

In 1625 Grotius condemned pirates as "the common enemy of mankind." [19] But, except for denying them the benefit of international law's requirement of *bona fides* in political relations [20] and denying that they could form a political society cognizable in international law,[21] he attempted no closer analysis of their place in international relations. Although his views as to the legal inability of "pirate" groups to form a political society cognizable in international law may be thought to indicate a feeling on the part of Grotius that the relations of a "pirate" to some group which is cognizable in international law,

from the activities of the adventurers and privateers of Christian countries of Europe in that area at that time who were not considered to merit treatment as "pirates" by the Governments involved is impressively marshalled in Sir G. Fisher, *Barbary Legend* (Oxford, 1957), pp. 137 *et seq.*

[15] H. Grotius, *De Iure Praedae Commentarius* (Williams and Zeydel transl.) ed. of 1604 (Oxford, 1950), p. 327.

[16] *Id.*, p. 237.

[17] *Id.*, p. 327.

[18] Butler and Maccoby, *loc. cit.*, pp. 40-53. Grotius himself modified his views on the point somewhat. See Grotius, *De Jure Belli ac Pacis* (Kelsey and others transl.) ed. of 1646 (Oxford, 1925), p. 631. Cf. A. S. de Blecourt, "Grotius contra Mare Liberum?", 7 *Revue de Droit International* (1937) 429.

[19] Grotius, *Belli ac Pacis*, p. 373.

[20] *Id.*

[21] *Id.*, p. 631.

e.g., a state, was significant, Grotius did not pursue this line of reasoning or relate this feeling to an explicit definition of piracy.

Of the other European publicists of the seventeenth century, Pufendorf also mentions piracy, but, like Grotius, he merely draws legal results from attaching the label without attempting to define the facts from which those legal results were felt to flow.[22]

In England, Sir Leoline Jenkins attempted to define the English common law of piracy in a charge given to a jury at a session of Admiralty in 1668.[23] After explaining that their jurisdiction was limited strictly to the territory and sea within the Admiral's purview[24] he noted that under some circumstances the entire body of the seas could be considered as within Admiralty jurisdiction and said:

> You are therefore to enquire of all Pirates and *Sea-rovers*, they are in the Eye of the Law *Hostes humani generis*, Enemies not of one Nation ... only, but of all Mankind. They are outlaws, as I may say, the Laws of all Nations ...
>
> That which is called Robbing upon the Highways, the same being done upon the Water, is called Piracy: Now Robbery ... implies not only the actual taking away of my Goods, while I am, as we say, in Peace, but also the putting me in Fear, by taking them away by Force and Arms out of my Hands, or in my Sight and Presence; when this is done upon the Sea, without a lawful Commission of War or Reprisals, it is downright Piracy.[25]

In another charge before an Admiralty session at the Old Bailey Jenkins traced Admiralty jurisdiction over pirates in whatever waters found to the tacit agreement of "all sovereign Princes that have Ships and Subjects at Sea," and found this jurisdiction in international law to be exercisable by "all Nations and Sovereign Princes that meet with" pirates.[26] No evidence of the tacit agreement was presented, however; Jenkins found the competence of English Admiralty Courts not in international law but in the legislation of Henry VIII cited above.[27] Thus, since he apparently regarded that part of the statute of

[22] Samuel von Pufendorf, *De Jure Naturae et Gentium*, Bk. IV, ch. ii, Sec. 8.

[23] W. Wynn, *The Life of Sir Leoline Jenkins* ... (London, 1724), Vol. I, pp. lxxxv *et seq*. Jenkins was a very influential Judge of the Court of Admiralty of England, Ireland and the Cinque Ports and Privy Counsellor. See also Jenkins's charge to a Southwark Jury dated February 18, 1680, 167 E.R. 561, Burrell 255.

[24] Wynn, *loc. cit.*, p. lxxxvi.

[25] *Id.*

[26] *Id.*, p. xci.

[27] *Id.*, p. xciv. The Act 3 Jac. I c. 4 (1606) confirmed the statute of Henry VIII cited above.

Henry VIII which brought robbery-within-the-territorial-limits-of-admiralty-jurisdiction into the competence of Admiralty Courts in England as bringing the international law crime of "piracy" into the competence of those courts, he apparently equated the international law crime of "piracy" with the English common law crime of "piracy," and both with the English crime of "robbery" performed at sea.

Where the Crown was considered to have undoubtable sovereignty within its land territory and on certain portions of the seas,[28] and thus any act of force in those areas not authorized by the Crown must have constituted a breach of the King's peace, the situation on the seas beyond those considered to be within the Crown's dominions led to difficulties. The concept of piracy being a breach of the King's peace was firmly embedded in Jenkins's thought. In his view it was not merely the act which constituted "piracy," but the victim of the act he felt had to be either an Englishman or "a Foreigner . . . if he be *de Amicitia Regis*," and thus "*eo nomine* under the King's protection . . ." [29] Under this definition acts amounting to robbery as defined in English municipal law, committed at sea, could not be considered "piracy" unless committed against persons deemed under the protection of the King of England (which, by a legal fiction, might include persons on very distant seas who had never heard of England).

Similarly, the contemplation of "a lawful Commission of War or Reprisals" involves difficulties, since, unlike the situation within the dominion of the Crown of England, many sovereigns issue commissions effective upon the seas. Jenkins did not limit his reference to a commission to one issued by the King of England. Yet once it is acknowledged that a foreign sovereign may issue a commission authorizing depredations on the sea, and that by doing so a person committing acts otherwise deemed piratical can be protected from the legal consequences of committing the crime of piracy, it becomes logically impossible to dictate to the foreign sovereign the form of his commission or, to carry the argument one step further, to limit the foreign sovereign's right to intervene on behalf of his subject in whatever form he chooses to do so.

Both these difficulties were addressed by Jenkins in an official letter dated April 3, 1675. In that letter he drew a distinction between "a

[28] Jenkins regarded rather large areas of the seas as within English territorial jurisdiction. *Id.*, p. xc; Vol. II, pp. 699-700.

[29] *Id.*, Vol. I, p. xciv.

Pirate who is a Highwayman" and those on board "a lawful Man of War" sailing under the commission of a country, even though that Commission had been exceeded. In the latter case Jenkins felt that the Crown had a right to interpose on behalf of the King's subjects who were involved (they were Scots) even though the commission, as well as being exceeded, was issued by the sovereign of a foreign country. The distinction between a "Highwayman" and a ship exceeding its commission appears to be weak, but irrelevant to Jenkins's actual logic – which is positivist international law doctrine:

> ... [T]here is no third power that can give a law that shall be decisive or binding between two independent Princes, unless themselves shall please to do it (which seldom happens) and then cannot be extended beyond the cases expressed by that Treaty.[30]

It would thus appear that in Jenkins's view a "pirate" could be relieved of the legal consequences of his acts: (1) By showing that he acted under the commission of any sovereign authority (in which case it becomes a moot question whether he actually committed the crime of "piracy" and was exculpated, or never committed the crime at all since "absence of commission" may be regarded as a missing essential element of the crime); or (2) By the interposition of some sovereign authority on his behalf (*sed quaere*, if the "pirate" is not a subject of the intervening sovereign).

To the extent that this view was accepted as the international law of piracy in Europe,[31] therefore, failure to accord to non-European

[30] *Id.*, Vol. II, p. 714.

[31] Jenkins himself did consider the attitudes of other European powers in this context when advising the King in a letter dated February 11, 1680, that

> "Moors and Turks ... cannot be proceeded against as Pirates ..., but are to have the Privileges of Enemies in an Open War"

on the grounds that the rights of the Algerian Government were recognized

> "as well by several Treaties of Peace and Declarations of War, as by the Establishment of Trade and even of Consuls and Residents among them by so many Princes and States."

Id., Vol. II, pp. 790-791.

A broader definition of "piracy" is occasionally attributed to Justice Hedges in R. v. Dawson, 13 State Trials 451:

> "[P]iracy is only a sea-term for robbery ... committed within the jurisdiction of the Admiralty."

However, in the actual case no question of commissions or the interposition of any sovereign arose and, perhaps for that reason, Justice Hedges did not speak to the legal effect of such possible complications.

No other early definition of "piracy" has been found pertinent to this study. As will be seen, later European definitions of "piracy" differ substantially from those noted above.

sovereigns the right to issue valid commissions or otherwise to interpose on behalf of their subjects who had performed acts which might otherwise have been considered to merit the legal results of the label "piracy," would be significant. It would represent a refusal to accord to non-European political leaders rights accorded to European sovereigns, and thus imply a refusal to extend the rule of "international" law to all "nations."

II. Applying the Term "Piracy" in Malayan Waters

D'Albuquerque nowhere used the term or the concept of piracy in connection with the non-European polities with which his natural father came in contact in the sixteenth century.[32] Varthema, writing in 1510, mentioned "sea-robbers" in referring to the politically unorganized Sallates,[33] but did not attach that label to any politically organized group. Linschoten, writing at the end of the century, did not speak of piracy.[34]

The first use of the word "piracy" in specific connection with Southeast Asia appears to have been Grotius's use of it in 1604 to describe the Portuguese attempt to close the Straits of Malacca to Dutch vessels, attempting to justify Dutch counteraction.[35] Purchas, writing in 1625 attached the word to the Sallates apparently in saying that the Dutch attack on Malacca in 1608 was aided by fifteen "Frigats of Blacke Pirates [who] adjoyned themselves to the Hollanders."[36] It is, of course, possible that Johore ships were meant. The term was applied to the Dutch (!) by the Portuguese cleric Sebastien Manrique writing in 1649.[37] Bowrey appears to combine the precedents of Varthema

[32] Braz D'Albuquerque, *The Commentaries of the Great Afonso D'Albuquerque* (Birch transl.) ed. of 1774 (London, 1872-1884), *passim*. Afonso D'Albuquerque was the first Portugese Governor-General of India and the conqueror of Malacca in 1511.

[33] Ludovico di Varthema, *Travels* (Badger and Jones transl. and ed.) ed. of 1510 (London, 1863), p. 241. The "Sallates" (Malay "Orang Laut", men of the sea) were rather like canoe-born Gypsies active in Malayan coastal waters but not acknowledging the authority of any land-based chieftain.

[34] J. H. van Linschoten, *Voyage to the East Indies* (Burnell transl.) ed. of 1598, (London, 1885), *passim*.

[35] *Vide supra*.

[36] Samuel Purchas, *Hakluytus Postumus or Purchas His Pilgrims* (1625) (Glasgow, 1905-1907), Vol. V, p. 221.

[37] Fray Sebastian Manrique, *Travels* (Luard and Hosten transl.) eds. of 1649 and 1654 (Oxford, 1927), Vol. II, pp. 12, 18, 25.

and Purchas in referring to the Sallates as "absolute Piratts" [38] in 1679.

The first time the word "pirate" appears to have been applied unmistakably to a politically organised Malay polity seems to have been in 1717 when Dampier, writing of events in 1689, spoke of the Malayan predators of the west coast of the Malayan Peninsula as "... the Pirates who lurk on this Coast." [39] It was Dampier's view that the "so many petty robberies and Piracies as are committed by the Malayans on this Coast" were probably a reaction to Dutch actions restricting free trade.[40]

III. Background

At this point a detour is necessary to acquaint the general reader with the state of facts to which the label "piracy" began to be attached in Malayan waters.

Malacca became a nodal point of trade between the Far East and Europe during the fifteenth century.[41] The trade was in the hands of Moslem traders, primarily Indian and Arab, who spoke loudly in the councils of the Malay Sultan of Malacca.[42] In 1509 Diogo Lopez de Sequeira was sent directly from Portugal to Malacca.[43] Two years later, in 1511, the Portuguese conquered Malacca.[44] Their object was to monopolize the trade between the Far East and Europe.[45] In this they were not successful as the displaced Arab and Indian merchants made a rival trading power of Atjeh, a Sultanate at the northern end

[38] Thomas Bowrey, *A Geographic Account of Countries Round the Bay of Bengal, 1669 to 1679* (Temple ed.) (Cambridge, 1905), p. 237 note 2.

[39] William Dampier, *A New Voyage Round the World (Supplement)* (Masefield ed.) ed. of 1717 (London, 1906), Vol. II, p. 88.

[40] *Id.*, p. 87. "[W]here there is any Trade to be had, yet not sufficient to maintain a Factory ..., so as to secure the whole Trade to themselves, the ... [Dutch] send their Guard-Ships ...". *Id.*

[41] Christopher H. Wake, "Malacca's Early Kings and the Reception of Islam," 5(2) Journal of Southeast Asian History (hereinafter cited as *JSAH*) 104 *et seq.*; P. E. de Josselin de Jong and H. L. A. van Wijk, "The Malacca Sultanate," 1(2) *JSAH* 20 at p. 29 (excerpt from J. de Barros, *Decadas da Asia* (ed. of 1553)).

[42] Tomè Pires, *Suma Oriental* (A. Cortesaõ transl. and ed.) ed. of 1512-1515 (London, 1944), Vol. II, pp. 256-257.

[43] D'Albuquerque, *loc. cit.*, Vol. II, p. 31.

[44] *Id.*, Vol. III, pp. 125-127.

[45] Tomè Pires, *loc. cit.*, p. 287: "Whoever is lord of Malacca has his hand on the throat of Venice."

of Sumatra.[46] The Portuguese attempted to enforce a monopoly by blockading the Straits of Malacca whenever they were strong enough, which was rare. Intermittent filibustering, never denominated "piracy" in any contemporary writings consulted by this writer, was the rule between Portugal and several local Princes.

By the end of the sixteenth century British and Dutch trading vessels had begun to appear in Malayan waters. Where Malaya Governments were firmly in control, "factories" (i.e., trading stations in charge of a "factor") were established, occasionally by more than one European country's representative in a single village.[47] Competition among the European powers was severe and there were many bloody episodes.[48]

The Dutch attempted to secure monopoly trade in the area by concluding treaties with the Malay Sultans providing for exclusive Dutch rights to trade. The British, unwilling to make the same political commitment of their forces in the Malayan area as the Dutch, abandoned silimar attempts to conclude monopoly treaties and argued that such treaties were not legally effective.[49] The legal argument appears to have assumed the legal capacity of the Malay Sultans to deal internationally and concentrated instead on the question of whether a third State had the right to trade with a Malay treaty-breaker. Grotius, an advocate for the Dutch, in the arguments with the English recognized the "unequal"-ness of the Dutch-Malay bargains but supported their validity.[50] The English writer Richard Zouche, writing in 1650, also seems to have had some hesitations concerning these treaties and

[46] The growing rivalry between Portugese Malacca and Atjeh is traced in Frederick C. Danvers, *The Portuguese in India* (London, 1894), Vol. I, pp. 344 *et seq*.

[47] The early accounts mention several co-located factories. See, e.g., anonymous account of Sir James Lancaster's third voyage (1601-1603) in Purchas, *loc. cit*., Vol. III, pp. 147 *et seq*.; Sir William Foster, ed., *The Voyages of Sir James Lancaster* (London, 1940) pp. 75 *et seq*. esp. pp. 90 *et seq*.; R. A. C. de Renneville, *Recueil des Voyages* . . . (Amsterdam, 1702), Vol. I, pp. 305 *et seq*.

[48] Dutch and English voyages into the Malayan area began only at the end of the sixteenth century. By 1623 the rivalries had reached a peak with the Amboina massacre. See D. K. Bassett, "The 'Amboyna Massacre' of 1623," 1(2) *JSAH* (1960) 1. A good summary of Dutch-Portuguese rivalry at this time is in Purchas, *loc. cit*., Vol. V, pp. 197-226.

[49] See G. N. Clark, "Grotius's East India Mission to England," 20 Transactions of the Grotius Society (1934) 45 at p. 76.

[50] Grotius, *Belli ac Pacis*, pp. 130-136, 394-397, 403, 516.

others between European and non-European powers, finding them valid only in that

> ... no reason can be found why it should not be lawful to enter into treaties of commerce and the like with the heathen for the common advantage ...[51]

He did not address situations in which the advantages are not "common" and appears to have focussed on the legal effects *in Europe* of those treaties, and not on the extent to which the non-European partner was bound.

In 1641 the Dutch conquered Malacca from the Portuguese.[52] The usual monopoly treaties were concluded with some, but not all, of the Malay Sultanates in the area. Eventually, in 1668, the Dutch instituted a regular patrol of the Straits of Malacca.[53] The object of this patrol was stated to be:

> ... to prevent ships and vessels from passing Malacca without first calling there and paying the customary dues.[54]

It was enforced against all comers, including Portuguese and Arabs, except for the English and for Malays trading from one part of the Sultanate of Johore to another.[55] The use of violence was authorized against "illegal" traders of all internationalities.[56]

Although the Malay Sultans certainly did have a concept of treaty as a binding expression of intention,[57] they, as well as the English, ap-

[51] Richard Zouche, *Iuris et Iudicii Fecialis, Iuris Inter Gentes et Questionum de Eodem Explicatio* (Brierly transl.) ed. of 1650 (Baltimore (U.S.A.), 1911), p. 101.

[52] P. A. Leupe, "The Siege and Capture of Malacca ..." (Mac Hacobian, transl.) 14(1) *Journal of the Royal Asiatic Society Malayan Branch* (*JRASMB*) (1936) 1 at p. 48.

[53] Balthasar Bort, "Report of Balthasar Bort on Malacca, 1678" (Bremner, transl.) 5(1) *JRASMB* (1927) 1 at pp. 180-183.

[54] *Id.*, p. 179.

[55] *Id.*, p. 182. Johore at this time had Sumatran dependencies.

[56] *Id.* The Treaty of Breda, ending the Second Anglo-Dutch War, had been concluded in July, 1667. The Third Anglo-Dutch War did not begin until 1672.

[57] *Cf.* the account of negotiations between Captain Lancaster and the authorities of Atjeh in Foster, *Lancaster*, pp. 94 *et seq.*, 155 *et seq.* On the other hand the concept of treaty being binding for an indefinite period, or binding the state rather than merely the person of the ruler, was alien to Malayan practice. The first example of a treaty solely between Malayan parties which was reduced to writing appears to date in the 1640s. See Francois Valentijn, "Description of Malacca" (Hon. D. F. A. Vervey, transl.) ed. of 1726, Part IV, 22 *Journal of the Straits Branch of the Royal Asiatic Society* (1892) 225 at p. 237. Even in that case the hand of Dutch drafters is clear.

parently disagreed with the Dutch assertions of right to monopolize trade through the Straits of Malacca. English trade with Kedah seems to have been maintained at a moderate level after 1668; an English attempt to establish a factory there was abandoned in 1674.[58] In 1675 the English demanded satisfaction of the Sultan of Kedah (to no avail) for the taking of an English vessel near Kedah roadstead by Sallate marauders.[59] In 1689 the English were welcome at Atjeh.[60]

The Dutch blockade, although not enforced against the English for reasons involving the relations of England with the Netherlands in Europe, was enforced with vigor against all other nations' traders. A blockade of the Straits of Singapore, at the southern entrance to the Straits of Malacca, was to be enforced in 1678 against Chinese, Japanese and Philippine vessels. Intercepted vessels were to be "brought to Malacca to trade there" in order to "deprive Johor [Johore] of that traffic." [61] Since the Governments of China and Japan at that time were equally concerned to prevent their people from engaging in foreign trade,[62] and since relations between the Netherlands and Spain were determined in Europe and not in the Far East in the seventeenth century (the Philippines were nominally under Spanish control), the only parties on the international level who felt outraged by these Dutch actions and who lacked effective peaceful recourse were the Malay Sultans (including those of the Southern Philippines).

The Dutch did not scruple to use force to obtain monopoly treaties in the Malayan area. As has been seen, they did not scruple to use force to enforce treaty rights once obtained. In fact, it appears that during the last half of the seventeenth century the Dutch began less and less to differentiate between the use of force for the one purpose and for the other. Both purposes sufficed to justify the use of force in the international law applied in Europe at this time. Furthermore, imposing trade monopolies by the use of force was consistent with the practices of the Malay Sultanates and their Southeast Asian predecessors and neighbours such as Sri Vijaya and Siam. Where the activities of the Europeans differed from those of the other powers in the area

[58] Bowrey, *loc. cit.*, p. 267 note 1.

[59] *Id.*, pp. 262-263.

[60] Dampier, *loc. cit.*, Vol. II, p. 62.

[61] Bort, *loc. cit.*, p. 187. See also H. B. Morse, *The Chronicles of the East India Company Trading to China* (Oxford, 1926-1929), Vol. I, pp. 44 *et seq.*

[62] G. B. Sansom, *The Western World and Japan* (London, 1950), pp. 149-150, 181.

until the late seventeenth century seems to have been more in the degree of success which greeted their efforts and the use of sophisticated political organizations to exploit those successes than in the application of new concepts of justifiable international behaviour.

Although Atjeh, like the Sultanate of Malacca in the fifteenth century, prospered largely through the efforts of Arab and Indian traders, in the smaller Malay Sultanates the first, and often the only, merchant in his country was the Sultan himself.[63] Of course, within the areas served by some river systems in the Malay Peninsula there was trade by Malay smalltraders some of whom did, upon paying a proper amercement to the appropriate riverine Sultans, engage in wider trading ventures. It appears that some Peninsular produce was traded by Malay traders to Siam for rice.[64] Bugis traders, Malays from the Celebes, began to play a large part in the economic and political life of the Peninsula towards the end of the seventeenth century.[65] All of this activity was regarded by the Dutch as violative of their treaty rights or their customary rights as possessors of Malacca and the small-traders were compelled to call at Malacca whenever possible. The disruption of the authority of the Malay Sultans over their subjects and trading partners appears to have been great.[66]

Deprived of their accustomed courses of trade and part of their profits by the Dutch-imposed need to spend time and money at Malacca, and released to some extent from the restraining hand of their Sultans, some of the Malay small-traders turned to depredation against European shipping when possible, and against Malay shipping when available, as a means of livelihood.[67] Far more significant, the Sultans themselves appear to have turned to a kind of guerrilla warfare at sea against the Dutch.[68] Both types of depredation were denominated "piracy" by the Dutch at the beginning of the eighteenth century.[69]

[63] John Crawfurd, *History of the Indian Archipelago* (Edinburgh, 1820), Vol. III, p. 152.

[64] *Id.*, p. 185.

[65] *Id.*, Vol. II, p. 60, Vol. III, p. 149; Dampier, *loc. cit.*, Vol. II, p. 38; Alexander Hamilton, *A New Account of the East Indies*, ed. of 1727 (London, 1930), Vol. II, pp. 82, 84.

[66] Crawfurd, *loc. cit.*, Vol. III, pp. 312 *et seq.*

[67] Dampier, *loc. cit.*, Vol. II, pp. 86-88.

[68] *Id.*, p. 88.

[69] *Cf.* Thomas Braddell, "The Europeans in the Indian Archipelago in the 16th and 17th Centuries," 2 *Journal of the Indian Archipelago* (*Logan's Journal*) (New Series) (1858) 313 *et seq.* Bernhard H. M. Vlekke, *Nusantara* (The Hague, 1959), pp. 206-208, denies that the "piracy," which he regards as first

IV. Foreground

European force did not dominate Malayan waters during the eighteenth century. But early in the nineteenth century growing European self-confidence and the drive for political expansion brought to issue the growing tendency of European administrators in Southeast Asia to consider Malay Sultans to be sovereigns or pirate chieftains as suited the need of the moment for legal argument. Even when the Malay Sultan was to be considered sovereign (usually in order to conclude a treaty with him) the tendency was marked to label his military arm as "pirates."

In 1811 Thomas Stamford Raffles, the brilliant young British Lieutenant-Governor of Java and later to be founder of the Colony of Singapore, wrote to Lord Minto, Governor-General of India, about the problem of "piracy" in the Malay area.[70]

> [T]he Dutch have been altogether unable to oppose any effectual restraint to the ravages of the Lanuns [*Ilanuns*] and other pirates ... They are privately encouraged by the Sultan of Lingen [*Lingga*] and almost openly by the Rajah Mudah of Rhio [*Riau*], and no Malay hesitates to admit that these chiefs ... are the real heads of the Lanuns. ... It is unfortunately the practice in some of the Malay states rather to encourage the young nobles of high rank, especially those of the Rajah's own extraction, whose maintenance would otherwise fall upon the Rajah himself, to subsist themselves by piratical practices than to discourage such proceedings.[71]

Raffles's recommendations to end this situation involved active British

"noticed" by Europeans in the area in the early eighteenth century, was a result of the Dutch monopoly system and suppression of customary trade. He argues that denominating the Malayan magnates "pirates" was the result of Europeans beginning to differentiate between honest trade and robbery. He points out that some "pirate" communities, *e.g.*, those of Sulu and other remote areas, were beyond the reach of Dutch blockades. However, it is not clear that customary lines of trade are unaffected merely because remote from the disruption of trade round the collection points. It is also not clear why the Sulu magnates should have been considered "pirates" while the magnates of Algiers were not. Vlekke does not explain why the politically unorganized Sallates were denominated "pirates" as early as 1510 while the organized Malayans were not given that label by Europeans until nearly two hundred years later. The evidence is overwhelming that petty robbery at sea increased vastly in the Malayan area in the last years of the seventeenth century.

[70] Lady Sophia Raffles, *Memoir of the Life and Public Services of Sir Thomas Stamford Raffles* ... (London, 1830), pp. 39 *et seq*.

[71] *Id*., pp. 45-46. On page 45 Raffles noted that "the name Lanuns ... has been extended to almost all the sea-rovers of the East ...".

steps to "oblige every Rajah to refuse to every description of pirates and Lanuns any sort of assistance or protection in his own territories." [72] This he openly regarded as a means of laying the legal basis for a British use of force to compel a radical change in Malay custom. British force would support "legitimate authority," mediate dynastic disputes, suppress "piracy" by holding the Sultans personally responsible for the acts of their subjects, end slavery, revise and codify Malay law in general, especially its commercial provisions,[73] and remove the Sultans from their interest in monopoly trade.[74] Aware that in 1811 "to go a-roving . . . implies no dishonour in the present state of the Malay morals," [75] Raffles must have been aware that his plan involved a radical change in the political and economic organization of the Sultanates. He did not consider the legal ramifications of his proposals, apparently involving, as they did, treating with the Sultans as heads of states and, at the same time, asserting rights to use force to control their activities which would seem so far reaching as to be inconsistent with their continued independence as sovereign heads of states.

One obstacle to the realization of Raffles's plans was the reluctance of British judges to regard their writ as running to the Sultans' territories. In 1813 two Malays were apprehended and brought to trial in Penang, a British colony off the coast of Kedah. They were found guilty of robbery for actions occurring in Province Wellesley, a strip of British territory on the mainland of the Peninsula opposite Penang. Upon the testimony of the Malay Chief of Kurau that the place within which three associated killings took place was "within the King of Pera's [Perak's] Territories," however, they were relieved of the accusation of murder. It was the court's view that no jurisdiction could be asserted by the British over the killings since they occurred "within the jurisdiction of a foreign State." This opinion was upheld on appeal to Madras 3-0 and on ultimate appeal to Calcutta 2-1.[76] Unfortunately, the dissenting opinion appears not to have been published.

[72] *Id.*, p. 48.

[73] Raffles's ideas of Malay law in 1811 were not entirely accurate. He seems to have confused local custom with Muslim religious law and local codes. H. Westra, "Custom and Muslim Law in the Netherlands East Indies," 25 *Transactions of the Grotius Society* (1940) 151 *et seq.*

[74] Raffles, *loc. cit.*, pp. 77-82.

[75] *Id.*, p. 48.

[76] R. v. Lebby Lundoo and Another, 2 Kyshe 6.

In strictly political action Raffles was not so hampered at first. In 1812 an expedition which he sent out of Batavia razed the shore fortifications of "pirates" in Borneo.[77] But where the Malays were more sophisticated it was more difficult to make the accusation of "piracy" serve as a sufficient justification for forcible action. In this regard it will be instructive to examine the role of the accusation of "piracy" in justifying British interference in the affairs of Atjeh.

In 1808 the British Resident of Malacca seized an Atjeh ship, claiming it to be properly considered Danish and condemning it as prize.[78] The remonstrances of the Sultan of Atjeh's French agent in Penang were disregarded, much to the damage and indignaton of the Sultan.[79] Some time later the Sultan of Atjeh had a Penang Malay's vessel and a British ship seized at Atjeh for respectively breach of port regulations and as security against or reprisal for (the report is not clear) breach of contract. These acts of Atjeh were denominated "piracies" by the Penang officials.[80]

In 1813 the Sultan of Atjeh seized a Coromandel (Indian) ship which had been trading in ports of Atjeh the closure of which to foreign shipping had been proclaimed in Penang some time before by the Sultan's agents. This seizure was denominated "piracy" by the Penang authorities.[81] On August 26, 1813, the Governor of Penang recorded his opinion that it would be necessary to "check" the "piratical" conduct of the Government of Atjeh which was interfering with the trade of British subjects in its territory.[82] A British naval vessel was dispatched which took the Coromandel ship and brought it into Penang, where it was presumably returned to its owners.[83] Whether the re-capturing ship received a share of the recovered valuables, and, if so, on what theory of law, if any, is not reported.

[77] S. Baring-Gould and C. A. Bampfylde, *A History of Sarawak Under Its Two White Rajahs* (London, 1909), p. 92.

[78] The British were at war in Europe with Denmark, which was allied with Napoleon, at the time. H. A. L. Fisher, *A History of Europe* (London, 1936), p. 878; A. T. Mahan, *The Influence of Sea Power upon the French Revolution and Empire, 1793-1812* (London, 1892), Vol. II, p. 277.

[79] John Anderson, *Acheen and the Ports on the North and East Coast of Sumatra* . . . (London, 1840), pp. 35-36.

[80] *Id.*, p. 37 note.

[81] *Id.*, p. 47 note.

[82] J. Low, "An Account of the Origin and Progress of the British Colonies in the Straits of Malacca" 4 *Logan's Journal* (1850) 17.

[83] Anderson, *Acheen*, p. 45; C. D. Cowan, "Early Penang and the Rise of Singapore, 1805-1832" 23(2) *JRASMB* (1945) 1 at pp. 49-50.

On September 10, 1813, the Supreme Government wrote to Penang:

[T]he right of the King of Acheen [*Atjeh*] to regulate the Trade of the Country actually under his authority cannot be disputed, but his pretensions . . . with respect to Countries which are only nominally a part of his Dominions cannot be admitted. . . . [T]he seizure by the King of Acheen of Vessels trading to those Countries on the pretence of it being a violation of the Laws of his Kingdom is little short of piracy.[84]

The use of the term "piracy" in these episodes is particularly interesting since the full legal results which were, in the heat of British colonial indignation, felt to flow against the Sultan of Atjeh from this classification were not, in fact, asserted; the Sultan was not hunted down as a common enemy of mankind and his ships were not attacked generally. Instead, classifying the actions of the Sultan of Atjeh as "piracy" seems merely to have removed from the Sultan and his commissioners the protection of the normal rules of international intercourse and his power to make rules for the governance of his own territory was impugned. A British official, known for his own brand of high-handed action as Governor of Penang in the 1820's, commenting on this action called it "the complete demonstration of our own arrogance." [85]

The label "piracy" had been used by the Government of Penang to justify action in Atjeh in a way quite inconceivable in European intercourse. The recognition of a rebel government as *de jure* independent before a situation stability has arisen to make such a recognition consistent with the facts was an intervention in internal affairs not warranted in normal relations among states in Europe in the early nineteenth century.[86] Furthermore, the use of blockade, if properly declared as this apparently was, to restrict the freedom of commerce of neutral third states with belligerent areas seems also to have been beyond question permissable at that time.[87] In short, in calling the

[84] Cowan, *loc. cit.*, p. 51.

[85] Governor Fullerton, quoted in Anderson, *Acheen*, p. 47 note.

[86] J. B. Moore, *Digest of International Law* (Washington, 1906), Vol. I, p. 73; H. Lauterpacht, *Recognition in International Law* (Cambridge, 1947), pp. 11-12.

[87] Blockade was a proper legal practice at this time even with regard to ports over which the blockading authority had no color of right to make regulations. The Hurtige Hane (1801) 3 C. Rob. 324, 165 E.R. 480; The Fortuna (1800) 2 C. Rob. 92, 165 E.R. 250. These decisions by Lord Stowell (then Sir William Scott) involved Moslem claimants operating out of Algiers in breach of the British blockade of Napoleon's France. The blockade, which was enforced against the Algerian shippers had apparently never been properly proclaimed in Algiers.

Sultan's actions "little short of piracy" a different yardstick was being used to measure the propriety of his acts than was used in measuring the propriety of European sovereign's actions by the international law of the early nineteenth century. In Europe at this time states were acknowledged the right to restrict within their own borders other states' "imperfect right" to free commercial intercourse; [88] in Malayan waters the sovereign who attempted the same restrictions ran a risk of being considered a pirate. The British authorities in Penang, the most influential and active European officials in the area of the Straits of Malacca at this time were prepared to act in some ways against such sovereign "pirates." The British authorities in Bengal (called in contemporary documents the "Supreme Government") were prepared to approve Penang's actions.

The Sultan of Atjeh appealed to the Supreme Government for satisfaction and a British officer was sent to Atjeh in 1814 to investigate. His visit to rebel chieftains, who had been otherwise effectively blockaded by the Sultan, was taken by those chieftains as an encouragement to rebellion; the Sultan was less than hospitable to the British officer when that officer got around to visiting him.[89] The result was that the British officer's report, objective as to the facts indicating that some significant areas of Atjeh were not effectively controlled by the Sultan, did not indicate that this political situation was unstable and that the Sultan had a fair chance of regaining full control over Atjeh.[90] In 1815 a party of Atjeh magnates wrote to Penang to ask permission to rebel against the Sultan, alleging as their aim the ouster of a British adventurer who seems to have been the Sultan's principal adviser in attempts to regulate and order Atjeh's trade.[91] The British had already found this man's presence in Atjeh so embarrassing (and, presumably, such an obstacle to profitable trade) that his continued residence in the Far East had been forbidden by Penang.[92] Nonetheless, a noncommital answer was returned to this request for "permission." However, a key Arab figure in the Atjeh intriques was permitted to fit out five ships in Penang for defense against "pirates," and this fleet seems to have attacked vessels of the Sultan of Atjeh. The Penang-based

[88] E. de Vattel, *The Law of Nations* (Fenwick, transl.) ed. of 1758 (Washington, 1916), pp. 121-122.
[89] Anderson, *Acheen*, p. 49.
[90] *Id.*, pp. 50-51.
[91] Low, *loc. cit.*, pp. 17-18.
[92] Anderson, *Acheen*, pp. 51-52; 1 Kyshe xliv, xlvii.

vessels flew British colours and some British subjects took part in the attacks.[93] The Sultan of Atjeh brought this situation to the attention of the Supreme Government, which eventually decreed a strict policy of non-intervention.[94]

At this juncture a very rich Arab merchant in Penang had the rebellious magnates declare his son, a British subject by virtue of his birth in the Colony, "Sultan" of Atjeh.[95] The former Sultan continued his battle, but took great care to avoid any action that might again bring upon him the accusation of "piracy." Now the new Sultan appears to have made the mistake of seizing some trading ships on the plea that they belonged to the former Sultan.[96] For this action his father, the Penang merchant, was actually gaoled on a charge of "piracy"! He was released apparently only after considerable political pressure had been applied in his behalf by the Moslem community in Penang against the British Governor.[97]

By the end of 1816 the former Sultan seems to have regained his place in the town of Atjeh. In February, 1817, the Governor of Penang proposed a treaty by which the British would get a favourable tariff rate and other concessions from him.[98] There appears to have been no embarrassment felt at the prospect of treating with this "pirate" as a sovereign once again. The Supreme Government overruled the attempt to gain commercial concessions, but directed that should the Sultan be able to re-establish himself throughout Atjeh again an indemnity should be demanded of him for injuries which the rebellion in Atjeh had caused to British subjects (presumably including the pretender), and an acquiescence in the other non-commercial terms of the treaty proposed by Penang should be obtained. Failing this, the Supreme Government agreed that "ulterior measures must be taken" and contemplated sending troops into Atjeh to establish a permanent political connection between Penang and Atjeh.[99]

At this delicate point the resources of the Arab pretender's Penang merchant father began to run dry and the real Malay leader of the rebellion, the Chief of Pedir, switched allegiance back to the former

[93] Anderson, *Acheen*, pp. 56-58.
[94] *Id.*, p. 76.
[95] *Id.*, pp. 65, 75, 81.
[96] *Id.*, p. 78.
[97] *Id.*, pp. 79-80.
[98] *Id.*, p. 82.
[99] *Id.*, pp. 82-83.

Sultan of Atjeh.[100] Unfortunately, the British officer sent into Atjeh late in 1817 to report on matters appears to have committed Penang to assist the pretender further and wrote two reports, in January and February 1818, favourable to his claims.[101] Matters were set to rights by Raffles's personal intervention and the British confirmed the "legitimate" Sultan in his old office and forced the pretender to retire to Penang.[102] By this time, however, it was too late to prevent further deterioration of the political situation in Atjeh and by 1820 Penang's trade with Atjeh was ruined and the Supreme Government was again considering direct action.[103] In fact, no direct action was taken by the British, the pretender ended his life in Penang a stipendiary of the Sultan of Atjeh,[104] and the restored Sultan died in 1824 still at odds with his magnates, who, as was their right under Malay law, selected a more distant relative than his heir apparent to succeed him in regal dignity.[105]

The use of the word "piracy" to justify British authorities in Penang taking action in Malayan political affairs in circumstances when similar action would not have been considered justifiable against European sovereigns by the international law of the early nineteenth century was also evident in events in the Peninsula. In January of 1816 the Governor of Penang wrote to the Sultan of Kedah that the British had heard that the Sumatran polity of Siak was planning to attack Perak in the Malay Peninsula. Suspecting that the Sultan of Kedah intended to participate in the attack, he wrote, "Though not bound by treaty to protect Perak from invasion by sea, as in the case with Quedah [Kedah],[106] I shall treat as pirates any whom I find

[100] *Id.*, pp. 84-86.

[101] *Id.*, pp. 145, 108-119, 126-127.

[102] *Id.*, pp. 131, 144; C. E. Wurtzburg, *Raffles of the Eastern Isles* (London, 1954), pp. 508-509, 518. See C. A. Gibson-Hill, "Raffles, Acheh and the Order of the Golden Sword." 29(1) *JRASMB* (1951) 1.

[103] Cowan, *loc. cit.*, pp. 68-72, 110-111.

[104] Anderson, *Acheen*, p. 150. The stipend had been part of the settlement of 1818.

[105] *Id.*, p. 152.

[106] Whether the British actually had such a legal obligation to Kedah is open to question. The obligation was considered by the British to grow out of what purport to be treaties. See Sir W. G. Maxwell and W. S. Gibson, *Treaties and Engagements Affecting the Malay States and Borneo* (London, 1924), pp. 95-100. An adequate discussion of the transactions giving rise to the "treaties" and the conflicting interpretations of them would require a disproportionate amount of space and is therefore not included in this paper.

waging hostility so near to this island [Penang] as any part of the Perak territory." [107] To the Sultan of Siak, however, he wrote merely that he would consider any who took part in hostilities against Perak "as enemies to the British Government." [108]

The letter to the Sultan of Siak is clearly ambiguous in the context of this investigation. Enemies of the British Government need not be "pirates" in order to be subject to retorsion, reprisal, self-defense actions or war.[109] "Pirates," as *hostes humani generis*,[110] may certainly be treated as enemies of a particular government.

The letter to the Sultan of Kedah is not ambiguous in this context. The highest authority of the British Government in the area indicated in a letter to the acknowledged chief of a state with which the British were tied by treaty that no plea of state authority or commission, and no representations by the sovereign, would be considered valid to stand between any person "waging hostility" in Perak and the legal results of his being labeled a "pirate." Three aspects of this development are worth noting specially: (1) The British were proposing to attach the label "piracy" to acts which would not have been considered to merit that label under the customary international law of piracy applicable in Europe at this time; (2) The British were proposing to deny to accused "pirates" the defenses which were available to Europeans accused of "piracy" and their sovereigns; and (3) the British were proposing to accord to a foreign sovereign treatment which they would have considered improper had the foreign sovereign offered identical treatment to British commissioners in equivalent circumstances.

As to the first point, without analyzing all the differences it is necessary to point out merely that in proposing to treat as "piracy" acts taking place wholly within the land territory of a foreign independent sovereign (indeed, a sovereign whose independence was at issue in the case, with the British attempting to support it) the political arm of the

[107] Anderson, *Acheen*, p. 73.

[108] *Id.*

[109] On the law of retorsion and reprisal in the late eighteenth to early nineteenth centuries see Vattel, *loc. cit.*, Bk. ii, secs. 341-354. Self-defense is discussed in *id.*, secs. 49-53, 119-121; the classic formulation of that doctrine did not come until the British-American correspondence concerning the sinking of the *Caroline* by Canadian authorities in the United States in 1837. See R. Y. Jennings, "The Caroline and McLoed Cases," 32 American Journal of International Law (1938) 82 *et seq*. The justifications for war at this period are noted in Butler and Maccoby, *loc. cit.*, pp. 107 *et seq*.

[110] See Part I above.

British Government was advancing on a course which had already run into legal difficulties just three years before.[111] If, now, using the label "piracy" would help to overcome the reluctance of British judges to assert British jurisdiction over acts occurring wholly in the territory of foreign sovereigns, or if, by use of the concept of "piracy," legal results could be attached to foreigners' behaviour without the need to have the applicable law considered by a municipal law tribunal, British policy makers would be relieved of a wide range of legal restraints, both in international law and British constitutional law, in determining on action in Southeast Asia.[112]

As to the second point, there is no evidence that the rights of a sovereign to protect his subjects accused of "piracy" were ever diminished in Europe. As noted above, since at least 1675 in England

[111] See above, events of 1813. But, per contra, see R. v. Noquedah Allong and Others (1811) 2 Kyshe 3 in which the defendants, accused of robbery and murder committed in the waters just off Penang, were shipped off to Calcutta for trial along with the witnesses. It appears that although the courts would not extend their writ into the territory of foreign Malay sovereigns, there were ways of hanging those sovereigns' subjects for acts committed at sea, even without charging "piracy." Note that at this time British territorial waters did not carry territorial jurisdiction with them. See R. v. Keyn ("The Franconia") cited note 7 above.

[112] An example of the freedom of action felt to have been achieved by this use of the label "piracy" is the following:

In January 1827 a British officer was sent on a "piratehunting" expedition into the Malay Peninsula. For this the Penang Government was roundly reprimanded by the Supreme Government:

> "... [U]nder ... the laws of all civilized nations, his [the offending Malay chieftain's] conduct should have formed the subject of representation and remonstrance to his own Government. If that Government refused redress, the question of the proper course to be pursued would then have naturally attracted the grave and deliberate consideration of your Board and of the Supreme Government."

The defense set out by Governor Fullerton and his Council at Penang was that they were bound by international law to "destroy" the "noted pirate, one of the common enemies of mankind." The reason given for not capturing him and taking him to Penang for trial was that the court at Penang did not have jurisdiction over "piracy." Neither argument seems to make a compelling case since (a) it is not self-evidently proper or common practice to pursue "pirates" into the territory of a foreign sovereign without that sovereign's permission, and (b) as noted in note 111 above the lack of admiralty jurisdiction in the courts of Penang did not hamper it sending accused sea robbers back to Calcutta for trial. Nonetheless, the Supreme Government accepted Penang's reasoning and the matter dropped. The Penang authorities were more careful in the years that followed in any event. Correspondence concerning this affair occupies a large part of Colonel Henry Burney, *The Burney Papers* (Bangkok, 1910-1914), Vol. II, Part VI.

sovereigns were considered to have the right to protect at least their own subjects from being treated as pirates either by issuing commissions or by otherwise interposing their sovereignty between the accused and the sovereign seeking to punish them.

As to the third point, it is hardly necessary to find precedents to support the proposition that the British would have been anguished indeed by the thought that a Malay Sultan had the right to treat as a "pirate" a British Naval Officer doing his duty, particularly if the acts complained of occurred on the high seas or within the boundaries of a third state.

V. Conclusion

We have seen how European authorities began to manipulate the concept of "piracy" at international law to suit political needs in Malayan waters at the beginning of the eighteenth century. We have also seen how, by the beginning of the third decade of the nineteenth century the label "pirate" was used by British authorities to avoid restraints placed on them by international law and by British municipal law. In so using the label, as we have seen, the British authorities appeared to be applying legal classifications and drawing legal conclusions to acts and relations which would not have borne the same legal classifications or results in Europe. From this it might be concluded that the "international law" applied in Southeast Asia by European (or, at least, British) authorities was different in substance from the "international law" applied in Europe; *i.e.*, that a sovereign's actions in Europe bore different legal consequences than the same actions in Southeast Asia done by an authority which would have been considered "sovereign" had it possessed the same incidents of authority in Europe. It might be argued that the substantive rules of "international law" remained the same in Southeast Asia as in Europe, but that under the press of exciting events in times when European power was not as preponderant as it was to become, administrators far removed from cool counsel improperly spoke of "piracy" while intending merely to express political, rather than legal, views. Nonetheless, even if used to mask political action primarily, it must be observed that when words are used to *justify* action as is done in the incidents described above, the correspondence is by definition legal whether or not it is also political. An *opinio juris* is being expressed.

It is difficult to ignore an *opinio juris* expressed by the highest authorities of the most powerful government in an area as a statement of applicable international law. The concept of "piracy" was in fact taken up by highly respected judicial authorities in Great Britain at least and applied quite consciously to some non-European political leaders.[113] This was coupled with some ruthless efforts to suppress "piracy" in some areas in which the presence of marauding Malayan state enterprises was embarrassing to policy makers seeking to expand their political influence.[114] Those wishing to believe the substance of international law remained the same in Asia as Europe during the nineteenth century were comforted some fifty years later to discover a theory by which the apparent contradiction could be explained. In his division of states into fully sovereign and less than fully sovereign (corresponding generally with European and non-European) Lorimer [115] preserved the unseamed garment of international law by denying to such as the Malay Sultans the right to equal treatment with European sovereigns under that "universal" law.

On the other hand, it should not be forgotten that these developments were not unanimously accepted; the treatment of non-Europeans under the international law of the nineteenth century was not in all cases as discriminatory as the foregoing evidence might indicate.

[113] See the Serhassan Pirates, (1845) 166 E.R. 788, 2 W. Rob 354. In his opinion on The Magellan Pirates (1853), 164 E.R. 47, 1 Spink Ecc. & Ad. 81, Dr. Lushington wrote:

> "Even an independent state may, in my opinion, be guilty of piratical acts. What were the Barbary pirates of olden times? What many of the African tribes of this moment? . . .".

In fact, the "Barbary pirates of olden times" were not considered to be "pirates" by their contemporaries specifically because they held commissions of a sovereign. See note 31 above.

[114] Sir James Brooke, for example, owed a large part of his political success in Borneo to the suppression of rival Rajahs' forces as "pirates." See *Parliamentary Papers* 1854-55, Vol. XXIX, "Report of the Commissioners Appointed to Inquire into Certain Matters Connected with the Position of Sir James Brooke," esp. pp. 435-437; Admiral Sir Henry Keppel, *A Sailor's Life Under Four Sovereigns* (London, 1899), Vol. I, chs. XXVIII and XXIX.

[115] J. Lorimer, *The Institutes of Law* (Edinburgh, 1872); Prolégomènes d'un Système Raisonné de Droit International," 10 *Revue de Droit International et de Législation Comparée* (1878) 339; "La Doctrine de la Reconnaissance," 16 *id.*, (1884) 333. It is astounding to the modern reader that these works, so frankly and naively keyed to "race" (Lorimer divided the population of the world into "Aryans" and "Shemites," with "Buddhists" falling slightly on the Aryan side), and so completely wrong in their "facts," could have achieved the influence they undoubtedly did.

In 1840 the British court in Penang held innocent of piracy a Malay rebel involved in political intrigues in Kedah.[116] The holding was placed squarely on the ground of "piracy" being a concept inapplicable to political action.[117] In 1847 the Law Officers of the Crown advised the British Government that British naval authorities lacked the right in international law to pursue Turkish "pirates" into Turkish rivers, or seize on the high seas vessels that have been involved in depredations solely within Turkish territory.[118] In 1848 the Law Officers of the Crown gave their view that a ship under control of a rebel group is not a pirate ship even if friendly relations are maintained with the old government against which the rebels were fighting.[119]

In summary, it appears that once the concept of "piracy" had become so removed from universal applicability that it threatened to become merely an excuse for political action rather than a definitive legal justification for such action, the concept became more and more elusive as a matter of law. It is not possible to say even today that a clearly defined, useful concept of "piracy" remains in international law.[120]

[116] R. v. Tunkoo Mahomed Saad and Others (1840) 2 Kysbe 18.

[117] *Id.*, p. 72.

[118] Sir A. D. McNair, *International Law Opinions* (Cambridge, 1956), Vol. I, p. 270. This position was reiterated in 1879 but modified in 1881 to justify counter-action in Turkish territory apparently as a political measure - and without reference to the law of "piracy." *Id.*, Vol. II, pp. 273 *et seq.*

[119] *Id.*, Vol. I, p. 270.

[120] There have been many attempts, even in this century, to apply the legal consequences of the classification "piracy" to political acts. The most recent attempt to codify the customary international law of piracy (Article 15 of the Geneva Convention on the High Seas (1958)) provides that the depredation must be "committed for private ends." It should be noted, however, that even this Convention has been justly criticized for its lack of precision. B. Forman, "International Law of Piracy," 15 JAG Journal (1961) 143 *et seq.*

PROF. DANIEL TURACK

University of Mississippi

Early English Restrictions to Travel

"Moreover I said unto the King, If it please the King, let letters be given me to the governors beyond the river, that they may let me pass through till I come unto Judah."

Nehemiah 2 : 7 Old Testament, Revised Version

I.

Through the centuries, scholars have been divided as to whether or not the subject was entitled by the common law to leave England. Fitz-Neal, Glanvill and Bracton, three of the earliest writers on the common law did not deal with the question. Fleta,[1] and Britton,[2] both writing about the time of Edward I maintain that the subject could only leave the country after securing the required licence from the monarch. Fitz-Herbert,[3] writing in 1534 was of the opinion that the subject was at liberty to leave without a licence. Coke [4] disagreed with Fitz-Herbert, while Hale [5] and Blackstone,[5a] who followed him, found

[1] Fleta, (1647 edition) pp. 382-3 speaks of the "*Essoin de ultra mare*" and warns that it would be ill advised and wrong for anyone to leave the realm without first obtaining the king's permission. See also J. Beames, *The Writ of Ne Exeat Regno* (New York, 1921) p. 4, and C. M. Whelan, "Passports And Freedom of Travel: The Conflict Of A Right And A Privilege," 41 *Georgetown L.J.* (1952) 63.

[2] Britton, Book VI, chapter VII, writing of the "*Essoin de ultra mare*" says that "no great lord or knight of our realm ought to travel forth of it without our licence, since by that means the kingdom might be left destitute of able persons . . ." Britton, (revised and translated) by F. M. Nichols (2 vols., Oxford, 1865) Vol. 2, p. 349.

[3] Sir Anthony Fitz-Herbert, *The New Natura Brevium* (London, 1666) ch. 85, p. 204 stated: "By the Common Law every man may go out of the Realm to Merchandize, or on Pilgrimage, or for other cause he pleaseth, without the King's leave; and he shall not be punished for so doing: . . ."

[4] Sir Edward Coke, *The Third Part of the Institutes of the Laws of England*, (4th edn., London, 1669) p. 178, stated that the 4th Constitution of Clarendon of 1164 ". . . appeareth in it self to be but a recognition, or declaration of the Common Law."

[5] Sir Mathew Hale, *A Treatise In Three Parts, Part 2, De Portibus Maris*, found in F. Hargrave, *Collection of tracts relative to the law of England* (Dublin, 1787) p. 91, stated: "At common law any man might pass the seas without licence, unless he were prohibited; . . ."

[5a] William Blackstone, *Commentaries On The Laws of England* (4 vols., Oxford, 1765) Vol. I, p. 265, stated:

merit in Fitz-Herbert's view. The early legal giants of the common law were divided.

More recently, the younger Chitty [6] writing in 1820 was of the opinion that the King's permission was required while Beames [7] writing a year later disagreed. In this century, Sibley,[8] an expert on passports, writing in 1906 supported the view that the common law prohibited the subject leaving the realm without a licence, a view also taken by Holdsworth [9] in his examination of the whole of the history of English law. Without disclosure of which camp appears to be right, it might be advisable to examine where the foundation stones of the topic lay.

Review of the Anglo-Saxon practices in England on the subject draws a blank. The topic appears to have its genesis in the years following the Norman conquest of England. As the Norman Church lay firmly under the control of the Norman dukes,[10] it is not surprising to find William the Conqueror asserting a similar authority over the English Church. In ecclesiastical matters, William proposed to maintain the English Church as a national, self-governing institution amenable to his temporal power. William, however, was to find a challenger to his control over the English Church in the person of the Pope. The concept of a centralized church regulated in all aspects by the Pope was untenable to the Conqueror, who regarded such a policy as contrary

"By the common law, every man may go out of the realm for whatever cause he pleaseth, without obtaining the King's leave; provided he is under no injunction of staying at home..." A barrister of Lincoln's Inn, Timothy Brecknock, writing a year earlier than Blackstone, followed Britton - *Droit le Roy* (London, 1764) p. 81.

[6] J. Chitty the Younger, *A Treatise On The Law Of The Prerogatives of The Crown* (London, 1820) p. 21 states "The King's right to keep his subjects within the realm, which exists at common law, ..."

[7] J. Beames, *The Writ of Ne Exeat Regno* (New York, 1821) p. 1 speaking of the writ stated that "It appears to have been unknown to the ancient Common Law, which in the freedom of its spirit, allowed everyman to depart the Realm at his pleasure."

[8] N. W. Sibley, "The Passport System," VII *Jour. of The Soc. of Comp. Legislation, N.S.* (1906), p. 32. This was the view taken as recently as 1946, see K. Diplock, "Passports And Protection In International Law," *The Grotius Society*, vol. 32 (1947) p. 44.

[9] Sir William Holdsworth, *A History Of English Law* (Vol. X, London, 1938), p. 390 stated "At common law the King had certain powers to control the movements of his subjects."

[10] C. H. Haskins, *Norman Institutions* (Cambridge, Mass., 1925) p. 30f.

to his tradition and an attempt to encroach upon his secular authority. William envisaged himself as an absolute monarch which included his mastership over clerics in his dominions. Recognition of the papal headship of the Church was acceptable as long as papal contact with the English Church did not seek to restrict the King's authority over his subjects. William's concern proved to be well-founded as Pope Gregory VII was to call for the exemption of the English Church from secular administration and the subjection of the King to the power of the Roman See.[11] As the Roman Church sought to extend its influence and power, the hitherto peaceful harmony which prevailed between church and state prior to the conquest was destined to erupt into a clash between the king and the Pope.

It is to the king's line of action for the containment of the Roman influence that we are directed.[12] Without reference to former law or custom, William innovated a series of edicts designed to accomplish his purpose.[13] Among the new laws were to be found the restrictions that (a) no appeals to the Papal Court were allowed without the king's permission save in matrimonial and testamentary matters; [14] (b) no papal legate a *latere* was to set foot in England without first obtaining the king's licence, and providing security or taking an oath not to do anything against the king's will; [15] (c) no papal bull, constitution or

[11] E. A. Freeman, *History of The Norman Conquest of England* (6 vols., Oxford, 1867-1879) Vol. IV, pp. 432 and 433. For a full discussion on this question see Z. N. Brooke, *The English Church And The Papacy* (Cambridge, 1931), p. 132 seq. and A. J. MacDonald, *Lanfranc: a Study of His Life, Work and Writing* (Oxford, 1926) pp. 220-231. See also Pope Gregory VII's letter to William dated May 8, 1080 in which he makes a formal demand for William's fealty, found in D. C. Douglas & G. W. Greenaway, eds., *English Historical Documents 1042-1189*, Vol. II (London, 1953) p. 646.

[12] *Eadmeri Historia Novorum in Anglia*, ed. M. Rule (Rolls Ser., London, 1884) Bk. I, p. 10 (hereafter referred to as *Eadmer*); G. Bosanquet, *Eadmer's History of Recent Events in England* (translated), (London, 1964) pp. 10-11.

[13] F. Barlow, *The Feudal Kingdom of England 1042-1216* (London, 1955), p. 131.

[14] For an excellent discussion of this restriction see F. Makower, *The Constitutional History And Constitution of the Church of England* (translated, London and New York, 1895), pp. 225-232. Also see T. B. Ingram, *England and Rome* (London, 1892) pp. 24-47; H. G. Richardson and G. O. Sayles, *The Governance of Medieval England From The Conquest To Magna Carta* (Edinburgh, 1963) pp. 295-302; W. Stubbs, *The Constitutional History of England* (3 vols., Oxford, 1874-78) III, p. 348 ff. (referred to hereafter as *Const. Hist.*

[15] F. Makower, *op. cit.*, pp. 232-235; T. B. Ingram, *op. cit.*, pp. 15-24, Stubbs, *Const. Hist.*, *op cit.*, III, pp. 298-301.

letter could be received or brought into England unless it was approved by the king; [16] (d) no Pope was to be recognized in England without the king's consent; [17] and (e) no ecclesiastic was to leave England without the king's permission, as well as other restrictions.[18] In time these *leges* of the Conqueror were to become known as the *avitae consuetudines* or the ancestral customs. It is this last specific restriction with which we are most concerned, but in some instances, it will be necessary to examine the question of appeals, (a) above, which bears a special relationship to the limitation on travel.

As the actual edict of William, which called for the king's licence before an ecclesiastic could journey beyond the seas, is lost in the mist of time, it becomes necessary to prove the case of its existence by sifting the evidence provided by the Conqueror's actions. William's actual enforcement of this restriction is attested to by several church historians.[19] The initial exercise of the prerequisite to leaving the country is deemed to have taken place in 1071 when William granted his permission to Lanfranc, the Archbishop of Canterbury, and Thomas, the Archbishop of York to proceed to the Apostolic See to receive their pallia from the Pope. Prior to the conquest, the Anglo-Saxon kings allowed an archbishop to travel to Rome for the pallium without special leave of the king.[20] The king's licence or passport was probably contained in a document sealed under the Great Seal in a form similar to what subsequently became the *licentia transfretandi.*[21]

In a letter addressed to Archbishop Lanfranc, dated 25 March 1097, Pope Gregory VII ventured a guess as to the archbishop's failure to visit Rome. He wrote,

> Verily, as we have ascertained from a reliable source, your presence has been denied to us ... through fear of the king ... [who] has taken this measure against the holy see ...

[16] F. Makower, *op. cit.*, pp. 235-239.

[17] J. T. Ellis, *Anti-Papal Legislation In Medieval England (1066-1377)*, (Washington, 1930), p. 9.

[18] W. Stubbs, *Const. Hist., op cit.*, I, pp. 285-6.

[19] N. F. Cantor, *Church, Kingship And Lay Investiture in England 1089-1135* (New Jersey, 1958) p. 77; W. Waterworth, England and Rome (London, 1854) p. 253.

[20] G. O. Sayles, *The Medieval Foundations of England* (London, 1948) p. 194. Archbishops of Canterbury went to Rome for this purpose as early as 925 while the archbishops of York went from 1026.

[21] See Sir Francis Palgrave, *The History of Normandy and England* (4 vols., London, 1851-65) iv, p. 106.

and Lanfranc was directed to

> counsel him not to presume unjustly against the Roman Church . . . nor to restrict further you or any other devoutly desiring to visit the apostolic see.[22]

Not long afterwards, in a letter addressed to Hubert, subdeacon of the Roman Church, dated 23 September 1079, Pope Gregory expresses his indignation as to the king's malevolent practice in these words:

> For none of all the kings, not excepting those that are heathen, has dared to act against the apostolic see in the way he has unblushingly done; none has been so irreverent or shameless as to forbid the bishops and archbishops to frequent the threshold of the apostles.[23]

One view which seeks to explain the remarks in these letters is offered by the church historian, Waterworth.[24] He suggests that these letters were written by the pontiff after William had ignored repeated solicitations by Lanfranc for the king's licence to journey to Rome. I would add that the reference to *bishops and archbishops* in the second letter is more realistic, as others aside from Lanfranc would be expected to visit Rome.

Following William's receipt of the Pope's letter of 8 May 1080[25] which calls for William's fealty to Gregory VII, and William's explicit refusal[26] in words which led the historian, Stenton,[27] to relate "No statesman has ever settled a major issue in fewer words, or more conclusively," the Conqueror would ensure that stringent measures were maintained to enforce his policies. The directness of the papal ambitions and their utter rejection by William left little chance for relaxation of the Conqueror's policy to limit freedom of access by his bishops to Rome. Witness to this proposition can be shown from Lanfranc's failure to journey to Rome despite a papal command in 1082 which carried with it the threat of suspension from all episcopal function if Lanfranc disobeyed.[28]

[22] D. C. Douglas and G. W. Greenaway, ed., *English Historical Documents 1042-1189*, vol. 2 (London, 1953) p. 643. Reference to this letter is also found in W. Waterworth, *op cit.*, p. 254; Z. N. Brooke, *op. cit.*, p. 137. E. A. Freeman, *op. cit.*, vol. IV, p. 435, n. 1 contains the Latin text of the letter.

[23] D. C. Douglas and G. W. Greenaway, *op. cit.*, pp. 643-4. See also, Z. N. Brooke, *op. cit.*, p. 137.

[24] W. Waterworth, *op. cit.*, p. 253.

[25] See note 11.

[26] D. C. Douglas and G. W. Greenaway, *op. cit.*, pp. 646-7.

[27] F. M. Stenton, *Anglo-Saxon England* (Oxford, 1943) p. 667.

[28] A translation of the letter from Pope Gregory to Lanfranc is found in D. C. Douglas and G. W. Greenaway, *op. cit.*, p. 648.

Another rationale which provides for the emergence of travel restrictions upon English prelates has its origin in the events which ensued on the death of Pope Alexander II. Rival popes, Gregory VII and Clement III, emerged as heirs to the throne of St. Peter. William adopted a policy of neutrality in refusing to acknowledge either candidate until he called a Council of the English Church to consider the matter, a move which he unhesitatingly deferred until Gregory's expulsion from his see by Emperor Henry IV in 1080. Until William formally accepted Gregory as the legitimate Pope the travel restrictions on English ecclesiastics served to save the king the embarrassment of rendering recognition before he had made up his mind.[29] Moreover, the deferment of recognition gave William the opportunity to strengthen his ecclesiastical policies. The theory, however, can only account for the development of the restraint on ecclesiastics going beyond the seas from the time of the death of Alexander II in 1073, when Pope and anti-pope made their appearance. As has been already noted, both archbishops Lanfranc and Thomas secured the king's permission before their departure in 1071.

Sir Francis Palgrave supports the view that the impediment to travel in this era did not rest solely upon the English clerics but that the king exercised this prerogative to prevent any of his subjects from leaving the realm.[30] Anglo-papal relations also found foreign ecclesiastics regarded with great suspicion by William. Such individuals had to receive William's permission before attempting to enter England as witnessed by Lanfranc's caution to Hugh the Cardinal in 1084, "I do not recommend your coming to England unless you first obtain permission from the king of the English." [31] Hence, at the close of the Conqueror's reign the practice of forbidding English clergy if not all English subjects from departing the realm without the king's licence is firmly entrenched.

Whether we agree or not that the initial appearance of the travel prerequisites occurred in the Conqueror's time, his successor exercised this tether upon his English subjects. Selden [32] was of the opinion that

[29] G. Slocombe, *William The Conqueror* (London, 1959) pp. 230-1.

[30] Sir Francis Palgrave, *op. cit.*, vol. IV, p. 106.

[31] D. C. Douglas and G. W. Greenaway, *op. cit.*, p. 649.

[32] *Joannis Seldeni Jurisconsulti Opera Omnia, Tam Edita quam Inedita*, Vol. 2 (London, 1726) p. 1010 where he states:

"*Archiepiscopis, episcopis, & personis regni non licet exire regnum absque licentia D.R. & si exierint, si regi placuerit, assecurabunt eum, quod nec in* the development of the restraint against ecclesiastics and other subjects enjoying freedom of travel was attributable to William Rufus, a view also shared by Beames.[33]

An excellent illustration of the complications encountered by an ecclesiastic who desired to depart the realm is brought to light in the *Trial of William of St. Calais, Bishop of Durham.*[34] Briefly, the bishop who also happened to be lord of the fief, had been indicted for treason. The bishop requested trial by compurgation which was refused. He asked for leave to appeal to the Papal Curia on the basis that it was a competent tribunal to try a bishop. Leave, in this situation, included the king's authorization in the form of the licence necessary to depart. Rufus responded to the request with an order to confiscate the bishop's temporalties. The bishop finally left the castle on receipt of a safe-conduct[35] from the king. The castle was surrendered to the king, and the bishop received a licence to enable him to cross the sea. The licence read:

"William, King of the English, to all his liegemen in all England greeting. Know that the bishop of Durham and all his men have my peace throughout the whole kingdom of England, and that they have my permission to cross the sea. Wherefore I forbid all men under my authority to do them harm." [36]

Noteworthy are the points that the document could be used as a

eundo, nec in redeundo, vel moram faciendo, perquirant malum sive damnum D. regi. Huc referas, an cum Polydoro ad Rufum an posteriora ad tempora rescriptum quod in regesto, Ne Exeas Regnum, habetur, haut ita multum interest, nec quaestionem accurare pretium erit operae."

[33] J. Beames, *op. cit.*, p. 1.

[34] For a more detailed account see *De injusta vexatione Willelmi episcopi primi, per Willelmum regem filium Willelmi magni regis, in Symeonis monachi Opera omnia*, ed. by T. Arnold, (2 vols. Rolls Series, London, 1882), Vol. I, p. 170 ff.; D. C. Douglas & G. W. Greenaway, *op. cit.*, Vol. II, pp. 609-624 and authorities cited therein; A. L. Poole, *From Domesday Book To Magna Carta 1087-1216*, 2d. edn. (Oxford, 1955) p. 103.

[35] F. Barlow, *The Feudal Kingdom of England 1042-1216* (London, etc., 1955) p. 145 contains the reference that the bishops never appeared before the king without a safe conduct. The document referred to was issued for the safety and protection of the holder in internal travels.

[36] D. C. Douglas & G. W. Greenaway, *op. cit.*, Vol. II, p. 622. The contemporary writer, Symeon of Durham, in his account stated the licence to be:

"*Willelmus rex Anglorum omnibus, fidelibus suis per totam Angliam salutem. Sciatis Dunelmensem episcopum et omnes suos homines pacem meam habere per totum regnum Angliae, et licentia et pace mea mare transire: ideoque defendo omnibus meae potestatis hominibus, ne aliquid mali eis faciant.*", T. Arnold, *op. cit.*, Vol. I, p. 192.

single passport by the bishop named specifically and as a collective passport for the benefit of the bishop and his retinue. Also, that the licence gave royal protection [37] for those mentioned therein to be enjoyed whilst in England. Lastly, the licence served to acknowledge the granting of the king's leave for departure from the realm.

I would add that the document described would be of little use to the traveler on reaching foreign soil, as a safe-conduct from the foreign sovereign would be required to assure the traveler some measure of safety. Despite the possession of the licence, the bishop and his retinue were delayed before the king gave his final approval to the departure.[38]

The sanctions to which the subject was exposed for leaving England without the requisite authorization during the reign of William Rufus are aptly demonstrated by the case of Herbert Losinga, Bishop of Norwich. In 1093, the bishop went to Rome to secure papal absolution for his sin of simoniacal purchase of his see. He neglected to acquire the necessary licence to embark upon the trip. Upon his return, Rufus withdrew the bishop's pastoral staff as punishment for his disobedience.[39]

The death of Lanfranc in 1089 created a vacancy in the archbishopric which remained empty until the election of Anselm on 6 March 1093, when he was both elected and invested as Rufus lay supposedly on his death-bed faced with the contingency that he might perish in body and soul if he died with the see still in his possession.[40] Thereafter Anselm sought the king's permission to journey abroad that he might receive the pallium without which he lacked the fulfilment of his office and could neither consecrate a bishop nor hold a council.[41] It was to make this point and secure the king's licence that Anselm went to Rufus at Gillingham in January 1095.[42] Anselm's plea fell upon deaf ears. The matter was discussed again at a meeting of

[37] The reference to *protection* here does not mean the immunity from suit as in the *litterae de protectione* which frequently appears in the Patent Rolls.

[38] T. Arnold, *op. cit.*, Vol. I, pp. 192-4; D. C. Douglas & G. W. Greenaway, *op. cit.*, Vol. II, pp. 622-4.

[39] N. F. Cantor, *op. cit.*, p. 77.

[40] *Eadmer*, pp. 30-31; N. F. Cantor, *op. cit.*, p. 53. A translation is to be found in D. C. Douglas & G. W. Greenaway, *op. cit.*, Vol. II, pp. 650-673. Anselm did homage to Rufus in September and was consecrated 4 December 1093.

[41] R. W. Southern, *Saint Anselm And His Biographer* (Cambridge, 1963) p. 154; A. L. Poole, *op. cit.*, pp. 173-4. Unless the pallium were obtained within a year of consecration, Anselm could be deprived of his archbishopric.

[42] Rufus was against Anselm's journey to receive the pallium because the

the *curia regis* in its fullest aspect which opened at Rockingham on 25 February 1095. The *curia regis* failed to settle the issue and Anselm again requested the king's permission to leave the realm, but without success.[43] The pallium was subsequently brought to England by the papal legate, Cardinal Walter of Albano.[44]

Anselm was already conversant with the practice of obtaining the king's licence to leave England before the issue over the pallium arose. He had arrived in England on 7 September 1092 as a visitor at the invitation of Earl Hugh of Chester. After staying a time, Anselm asked for the king's permission to leave the realm in order to return to Normandy but Rufus, without giving any reason refused to issue the passport and Anselm was compelled to follow the royal court.[45]

As Anselm promised to observe the "*avitae consuetudines*" in 1095[46] this could only mean that he acknowledged the right of Rufus to enforce the *leges* of the Conqueror. Selden probably viewed the emergence of the restraint on foreign travel by ecclesiastics during Rufus' reign in connection with the question of papal recognition.[47]

By 1097, Anselm could no longer tolerate the king's obvious spoli-

king had not yet recognized Clement III or Urban II as Pope following the death of Gregory VII in exile in 1085.

[43] R. W. Southern, ed., *The Life of St. Anselm by Eadmer* (London, etc., 1962) p. 87. The meeting of the curia regis at Rockingham was to consider the primary question of recognition of the Pope which would influence the decision by the king to allow Anselm to depart.

[44] *Ibid.*, p. 87. Anselm received the pallium at Canterbury on 27 May 1095 but without meeting the legate, *ibid.*, p. 87, n. 2; A. L. Poole, *op. cit.*, p. 175; Sir Francis Palgrave, *op. cit.*, Vol. IV, pp.206-207; R. W. Southern, *Saint Anselm And His Biographer, op. cit.*, p. 131.

[45] Sir Francis Palgrave, *op. cit.*, Vol. IV, p. 107; E. A. Freeman, *The Reign of William Rufus* (2 vols., Oxford, 1882), Vol. I, p. 388. In *Eadmer, op. cit.*, p. 29 we find: "*Post haec in Normanniam regredi volens, negata a rege licentia copiam id agendi habere non potuit.*" No doubt Anselm was well aware of the restrictions on everyone wishing to leave the realm and had to meet the situation from the time of his initial visit in 1079 and his numerous subsequent visits, R. W. Southern, *The Life of St. Anselm, op. cit.*, p. 57; Sir Francis Palgrave, *op. cit.*, Vol. 4, pp. 106-7. It also seems reasonable to conclude that he would not leave England without first obtaining the prior permission as he was aware of the treatment of Herbert Losinga, N. F. Cantor, *op. cit.*, p. 77, n. 169.

[46] F. Makower, *op. cit.*, p. 22, n. 41 where he cites *Eadmer*, op. cit., p. 84.

[47] Selden relates: "*Publico . . . edicto vetuit unumquemque sive commeatu suo ex Anglia egredi. Veluisse Anselmum, ne Urbanum PP. inviseret legimus; universos hoc complexum edicto, quam apud Polydorum, legendo me comperisse dissiteor, Joannis Seldeni Jurisconsulti Opera Omnia, Tam Edita quam Inedita, op. cit.*, Vol. II, p. 1005.

ation of Church property over the issue of knight service, or the degeneration of religious discipline and endeavoured to seek authoritative advice in Rome. On three occasions Anselm requested the king's permission to make the journey abroad. On the third occasion his persistence met with success and the licence was issued in October 1097.[48] Anselm recognized the right of the king to exercise his prerogative, for on the occasion of the second refusal, he said:

> He has the power: he says what he pleases. But if he refuses now, perhaps he will agree at another time. I shall keep on asking.[49]

At the time of Anselm's third request, the king answered [50] in a manner which cast little doubt as to the measures that would follow if the archbishop left without his licence as Anselm had indicated that he might leave the realm without the king's permission. Faced with the realization of Anselm's possible course of action, the king offered the ageing Archbishop a choice of either taking an oath never to appeal to Rome or to depart from England as quickly as possible and take nothing with him without the king's permission.[51] Such was the king's reluctance to allow freedom of access to Rome. Anselm chose to leave, and despite the issuance of the licence, the actual departure was delayed until a thorough search was completed lest the king be deprived of any riches.[52] The decision to travel meant exile to Anselm as well as confiscation of the church lands. His exile lasted until September 1100 when he returned at the invitation of a new sovereign, Henry I.

The return of Anselm to England did not mean a change in the application of the law or easing of the restriction on travel as shown by Henry's letter of October 1101 to Pope Paschal II.[53] Following the

[48] R. W. Southern, *The Life of St. Anselm By Eadmer, op. cit.*, pp. 91-92, and references contained in the footnotes. See also, G. Bosanquet, *op. cit.*, pp. 83-90; G. O. Sayles, *op. cit.*, p. 267. Some authorities felt that Anselm departed the realm without the permission, see A. L. Poole, *op. cit.*, p. 176. The explanation for this occurrence is found in R. W. Southern, *op. cit.*, p. 91, n. 2.

[49] R. W. Southern, *Saint Anselm And His Biographer, op. cit.*, p. 160.

[50] Rufus said, "As for his reasons I refuse to listen to them. But if he goes, he can be quite sure that I shall take back the whole of the archbishopric into my own hands and will never again receive him as Archbishop," G. Bosanquet, *op. cit.*, p. 84. See also Ingram, *op. cit.*, p. 31.

[51] R. W. Southern, *The Life of St. Anselm By Eadmer, op. cit.*, p. 92.

[52] *Ibid.*, p. 98; *Eadmer, op. cit.*, p. 88. See also, G. Bosanquet, *op. cit.*, pp. 87 and 91.

[53] The letter read in part: "That he had hoped the Pope would send the

death of Anselm in 1109 the see was left vacant by the thrifty king until 1114, and a virtual breach with the papacy prevailed as no appeals went to Rome. On the death of Thomas, Archbishop of York, Henry filled the vacancy by elevating Thurstan. Subsequent to Thurstan's election, Ralph d'Escures, the Archbishop of Canterbury summoned him to Canterbury to be consecrated. Thurstan wished to avoid this profession of obedience and proceeded instead to Rouen, where the king resided at this time, to request his permission to journey to Rome where he might submit the question of profession to the Pope. Henry refused to issue his licence.[54]

At this juncture, reference may be made to *Quadripartitus*, a law book written about 1114, which lends its authority to the proposition that the restraint upon individuals in England to secure the king's licence before departure did not merely encompass ecclesiastics as a class but applied to all persons.[55]

In 1115, Thurstan again applied for the king's permission so that he might proceed to Rome, but met with the same negative response.[56] Thurstan renewed his request in 1116 just after Easter but to no avail although Henry promised to let him go in the future.[57] At a later date Thurstan in disguise stole out of England from Dover [58] and crossed to Normandy where Henry was located and requested permission to

pallium to Gerard, Archbishop of York without insisting on a personal visit from the archbishop ..." - contained in *Regesta Regum Anglo-Normannorum 1066-1154*. Vol. II *Regesta Henrici Primi* 1100-1135 ed. by C. Johnson & H. A. Cronne (Oxford, 1956) p. 15 (hereafter referred to as *Regesta*).

[54] *The Historians of The Church of York And Its Archbishops By Hugh The Chantor*, ed. by J. Raine, (2 vols., Rolls Series, London, 1886) II, p. 131.

[55] "*Regem Anglie singulari majestate regni sui dominum esse, manifeste veritatis intuitus et singulorum denique cognovit effectus. Quod cum inclita bonitate regis et iure debita subditorum fidelitate proveniat, situs quoque patrie confidenter adjuvat, nature beneficiis et maris vicinitate conclusus, ut sine gratuita dominorum licencia nullus exitus, nulli relinquatur ingressus.*" - *Quadripartitus* ed. by F. Liebermann (Halle, 1892), Bk. II, p. 176 (*Praefatio* 1 & 2).

[56] J. Raine, *op. cit.*, p. 133; C. Johnson, *Hugh The Chantor*, (translation, London, etc., 1961) pp. 38-39.

[57] J. Raine, *op. cit.*, pp. 143 and 145. C. Johnson, *op. cit.*, pp. 49 and 51-52. The ban on ecclesiastics travelling to Rome was not absolute as the Archbishop of Canterbury was to go in 1117, accompanied by Herbert, bishop of Norwich; Hugh, abbot of Chertsey, a physician and William of Corbeuil, canon of Canterbury.

[58] J. Raine, *op. cit.*, p. 50; C. Johnson, *op. cit.*, p. 57. It seems that no reprimand followed.

visit the Pope who was then at Tours. Henry refused.[59] At about this time the Archbishop of Canterbury applied for a passport to travel abroad for a visit with Pope Calixtus II and we learn that Henry gave his leave without reluctance.[60] It was at the king's whim whether an individual would receive the required permission to leave the realm. The legal impediments to travel in this age are demonstrated by the fact that despite Archbishop Ralph's licence from Henry, the Archbishop could not obtain the necessary safe-conducts from the French king and the Count of Anjou to cross their territories. Thurstan, on the other hand, was respected by the French king and the Count of Anjou and could secure the safe conducts – but lacked Henry's passport.[61]

As Pope Calixtus was cognizant of the English restrictions on travel, he wrote to Henry to inform him that a General Council was being planned to be held at Rheims and called upon Henry to grant both archbishops his licence to attend and also to extend to either of the archbishops a licence to visit the Pope prior to the Council.[62] We also know that when Pope Calixtus II met Henry at Gisors in 1119 following the Council, Henry confirmed the Conqueror's *leges.*[63] Such confirmation before the Pope is not really surprising as Henry had previously made a unilateral declaration of his position in more general terms in a letter addressed to Pope Paschal II written during January 1101, and the papal acceptance merely represented an act of diplomacy. In the aforementioned letter, Henry "promises the same obedience to the Pope as rendered in his father's time; provided that he is allowed to have the same customs which his father had. But he will not let the dignities and customs of the realm of England be impaired." [64]

During the reign of Stephen the papacy used the inherent weaknesses of the monarch and the secular government to further the in-

[59] J. Raine, *op. cit.*, p. 154; C. Johnson, *op. cit.*, p. 61.

[60] J. Raine, *op. cit.*, p. 155, C. Johnson, *op. cit.*, p. 62.

[61] J. Raine, *op. cit.*, pp. 157-158; C. Johnson, *op. cit.*, p. 65.

[62] J. Raine, *op cit.*, p. 159; C. Johnson, *op. cit.*, p. 66. Henry finally gave Thurstan a licence to leave England; J. Raine, *op. cit.*, p. 161; C. Johnson, *op. cit.*, p. 69.

[63] *Ordericus Vitalis Historiae Ecclesiasticae* ed. by A. Le Prévost, (5 Vols., Paris, 1838-1885) Vol. 4, 1852, p. 373. F. Barlow, *op. cit.*, p. 185 takes the position that it was the Pope who was persuaded to confirm the customs of the Conqueror, a view which I submit goes too far.

[64] *Regesta, op. cit.*, Vol. II, pp. 6-7. The reply of Pope Paschal to Henry is found in Eadmer, Hist. Nov. pp. 128-131. For a brief description of the physical problems of travel in that day painted in colourful tones see J. Raine, *op. cit.*, p. 212; Johnson, *op. cit.*, pp. 123-4.

terests of Rome. Nevertheless, Stephen, like his predecessors exercised his prerogative to restrict travel without licence. He allowed only five English prelates to attend the Second Lateran Council held in 1139.[65] The consequences of illicit travel were obviously known to the magnates of the realm and others for when the bishops proposed to send some of their number to Rome to complain of the treatment of John of Salisbury in 1139, Aubrey de Vere warned them that "if anyone went anywhere out of England contrary to his wish [the king] and the majesty of the Crown it might be difficult for him to return." [66]

We also know that Pope Eugenius III summoned a Council at Rheims in 1148, and Stephen refused to allow Theobald, Archbishop of Canterbury to attend. Stephen did, however, allow three bishops to attend [67] in order to excuse the absence of Theobald and others. In addition to the refusal to Theobald, Stephen took the precaution of having the seaports watched to prevent the archbishop from leaving the country illegally. Despite the alert, Theobald stole out of the country in a fishing vessel and attended the Council,[68] a move which ultimately resulted in the archbishop's exile and deprivation of temporalities.[69]

One hypothesis for the development of the practice of having English agents more or less permanently resident in Rome to act as counsel at the Papal Curia on behalf of English bishops, abbots and others, hinges upon the obvious difficulty the subject had in leaving

[65] *Chronicles of The Reigns of Stephen, Henry II and Richard I* ed. by R. Howlett (4 vols., Rolls Series, London 1884-89), Vol. III, 1886, pp. 176-7. See also the notes of R. L. Poole & W. Hunt in 38 *E.H.R.* (1923) pp. 61-63 and pp. 557-560 respectively, as to the English bishops who actuelly attended. Prior to the Norman Conquest, English bishops were able to attend papal councils overseas without the king's licence, G. O. Sayles, *op. cit.*, p. 194.

[66] *The Historia Novella* by William of Malmesbury (translated) by K. R. Potter (London, etc., 1955) p. 33. See also Richardson & Sayles, *op. cit.*, pp. 297-8.

[67] Robert, bishop of Hereford; William, bishop of Norwich and Hilary, bishop of Chichester. Actually other English subjects made the journey as well as the official representatives. Theobald received permission from Stephen to send members of his household to excuse his absence. These persons stayed with the Archbishop during his subsequent exile, A. Saltman, *Theobald, Archbishop of Canterbury* (London, 1956), p. 25. Also, sent some of his clerks to apologise for Theobald's absence, M. Chibnall, *The Historia Pontificalis of John of Salisbury* (translated), (London, etc., 1956) p. 7.

[68] *The Historical Works of Gervase of Canterbury* ed. by W. Stubbs, (2 vols. London, 1879-80), Vol. I, 1879, p. 134; A. Saltman, *op cit.*, pp. 25-30; Chibnall, *op. cit.*, pp. 6-7.

[69] W. Stubbs, *op. cit.*, p. 135.

the realm. John of Salisbury acted for a time in this capacity and represented Theobald before Pope Eugenius III in the archbishop's dispute with the monks of St. Augustine who were similarly represented.[70]

During the Norman line of kings, we have witnessed the establishment and exercise of a practice which originates either in the time of William the Conqueror or William Rufus depending which authorities one follows. The question now to be faced is whether the application of the principle which prevented individuals departing from England without the king's permission was a principle belonging to the common law.

As the restraint on travel was not of Anglo-Saxon vintage, its appearance under the Norman kingship meant that it could not have been part of the English customs or *consuetudines* but rather it belonged to the classification of king's legislation or *leges*. Here I call upon the authority of Professor Hazeltine, who informs us that "the fundamental English distinction in the middle ages is not between the 'unwritten' and 'the written laws,' but between the customs and the king's enactments, between 'customs' and 'laws'; and, at least until the statutes of the king in parliament acquire a position of prominence in relation to common law, neither customs nor the various forms of royal legislation are viewed as 'written law'." [71]

The application of the Roman jurisprudential dichotomy of law being either *ius scriptum* or *ius non scriptum* would be as inappropriate as the modern division of common law and statute law to determine whether the king's enactment was part of the common law during the English middle ages. This pertinent piece of the king's legislation, administrative in character, could have been based upon custom in the middle ages sense while being mindful of the words of Professor Plucknett that "we must recognize the possibility that much of the common law may be ultimately of legislative origin," and that this legislation could very well have been "completely dissolved in the swift-moving stream of the common law . . ." [71a] by this date. But this argument will

[70] H. G. Richardson & G. O. Sayles, *The Governance of Medieval England from the Conquest to Magna Carta* (Edinburgh, 1963) p. 298 and references contained therein.

[71] H. D. Hazeltine, *The Interpretation Of Law By English Medieval Courts* p. x written as the General Preface in T. F. T. Plucknett, *Statutes And Their Interpretation In The First Half Of The Fourteenth Century* (Cambridge, 1922).

[71a] T. F. T. Plucknett, *Legislation Of Edward I* (Oxford, 1949), pp. 8-9.

not find favour with those who view the common law as dating from the time of Henry II [72] or some later date.[73]

II.

The death of Pope Adrian IV in September 1159 was followed by the recurrent appearance of pope and anti-pope, Alexander III and Victor IV. King Henry II chose to follow a policy of neutrality until he should formally recognize one of the rivals. In furtherance of this policy, Henry borbade appeals to proceed abroad and precluded his clergy from leaving the realm for a purpose which might force him to make a premature decision on recognition.[74] Henry's official acknowledgement of Alexander III removed the ban on appeals [75] and presumably the travel restrictions were lifted.

On the death of Archbishop Theobald, Henry saw his opportunity to curb the papal influence in England by naming Becket to the seat of St. Augustine. Henry indicated to the papacy that a change was to occur, by not leaving Becket journey abroad to receive the pallium.[76]

When the Pope's Council was held at Tours in May 1163, the archbishops of Canterbury and York, Becket and Roger, were in the English delegation.[77] However, according to Rymer, Henry gave his

[72] Bishop Stubbs in his historical study of law said: "The history of Norman law is ... in a debatable land between Anglo-Saxon law ... and the common law of England, which dates its historical shaping from the reign of Henry II," The Laws And Legislation Of The Norman Kings, in *Lectures On Early English History by William Stubbs*, ed. by A. Hassall (London, 1906) p. 38.

[73] For a discussion on this point see Pollock and Maitland, *The History of English Law before the time of Edward* I, 2d. edn., 2 Vols. (Cambridge, 1911) Vol. I, p. 168.

[74] H. G. Richardson & G. O. Sayles, *op. cit.*, p. 297 and references contained therein. The authors point out that Henry must have addressed writs to the clergy to state his position and was obeyed "because disobedience, if brought to light, might have unpleasant consequences." This policy by Henry gave an early indication of his desire to return to the so-called *avitae consuetudines* of the Normans - see A. Saltman, *op. cit.*, p. 543 and the same author's comments in *Inst. of Hist. Resear. Bull.*,Vol. 22 (1949) p. 154.

[75] See "The Anstey Case" by P. M. Barnes, in *A Medieval Miscellany For Doris Mary Stenton* ed. by P. M. Barnes & C. F. Slade (Pipe Roll Society, N.S., Vol. 36 (1962) pp. 1-23.

[76] *Radulfi De Diceto Decani Ludoniensis Opera Historica* ed. by W. Stubbs (2 vols., Rolls Ser., London, 1876) I p. 307. John of Salisbury and four other commissioners were dispatched in July 1162 to collect the pallium from the Pope at Montpellier - C. C. J. Webb, *John of Salisbury* (London, 1932) p. 104.

[77] *Radulfi De Diceto, op. cit.*, p. 310.

licence to the English delegates to attend after receiving an assurance from the Pope that the decision would not be regarded as a precedent.[78] Henry used the issue of jurisdiction over criminous ecclesiastical clerks to press his policies.[79] He summoned a Great Council to meet at Clarendon in January 1164 at which time Becket and the bishops gave assent to observe the *avitae consuetudines* in general terms. Henry, however, sought to have these customs which concerned ecclesiastical matters that were operative in his grandfather's day, reduced to writing. A committee of Barons carried out the task; the resultant document being the Constitutions of Clarendon. The preamble to the Constitutions signified that these were customs and rights of the kingdom at the time of the king's ancestors ,which I suggest, were to continue unless expressly withdrawn. Clause 4 gave notice of the restriction on freedom of exit of all his subjects in these words:

"Archbishops, bishops and persons of the realm are not allowed to leave the kingdom without licence of the lord the king; and if they do leave, they shall, if the king so please, give security that neither in going nor in staying, nor in returning, will they seek the ill or damage of the lord or realm." [80]

Clause 8 [81] must be read in conjunction with clause 4 to fully ap-

[78] *Foedera, conventiones, litterae, et cuiuscunque generis acta publica inter reges Angliae et alios quosvis imperatores, reges, pontifices principes, vel com-*mission, 1816-1869) p. 44, (hereafter referred to as *Foedera*), cited by C. R. Cheney, *From Backet To Langton* (Manchester, 1956) p. 92.

[79] See C. Duggan, "The Becket Dispute And The Criminous Clerks," *Inst. Hist. Res. Bull.*, vol. 35 (1962) pp. 1-28 and authorities cited on p. 2. Duggan supports the view that the issue over clerical immunity was of lesser importance than "the everwidening jurisdiction of papal judges delegate, freedom of appeal from the English ecclesiastical courts to the papal Curia: the passage of bishops and papal legates between the island and the continent" - at p. 2.

[80] G. B. Adams & H. M. Stephens, *Select Documents of English Constitutional History* (London, etc., 1920) pp. 12-13. Latin text can be found in W. Stubbs, *Select Charters And Other Illustrations of English Constitutional History*, 9th edn. ed. by H. W. C. Davis (Oxford, 1913) p. 165. The full text of the Constitutions can be found in William of Canterbury's biography of Becket, the chronicles of Gervase of Canterbury, Roger of Wendover and Matthew Paris.

[81] "In regard to appeals, if they shall occur, they must proceed from the archdeacon to the bishop, and from the bishop to the archbishop. And if the archbishop fail in showing justice, they must come at last to the lord the king, that by his command the dispute be concluded in the archbishop's court, so that it must not go further without the assent of the lord the king." G. B. Adams & H. M. Stephens, *op. cit.*, pp. 12-13. Latin text in W. Stubbs, *Select Charters, op. cit.*, p. 165.

preciate Henry's efforts to restrict freedom of movement of the English clergy to Rome.

The reference to *avitae consuetudines*, I submit, was Henry's attempt to give historical justification for the laws. Becket subsequently excommunicated the authors of the Constitutions, who were primarily Richard de Luci, Joceline de Baillol, for "fabricating the heretical customs." [82]

Henry had been determined to come to grips with the papal influence which hindered his grand design of reform. He was aware of the practices of the past. Why not use the methods employed by antecedents and ascribe to them the title of ancestral customs now to be a substantive rule of law? But the Constitutions were in their own right rather than as the *avitae consuetudines* able to become part of the common law.

We know that on the issue of appeals to Rome, Henry did not seek their abolition but merely wished to eliminate abuses which had crept into the practice while such a move would also safeguard his own interests as temporal lord.[83]

For the usage of the fourth constitution, we must return to the course of events which followed the Constitutions enacted by the king. Under pressure Becket consented to the Constitutions,[84] then requested the king's permission to leave the realm in order to visit the pontiff. On Henry's refusal, Becket twice chanced to leave England without the king's licence which was, of course, contrary to what he had sworn.[85] The Council of Northampton was held in October 1164, after which Becket sent bishop Walter of Rochester, bishop Robert of Hereford and bishop Roger of Worcester to Henry in quest of a licence but the king procrastinated by refusing to give an answer. In this inauspicious atmosphere the archbishop went into hiding and stole out of England on All Souls' Day, 2 November 1164.[86]

[82] R. W. Eyton, *Court, Household and Itinerary of King Henry II* (London, 1878) pp. 94-95.

[83] C. R. Cheney, *op. cit.*, p. 89 and authorities cited therein; see also *Materials For The History Of Thomas Becket*, ed. by J. C. Robertson & J. B. Sheppard (7 vols., Rolls Ser. London, 1875-85) VI, p. 79f. (hereafter referred to as *Materials*).

[84] F. Makower, *op. cit.*, p. 22 and authorities cited therein; see also J. T. Appleby, *Henry II* (London, 1962) p. 92ff.

[85] *Materials*, III, p. 293. On the first abortive attempt contrary winds prevented departure while on the second Becket was recognized and had to withdraw for fear of reprisal, J. T. Appleby, *op. cit.*, p. 98.

[86] W. H. Hutton, *Thomas Becket* (Cambridge, 1926) p. 115.

It will be remembered that Henry sent the Constitutions to Pope Alexander III with a request for his concurrence, but the pontiff disallowed ten of the sitxteen constitutions as being contradictory to the canons,[87] an act which created little impression upon Henry. Henry applied the fourth Constitution when he thought fit and his subjects obeyed such as the Archdeacon of Canterbury, Geoffrey Ridel who on 24 June 1166, would not cross to Normandy without the king's licence.[88] The responsibility for supervising exits of ecclesiastics was in the hands of the judges, and Henry periodically reminded his subjects of the law as in an ordinance of 1169, lest his subjects think that the practice was inoperative: "*Item nullus clericus, vel monachus, vel conversus alicujus religionis, permittatur transfretare, vel redire in Angliam, nisi de transfretatione habeat litteras justitiarum, et de reditu litteras regis. Et si aliquis aliter inventus fuerit, capiatur et retineatur.*" [89]

Although Henry and Becket were formally reconciled and the Archbishop returned to England in December 1170 no arrangement was reached on the Constitutions which meant they remained operative.[90] In a letter written by John of Salisbury to John, bishop of Poitiers soon after Becket's death, we learn that Henry rigidly enforced the restrictions on freedom of travel so that news from the Apostolic See as to the formal canonization of Becket, could not reach England.[91]

The murder of Becket put a strain on relations between Henry and the Pope. However, a settlement was reached at Avranches in September 1172, which reconciled Henry to the Pope. Examination of the concordat [92] discloses an absence of direct reference to the Constitutions of Clarendon. The customs as they existed prior to Henry's reign

[87] F. Makower, *op. cit.*, p. 23. Henry's representatives and Becket met the Pope at Sens. The constitutions disallowed by the Pope were 1, 3, 4, 5, 7, 8, 9, 10, 12 and 15.

[88] R. W. Eyton, *op. cit.*, p. 95.

[89] Hoveden I, p. 231 cited by F. Makower, *op. cit.*, p. 240 n. 2.

[90] F. Makower, *op. cit.*, p. 90.

[91] C. C. J. Webb, *op. cit.*, p. 119.

[92] On Henry's oath at Avranches see *Diceto, op. cit.* Vol. I, pp. 351-2; *Gervase, op. cit.*, Vol. I, pp. 238-9. See also M. Cheney, "The Compromise of Avranches of 1172 and the Spread of Canon Law in England," *Eng. Hist. Rev.* LVI (1941), pp. 177-197 in which the author discusses the practice of appeals proceeding to Rome before and after 1172, and Z. N. Brooke, "The Effect Of Becket's Murder On Papal Authority In England," *Camb. Hist. Jour.* II (1928), pp. 213-228.

were to remain untouched.[93] Despite the restoration of appeals to the Papal Curia, Henry could demand a security from appellants as a guarantee that they meant no harm to the king or realm before issuing them with a licence to leave the realm.[94] As the Constitutions were not expressly withdrawn, their application was dependent upon the attitude of the king, who thought it diplomatic at the time to allow ecclesiastical appeals to proceed to Rome. Not until Magna Carta was the fourth Constitution expressly repealed.[95] To enforce the condition of security from those who wished to leave the realm, a writ was framed which was known as *De securitate invenienda quod se non divertat aliquis versus partes externas sine licentia regis.*[96] The writ had two forms; one addressed to the Sheriff or Justice of the Peace of the county in which the clergyman resided, that required the Sheriff to take security from the individual who proposed to leave the realm and not to proceed without special licence of the king.[97] The second

[93] F. Makower, *op. cit.*, p. 240, Douglas & Greenaway, *op. cit.*, Vol. II, pp. 773-4; H. W. C. Davis, *England Under the Normans And Angevins 1066-1272* (13th ed., London, 1949), p. 243. In the Brooke article cited in n. 92, the author states that "when Henry was reconciled... he made two concessions: (1) he renounced those customs that had been introduced in his own time to the harm of the Church; and (2) he allowed appeals to Rome" and concluded that since Henry regarded the Constitutions as being "old" customs the first concession meant very little, p. 213. Bishop Stubbs was of the opinion that Henry renounced the Constitutions, *Const. Hist.* I, 5th ed., 1891, p. 513.

[94] *Gesta Regis Henrici Secundi Benedicti Abbatis*, ed. W. Stubbs (2 vols., Rolls Ser., London, 1867) I, p. 32 (hereafter referred to as *Gesta Regis Henrici II*).

[95] W. S. McKechnie, *Magna Carta* (Glasgow, 1905), p. 474.

[96] T. B. Ingram, *op. cit.*, p. 36, n. 1, where he cites T. Rymer, *Foedera*, 2d. edn., (London, 1727-1735) vii, p. 592.

[97] The writ is set out in Fitz-Herbert, *op. cit.*, ch. 85 and J. Beames, *op. cit.*, Appendix I. See also T. B. Ingram, *op. cit.*, p. 36. It read: "*REX Vic', &c. Ouia datem est nobis intelligi, quod A.B. Clericus, versus partes exteras, ad quamplura nobis et quampluribus de populo nostro praejudicialia et dampnosa ibid'. prosequend', transire proponit: Nos, malitiae suae resistere volentes in hac parte, tibi praecipimus, firmit, injungentes, quod praed. A.B. coram te corporalit. venire fac', et ipsum ad sufficientes Manucaptores inveniend', qui eum manucatere voluerint, sub certa poena eis per te rationabilit. imponend', pro qua nobis respond. volueris;* OR THUS, *et ipsum A.B. ad sufficient. securitatem inveniend'. sub poena centum librar. ad opus nost. solvend. vel quilibet eor. sub poena, &c. quod ipse versus aliquas partes exteras sine licentia nostra speciali se non divertat, nec quodcunque ibid. prosequatur aut prosequi vel attemptari facere praesumet, quod in nostro contemt'vel praejudic' aut populi nostri dampn. cedere valeat, nec aliquem aut aliquos ibid' mittet ex hac causa, quovis modo compellas. Et si hoc coram te fac. recusaverit, tunc ipsum A.B. prox. Gaol. nostrae committas, in ead' salvo custodiend', quousque hoc gratis fac.*

form of the writ[98] demonstrated clearly that Henry maintained control of his subjects' exit from the realm. This second form of the writ which is addressed to the layman, requires no security as a prerequisite for departure but is designed to prevent the addressee's leaving without the king's licence.[99]

Henry continued to exercise his prerogative to preclude unauthorized persons[100] from proceeding abroad. He restricted the number of English bishops to attend the Lateran Council in March 1179,[101] and applied the "other customs"[102] mentioned in the conclusion of the Constitutions.

The truant monarch, Richard I, who succeeded Henry II, left little doubt as to whether he would continue his father's policies. In October 1189, approximately a month after his coronation, the king asserted control over *exeats* and refused Godfrey, the archbishop elect of York

voluerit. Et cum securitat. ill. sic ceperis, nos inde in Cancellar. nostr. sub sigillo tuo distincte et aperte sine dilatione redd. certiores, vel certifices indilate, hoc Breve nobis remittens. Teste," &c.

[98] The writ is set out in Fitz-Herbert, *op. cit.*, ch. 85 and J. Beames, *op. cit.*, Appendix 2. See also T. B. Ingram, *op. cit.*, p. 36. "*REX 1. de B. salutem. Quia datum est nobis intelligi, quod tu versus partes exteras absque Licentia nostra clam destinas te diverter', et quamplura nobis et Coronae nostrae praejudicialia ibidem prosequi intendis, in nostri contemptum et praejudicium, ac contra proclamationes et inhibitiones nostras inde saepius factas: Nos, hujusmodi contemptui et praejudicio obviare volentes, tibi districte sub periculo quod incumbit prohibemus, ne versus partes exteras absque licentia nostra speciali aliqualiter te divertas, nec quicquam ibidem prosequi attemptes, seu attemptari fac', quod in nostrum seu dictae Coronae nostrae praejudic' cedere valeat quovis modo, nec aliquem ibidem mittas et hac causa. Teste,"* &c.

[99] J. Beames, *op. cit.*, p. 9.

[100] "*Randulfus filius Walteri reddit compotum de xx marcis, quia exivit de terra Domini Regis,*" W. S. McKechnie, *op. cit.*, p. 474, n. 1.

[101] Henry allowed only the bishops of Durham, Norwich, Hereford and Bath to attend, to whom some include the bishop of Worcester, Eyton, *op. cit.*, p. 225. See also Cheney, *op. cit.*, p. 82. The restriction on the number of bishops did not affect the number of English abbots who could attend, *Chronica Magistri Rogeri De Houedene*, ed. W. Stubbs (4 vols. Rolls Ser., London, 1868-1871) ii, p. 171.

[102] For example, Cardinal Vivian the papal legate appointed to visit Scotland, Ireland and Norway was met upon his arrival in England by 2 bishops dispatched by Henry, who demanded to know by what authority he landed without the king's licence. Only upon taking an oath not to do anything contrary to the king's will or pleasure during his legation was he allowed to cross the country, R. W. Eyton, *op. cit.*, p. 205; F. Makower, *op. cit.*, p. 234; W. R. W. Stephens, *The English Church From The Norman Conquest To The Accession of Edward I, 1066-1272* (London, 1909), p. 191.

or his clerks, licence to journey to Rome for the pallium.[103] The king was even more reluctant to issue the licence if the individual making the request could not be adequately protected abroad, as the traveller exposed himself to arrest or capture for ransom, a practice most prevalent during the time of war.[104]

A comment may be offered on some salient points relating to the king's licence in this age. King John received his new Great Seal on 7 June, 1199 at which time he used the same to give authority to a law which revised the scale of fees charged during Richard's reign by Chancery for preparation and sealing of *litterae protectionis patentes*. Henceforth, a simple protection was to be issued for the reduced fee of 2 shillings. As the simple protection, the safe-conduct and the licence or passport were sister documents, the fee for such licence to leave the realm was 2 shillings.[105] The formula in the licence probably became standardized during this period. We know that John issued a safe-conduct on 9 September 1208, to the Archbishop of Canterbury, Stephen Langton, to come to England. Langton, however, refused to come as the safe-conduct carried only the small seal instead of the Great Seal.[106] The close affinity of this document to

[103] "*Eodem mense idem Gaufridus Eboracensis electus misit Adam de Thornovere canonicum Eboracensem et alios nuncios quamplures ad Romanum pontificem propter pallium; sed rex voluit permittere eos transfretare, et sic reversi sunt ad dominum suum.*", *Gesta Regis Henrici II, op. cit.*, pp. 91-92. See also C. R. Cheney, *op. cit.*, p. 92.

[104] See C. R. Cheney, *op. cit.*, p. 63 and authorities cited therein. Cheney also tells us that Richard applied the "other customs" of the Constitutions such as his refusal to admit papal legates, p. 63.

[105] T. Rymer, *Foedera, op cit.*, I, p. 76; H. G. Richardson, *The Memoranda Roll for the Michaelmas Term of the First Year of the Reign of King John, 1199-1200* (London, 1943), pp. xxxv-vii; S. Painter, *The Reign of King John* (Baltimore, 1949), p. 94; W. L. Warren, *King John* (New Yok, 1961), p. 134. The reversion to the Henry II fee scale was for the benefit of the magnates, merchants and ecclesiastics, who would use such documents.

[106] J. E. A. Jolliffe, *Angevin Kingship* (2nd edn., London, 1963) pp. 150-151. Two biographers of King John suggest that Langton did not come to England as the address in the safe-conduct was an affront to his dignity in addressing Langton as cardinal instead of archbishop, Painter, *op. cit.*, p. 177; J. T. Appleby, *John, King of England* (New York, 1959), p. 158. Painter also suggests that Langton had little faith in John's safe-conduct and sought additional security by way of letters from prominent magnates and ecclesiastics, p. 230. The safe-conduct read:

"The King, to all etc. Be it known that we grant Stephen Langton, a Cardinal of The Roman See, a safe and secure conduct to come to England as far as Dover and to remain there until St. Michael's Day, in the 10th year of our reign, for three weeks. Thus when the three weeks are up within the eight the licence suggests that the latter document also had an approved form. The style of the licence used by John appears thus:

"John, by the grace of God, King & etc., to all his faithful subjects. Know ye, that we have given licence to Sampson, the bearer of these presents, to go to Nantes and there to purchase lampreys for the use of the Countess of Blois. These letters are to be valid for one journey only and no more. Witness ourself at Baugé, on the 12th day of January, in the 3rd year of our reign." [107] It was also necessary for the individual to be assured of receiving the king's licence before letters of protection and attorney would be issued.

III.

Thusfar the restrictions on travel to be examined have related specifically to ecclesiastics and in general to all subjects of the realm. Another group specifically singled out for restriction were the merchants. Otherwise what need would there have been for King John's legislation of 1200 which read:

"John, by the grace of God, King of England, Lord of Ireland, Duke of Normandy and of Aquitaine and Count of Anjou, to the bailiffs of the port of Lynn greetings. Let it be known that we give to Robert son of Sunolf licence to take one ship load of corn into Norway. And therefore we command you that you allow him to take the ships thither without hindrance. And keep these letters in your possession. Witnessed ourself at Westminster, 19th April." [108]

Such legislation was for the benefit of the subject and was distinguishable from the king's charters which gave licence to foreign merchants to enter and leave England.[109] Although interpretation of chapter 41 of Magna Carta (1215) usually stresses the right in favour of foreign merchants [110] because the later portion of the chapter obvious-

following days let him return, unless a very strong wind detains him. And in witness of this matter we issue this letter patent to him. Witnessed by G. Fitz Peter at Silverstone, The 9th day of September, in the 10th year of our reign." - J. T. Appleby, pp. 157-8.

[107] T. D. Hardy, *A Description of the Patent Rolls in the Tower of London* (London, 1885), p. 65. Examples of the letters patent formulae for the safe-conduct, protection and internal passage are also contained therein. The formulae used previous to John lacked uniformity.

[108] *Rotuli Chartarum*, 1199-1216, ed. by T. D. Hardy (London, 1887) p. 60.

[109] See the charter of 5 April, 1200, found in *Rotuli Chartarum, op. cit.*, p. 60; D. Macpherson, *Annals of Commerce* (4 vols., London, 1805), I, p. 360.

[110] W. S. McKechnie, *op. cit.*, p. 464 ff. or 2nd ed., 1914, p. 398 ff.

ly pertains to this group, nevertheless the first portion reflects that the chapter is applied to both foreign and native merchants. The wording, "*Omnes mercatores habeant salvum et securum exire de Anglia, et venire in Angliam*" [111] as did its antecedent chapter 31 of the Articles of the Barons, "*Quod mercatores habeant salvum ire et venire . . .*," [112] demonstrates this point.

What was specifically provided for the merchants in chapter 41 was generally provided for all persons in chapter 42. Chapter 42 read: "*Liceat unicuique de cetero exire de regno nostro, et redire, salvo et secure, per terram et per aquam, salva fide nostra, nisi tempore gwerrae per aliquod breve tempus, propter communem ultilitatem regni, exceptis imprisonatis et utlagatis secundum legem regni, et gente de terra contra nos gwerrina et mercatoribus de quibus fiat sicut praedictum est.*" [113] The following observations may be offered: First, John's practice of using his licence to restrict travel of merchants, as verified by the converse, his act of 19 April 1200, was probably learned from his father. It is known that Henry II obtained 2 falcons in 1181, for granting his licence to Arnold, son of Mabel, to export corn to Norway.[114] Second, the ability to leave the realm even with a licence prior to the declarations in Magna Carta, was not always easy, as illustrated by a case which occurred in the Spring of 1207. After obtaining the king's licence to allow him to journey to Ireland, William Marshal, had to give his second son to John as a hostage (John already held the oldest son) before he could sail.[115] Third, as we have already noted, the restriction in the Constitutions of Clarendon was not considered a dead

[111] W. Stubbs, *Select Charters, op. cit.*, pp. 297-8. The English translation would be, "All merchants shall have safety and security in coming into England and going out of England . . ."

[112] W. Stubbs, *Select Charters, op. cit.*, p. 288. The English translation would be, "That merchants shall have safety to go and to come . . ."

[113] W. Stubbs, *Select Charters, op. cit.*, p. 298. A relevant part of the translation reads, "It shall be lawful in future for anyone . . . to leave our kingdom and to return, safe and secure . . ." An abbreviated version of chapter 42 was included in chapter 33 of the Articles of the Barons which read, "*Ut liceat unicuique exire de regno et redire, salva fide domini regis, nisi tempore werrae per aliquod breve tempus propter communem utilitatem regni,*" W. Stubbe, *Select Charters, op. cit.*, p. 288.

[114] *AErn filius Mabiliae debet ij Girfalcones, pro Licentia ducendi Bladum in Norweiam,*" 27 Henry II (Pipe Roll Soc. vol. 30, 1909) p. 88 cited by T. Madox, *History and Antiquities of the Exchequer of the Kings of England,* (London, 1711), p. 323. See also, W. S. McKechnie, *op. cit.*, p. 466.

[115] K. Norgate, *John Lackland* (London, 1902) pp. 145-6.

letter before 1215.[116] Chapter 42 formally repealed the fourth of the Constitutions of Clarendon.

John's death brought Henry III to the throne with the Earl of Pembroke as *Rector regis et regni.* The Great Charter reissued on 12 November 1216 contained certain alternations and omissions. Chapter 41 of Magna Carta now appeared as chapter 37, as follows: "*Omnes mercatores, nisi publice antea prohibiti fuerint, habere salvum et securum exire de Anglia, et venire in Angliam . . .*" [117] John's surrender of England to the Pope on 15 May 1213,[118] was to strengthen the papal prerogatives over England for the remainder of John's reign and the entire reign of Henry III. The 1216 re-issue of Magna Carta omitted chapter 42 as did the subsequent re-issues. Such a step was germane to the secular authorities' attempt to block infringements by the Roman See.[119] The omission meant a reversion to past practices. In the 7th year of Henry's reign, 1222-23, the following case was reported: "*Willielmus Marmion clericus profectus est ad regem Franciae sine licentia domini regis, et propterea finem fecit.*" [120] And at a time when favourable relations existed between Pope and King, Pope Honorius III found it necessary to express his indignation, in a letter written to Henry dated 18 January 1224, as to Henry's restriction against allowing his bishops to come to the Apostolic See.[121]

The 1216 re-issue endeavoured to account for the changes in the concluding clause that,

> Since, however, some of the chapters which were contained in the former charter seemed onerous and doubtful, among which were the clauses respecting . . . the liberty of all subjects to leave and return to our kingdom . . . the prelates and great men of the realm who are named above have agreed to a delay in Our decision upon them, until We can obtain

[116] A view also taken by A. L. Poole, *From Domesday Book To Magna Carta 1087-1216,* (2nd edn., Oxford, 1955), p. 447.

[117] W. S. McKechnie, *op. cit.,* p. 584. The translation reads, All merchants unless they have before been publicy prohibited, shall have safe and secure exit from England, and entry to England . . .

[118] W. Stubbs, *Select Charters, op. cit.,* p. 279; H. Gee and W. J. Hardy, *Documents Illustrative of English Church History* (London, 1896), p. 75.

[119] W. S. McKechnie, *op. cit.,* p. 474.

[120] W. S. McKechnie, *op. cit.,* p. 474, n. 1.

[121] *Royal And Other Historical Letters illustrative of the Reign of Henry III,* ed. W. W. Shirley (2 vols., Rolls Ser., London, 1862-1866) I, pp. 218-19. The English bishops to whom the Pope refers are the Bishop of Winchester and Peter de Rupilsus. See also, F. A. Gasquet, *Henry The Third And The Church* (London, 1905), p. 79.

more complete information about them. Then we shall act fully in these matters, . . .[122]

The failure of chapter 42 to reappear in the 1216 re-issue and subsequent re-issues did not mean a total restraint on travel. On the contrary ample evidence in the Calendars to the Close Rolls and Patent Rolls discloses a certain amount of foreign travel.[123] But those who held the reins of state control and later the king himself were determined to maintain an unfettered discretion in the matter of egress of the king's subjects. Despite the retention of chapter 41 of Magna Carta, the merchants who wished to sail abroad still required the king's licence,[124] and occasionally an entry [125] appears on the Rolls which indicates the application of the restriction. Henry, in some instances, deemed it necessary to issue a proclamation to restrain all persons *ne quis exeant regnum* without the king's licence [126] either due to a public danger or *pro hac vice*.[127] The implication being that ordinarily persons could leave the realm without a licence. Such a view would be inconsistent with the practice as witnessed in the Calendars to the Close Rolls and Patent Rolls.

Britton tells us of the conduct of his day, Edward I's reign, that

[122] The translation is given by C. M. Whelan, "Passports And Freedom of Travel: The Conflict Of A Right And Privilege," 41 *Georgetown L.J.* (1952) 63 at p. 67.

[123] For example, on 1 January 1238 the issue of a "Licence for Patrick de Chaurces to go beyond seas to visit his parents until Michaelmas," *Cal. Pat. Rolls*, 1232-1247, p. 207; on 16 October 1242, the issue of a "Licence until Easter for James son of Nicholas, William de Waltham with the sons of W. de Cantilupo, and all clerks born in the realm, who studied at Paris, Orleans or elsewhere in the realm of France, to return to their own parts; with mandate to the barons of the Cinque Ports not to make or permit any hindrance to them by sea or land," *Cal. Pat. Rolls*, 1232-1247, p. 331; and on 8 September 1237 the issue of a "Licence for Robert de Monasteriis and Bertram le Bigod to go beyond seas to sue for their lands with the king of France," *Cal. Pat. Rolls*, 1232-1247, p. 195. A prolonged excavation in the Calendars to the Patent Rolls and Close Rolls, the Rolls of Parliament, Rymer's *Foedera* and Nicholas' Proceedings and Ordinances of the Privy Council will give numerous examples of licences to travel.

[124] An example is given in the licence issued on 14 June 1237 "for Peter de Rivallis to go beyond seas on business, on condition that he be with the king in England on the morrow of All Souls, 22 Henry III, to do what he shall have to do touching those things which the king shall will to speak against him (*era eum*)," *Cal. Pat. Rolls*, 1232-1247, p. 186.

[125] See for example, the king's writ of 12 July 1234, *Cal. Close Rolls*, 1231-1234, p. 570-1.

[126] M. Hale, *op. cit.*, p. 91.

[127] W. Holdsworth, *op. cit.*, x, p. 390, and authorities cited there.

"... no great lord or knight of our realm ought to travel forth of it without our licence since by that means the kingdom might be left destitute of able persons ..." [128] This statement reflects one obligation which followed the impressive revolution in the English army during Edward's time.[129] It was a view which found successive merit with Fitz-Herbert, Coke, Hale and Blackstone.[130]

In 1290, the segment of the population which adhered to the Jewish faith were expelled from England. If the individual was free to leave the realm at the time, it would not have been necessary to equip the Jews with the proper documents which would entitle them to leave the realm. Some 16,500 passports were issued to carry out the expulsion. Moreover, it was necessary for the king to provide the following ordinance: "Letters Patent directed to the Bailiffs, Barons and sailors of the Cinque Ports granting a safe conduct for the Jews leaving the realm with their wives, children and goods, and asking that only reasonable charges should be made to the poor Jews so that their leaving the country should not be impeded 27 July, 1290." [131]

During the remainder of Edward's reign there is an intermittent use of restraint on travel which demonstrates the range of its applicability. Edward declared war on France in June 1294 and directed John Baliol, King of Scotland who had pledged homage to Edward to forbid the departure from his ports of any man or vessel going overseas,[132] presumably due to the public danger. On 31 July 1295, it was necessary for Pope Boniface VIII to request Edward to grant the bishop of Winchester a licence so that he could come to Rome.[133] It was obvious that the alliance between the Papacy and the Crown of England which thrived from the time of John ended with the accession of Edward.

On 31 January 1297, it was necessary for the King in Council to issue a proclamation "against leaving England without licence," probably to remind the clergy who had been put outside the king's protection the previous day. During March of the same year an ordi-

[128] See note 2.

[129] See generally, M. Powicke, *Military Obligation In Medieval England* (Oxford, 1962), pp. 96-117.

[130] Fitz-Herbert, *op. cit.*, ch. 85, p. 204; Coke, 3 *Institutes*, op. cit., p. 179; Hale, *De Portibus*, *op. cit.*, p. 91; Blackstone, *Commentaries*, I, p. 265.

[131] The Jews In England (Public Record Office, London, 1957) p. 16; The Jews were given 2 months to depart under the penalty of death. See also, Cal. of Pat. Rolls, 1281-1292, pp. 378, 381 and 382 and T. Rymer, *Foedera*, I, p. 736.

[132] T. Rymer, *Foedera*, I, p. 801.

[133] T. Rymer, *Foedera*, I, p. 823.

nance was issued in the same terms as the preceding proclamation.[133a] There is also Edward's mandate of 4 October 1304 to the Warden of the Cinque Ports, Robert de Kendale, to prevent the departure of all knights and esquires who might try to leave the realm.[134]

Before leaving the reign of Edward I, let us mention again Britton's reference, to prevent the lords from departing the realm without licence otherwise the realm might be destitute of able persons, and suggest that this statement demonstrates the transition of the King's Council into a settled institution. Bishop Stubbs judged that Edward "seems thus to have accepted the institution of a council as a part of the general system of government, and . . . to have given it definiteness and consistency." [135] Hence the king had to have a certain number of his councillors with him if not within reach for possible consultation,[136] a point twice raised in parliament during the reign of Edward II.[137]

Edward II followed a similar policy with respect to subjects leaving the realm as did his father. During the war with Scotland in 1309, Edward issued a proclamation that inhibited his nobility from leaving the realm.[138] On 5 November 1317, the king sent a mandate to the Warden of the Cinque Ports to prevent everyone from leaving without the king's special licence [139] which suggests that the subject desirous of going abroad had to present a special passport from the king. To maintain the safe defence of the realm, the king proclaimed on 26 April 1321 that no knight or man-at-arms was to leave England.[140] Edward also found it necessary on 15 August, 1325 to alert the Warden of the Cinque Ports that no abbots or other religious person was to leave the realm.[141] Just before resigning his throne, Edward ordered on 13 January 1326 that none of his subjects save merchants were al-

[133a] R. R. Steele, A Bibliography of Royal Proclamations of the Tudor and Stuart Sovereigns. And Of Others Published Under Authority 1485-1714 (Vol. 5, Bibliotheca Lindesiana, Oxford, 1910), p. clix.

[134] T. Rymer, *Foedera*, II, 58.

[135] W. Stubbs, *Const. Hist.*, *op. cit.*, II, p. 258.

[136] For the changes in the Council during Edward's reign see, J. F. Baldwin, *The King's Council In England During The Middle Ages* (Oxford, 1913), p. 69 ff.

[137] J. F. Baldwin, *op. cit.*, p. 397.

[138] The proclamation issued on 8 October 1309 can be found in Rymer, *Foedera*, II, p. 95.

[139] T. Rymer, *Foedera*, II, *op. cit.*, p. 347.

[140] T. Rymer, *Foedera*, II, *op. cit.*, p. 447.

[141] T. Rymer, *Foedera*, II, *op. cit.*, p. 604.

lowed to cross out of England.[142] The exercise of the king's prerogative during the emergency of a public danger is only reasonable and it is assumed that the effect of the legislation would lapse when the event which gave rise to its enactment passed, however, the answer is by no means clear as to the duration of effectiveness of the legislation enacted at other times.

The reign of Edward III opened with a number of royal proclamations designed to restrain various groups of his subjects from leaving the realm. On 3 April 1327, all religious persons were to be restrained if they did not carry the king's licence, while on 30 April 1327, English merchants were precluded from departing the realm until they joined a staple.[143] The last mentioned restriction was soon followed by the Statute of Northampton passed in 1328 which stated in part:

"Item, it is enacted, That the Staples beyond the Sea and on this Side, ordained by Kings in Times past, and the Pains thereupon provided, shall cease; and that all Merchant Strangers and privy, may go and come with their Merchandises into England, after the Tenor of the Great Charter; and that Writs thereupon shall be sent to all Sheriffs of England, and to Mayors and Bailiffs of good Towns, where need shall require." [144] Despite the Statute, the king was called upon to specifically order the Sheriff of Lincoln on 20 February 1329, to permit English and foreign merchants to enter or leave the country.[145]

The practice of leaving the realm without a passport must have existed in some parts of the country or the law was just not enforced for on 3 August 1328 and on 24 April 1329, Edward issued proclamations that no person was to leave the realm without his licence.[146] Yet two days after the proclamation of April 24th, letters had to be sent Bartholomew de Burghersh, Constable of Dover and Warden of the Cinque Ports, to the mayor of London and to the mayors and bailiffs of 25 other towns on the same subject.[147] In February 1331, the difficulties with France were set at rest for awhile and there was

[142] T. Rymer, *Foedera*, II, *op. cit.*, p. 618.

[143] T. Rymer, *Foedera*, II, *op. cit.*, pp. 701 and 705 respectively.

[144] 2 Edward III, c. 9, Statutes of the Realm, I (London, 1810) p. 259. For the subsequent history of this legislation during the reign see, W. Longman, *The History of The Life And Times of Edward The Third* (2 vols., London, 1869) I, p. 74 ff.

[145] T. Rymer, *Foedera, op. cit.*, II, p. 757.

[146] T. Rymer, *Foedera, op. cit.*, II, pp. 746 and 761 respectively.

[147] T. Rymer, *Foedera, op. cit.*, II, p. 761.

an interval of peace with Scotland so that it is somewhat surprising to find the orders from Edward and his Council issued to several Sheriffs and William de Clynton, Warden of the Cinque Ports on February 24th, to proclaim that men-at-arms, horses and armour were not to leave the realm without special licence from the king.[148]

On 10 June 1336, Edward ordered the Warden of the Cinque Ports to prevent any religious person from leaving England.[149] War with Scotland and the threat of a French invasion in 1336 were probably behind the travel restraints issued on November 6th and December 15th.[150] By 1340 England was impoverished due to the finance of the wars and it was necessary to encourage greater trade to resuscitate the treasury. To realise this aim confirmation of the rights and liberties of the merchants by chapter 41 of Magna Carta 1215, was rendered by Parliament in 14 Edward III, statute 2, chapter 2.[151] Throughout most of 1341 Edward was preparing for a renewal of war with France using the dispute over the succession to the Duchy of Brittany as his reason. To be in readiness for the invasion, Edward and the Council issued a proclamation on 20 December 1341 against persons going overseas and as the expectation of conflict drew closer on 20 February 1342, he wrote to all the Sheriffs that no Earl, Baron, soldier or other man-at-arms should be permitted to leave the country without his leave.[152] During the period 1344-1348 Edward was busy either in preparation for war, or fighting, a state of affairs which brought with it the usual run of warnings against different groups of his subject leaving the realm.[153]

The Black Death plague appeared in England during 1347 and gradually began to take its heavy toll of life until 1349. The pestilence caused Edward to issue a proclamation on 20 November 1348 to prevent his subjects from going overseas [154] and another on 1 December

[148] T. Rymer, *Foedera, op. cit.*, II, p. 810.

[149] T. Rymer, *Foedera, op. cit.*, II, p. 940.

[150] T. Rymer, *Foedera, op. cit.*, II, p. 950 respectively.

[151] *Statutes of the Realm*, I, 290.

[152] R. R. Steele, *op. cit.*, p. clxv and T. Rymer, *Foedera, op. cit.*, II, p. 1188 respectively. For the sequence of events in Edward's preparation to invade Brittany see, W. Longman, *op. cit.*, I, p. 194 ff.

[153] See Edward's orders dated February 9th 1344, March 25th 1344, October 15th, 1344, February 20th, 1345, March 10th, 1345, July 10th, 1346, October 18th, 1347, October 28th, 1347 and June 4th, 1348, found in T. Rymer, *Foedera, op. cit.*, III, parsi, pp. 4, 10, 24, 30, 32, 85, 140, 141 and 161 respectively.

[154] R. R. Steele, *op. cit.*, p. clxvi.

1349, probably to prevent emigration of the survivors. The proclamation of 1349 reads in part:

"Forasmuch as no mean part of our people of our realm of England is dead in the present pestilence, and the treasure of the said realm is mostly exhausted, and numbers of this our kingdom are daily passing, or proposing to pass, to parts over sea with money which they are able to have kept within the realm, Now we, taking heed that if passage after this manner be tolerated, the kingdom will in a short time be stripped both of men and of treasure, and so therefrom grave danger may easily arise to us and to the said realm, unless a fitting remedy be speedily appointed – [I] do command the mayor and bailiffs of Sandwich (and forty-eight other ports) to stop the passage beyond sea of them that have no mandate, especially if they be Englishmen, excepting merchants, notaries, or the king's envoys." [155]

Proclamations were again issued by Edward in 1350 [156] to keep the remaining populace from going beyond the seas.

[155] T. Rymer, *Foedera, op. cit.*, III, parsi, p. 191. Translation is from C. Creighton, *A History of Epidemics In Britain* (2 vols., 2d. edn., London, 1965) I, pp. 180-1.

[156] The king issued a proclamation on January 28, R. R. Steele, *op. cit.*, p. clxvi and the King and Council issued another on June 23rd, T. Rymer, *Foedera, op. cit.*, III, parsi, p. 199.

M. B. Hooker
Faculty of Law, University of Singapore

The East India Company and the Crown 1773-1858

The issue of Charters containing legal provisions to the great trading companies was the primary means of establishing the common law in the various colonies from the seventeenth to the mid-nineteenth centuries. As well as containing a statement of that portion of the common law felt suitable for "export" at that time, the background of the Charters also illustrates one of the most peculiar relationships in English legal history: that which existed between the Crown and the East India Company. It is the nature of this relationship which is the subject of this essay.

For present purposes, the legal history of this area, the East Indies including the Straits Settlements, may be roughly divided into two stages. The first comprises the period from Charles II's Charter of 1661 – the earliest one to provide for the exercise of judicial powers in the English settlements – to the grant of the *Diwani* of Bengal to the Company in 1765. The second stage runs from the Regulating Act of 1773 up until the third (Straits Settlements) Charter of Justice in 1855.

Specifically, the transfer of common law to alien soil appears to revolve around five main topics for consideration.

1. The basis of the Company's territorial sovereignty. This involves two separate questions:
   - (a) The distinction between the role of the Company as a trading corporation *simpliciter*, and as a political and executive sovereign.
   - (b) The actual transference of English law into conquered or ceded territory.
2. The definition of "British subject."
3. The conflict between the Courts and the Company as to the

former's jurisdiction in executive – mainly revenue – fields, and the territorial extension of this jurisdiction.

4. Conflict between the "Crown Courts" and the Company's "Adaulet Courts" as to their respective spheres of jurisdiction.

5. The extent of the powers of the Supreme Courts in the Presidencies as against the sovereignty of native rulers who were tied to the Company by treaty.

A brief historical review of the period 1600-1765 will commence then with some survey of the relevant constitutional history. This may be taken as beginning with the Charter of Charles II in 1661 (12 Car. 2, c. 4). Under this Charter the Governor and Council of each factory had the power to "judge all persons belonging to the said Governor and Company or that shall be under them, in all causes, whether civil or criminal, according to the laws of this kingdom, and to execute judgment accordingly." [1] This was in addition to the power to raise revenues for purposes of naval and military defence. Nothing much was done at that time so far as any administration of the law was concerned except that in 1678 it was resolved at Madras that some trials should be held. In 1669, the port and island of Bombay were granted to the Company by Charter, to be held of the Crown in what can only be described as feudal terms; "as of the manor of Greenwich in free and common socage." [2] The provisions of the Charter of 1669 show clearly the transition of the Company from a trading association

[1] C. P. Ilbert, *Government of India* (1907) 16.

[2] On the relationship between the Crown and Company expressed in feudal terms see also *R.* v. *Shaik Boodin* (1846) 4 *Indian Decisions* (Old Series) 397 and *Doe Dem. De Silveira* v. *Texeira* (1845) 4 *Indian Decisions* (Old Series) 529.

"Indian Decisions" are hereafter cited as *Ind. D.* The first five volumes of the Old Series contain the following reports:

Volume 1 – 1774-1846 (Calcutta)
Morton (Montriou) 1774-1841; Bignell 1830-31; Montriou 1846; Fulton 1835-44; Morton 1774-1841.

Volume 2 – 1847-1859 (Calcultta)
Taylor 1847-48; Taylor & Bell, 3 vols. 1848-50, '51, '53; Gaspar's Small Causes 1850-59.

Volume 3 – 1791-1860 (Calcutta)
Bulnois, 2 vols. 1853-58, 1859; East's Notes 1791-1819; Gaspar's Commercial Cases (Supreme Court) 1851-60; Gaspar's Commercial Cases (Small Causes) 1851-60.

Volume 4 – 1826-1852 (Bombay)
Perry's Oriental Cases 1842-1852; Perry's Notes 1826-1847.

Volume 5 – 1798-1816 (Madras)
Srtange's Notes 1798-1816.

to a territorial *sovereign*, vested with powers of civil and military government and (in 1677) power to coin money. Legal administration at Bombay, like that at Madras was limited, and though it appears to have been of frequent exercise, there are the allegations usual at this time (and for the next hundred years) of corruption and inefficiency.[3] Under the Charter of 1683, the Company could exercise martial law, it could raise forces and a Court of Admiralty was established. The King also authorised the Company to establish a court of judicature, to be held at such places as the Company might direct and to consist of "one person learned in the civil law, and two assistants," to be appointed by the Company. This court appeared to have civil and criminal jurisdiction within the limits of the Company's Charter. The setting up of this court was actually commenced with the appointment of a Dr. St. John. This man held his appointment under a commission from the King *and* under a commission from the Company but he never appeared to have much judicial effectiveness. An unimportant Charter of 1686 merely confirmed the powers and privileges already enjoyed by the Company.

However, in 1687, James II delegated to the Company, the power of establishing by Charter a municipality at Madras. It set up a municipality on the English pattern, complete with Mayor, Alderman, and Burgesses, and established Mayor's courts having civil and criminal jurisdiction. This was the last of the Stuart Charters and the constitutional history of the Company up to 1688 shows the existence of a body ostensibly for trading and commercial purposes, incorporated and holding joint stock and yet possessing many of the trappings and powers of sovereignty. By a resolution of 1689 [4] the Company expressed itself determined to preserve its commercial supremacy on the basis of territorial sovereignty.

In 1698 the old company was induced to surrender its Charter, its corporate capacity was terminated, and its members were admitted into another company which had been constituted not by the Crown alone but by act of Parliament and by letters patent issued in pursuance of the act. This act was 8 & 9, Will. III, c. 44 entitled "An act for raising a sum not exceeding two millions, upon a fund for payment

[3] C. Fawcett, *The First Century of British Justice in India* (1934) Chapter VIII.

[4] C. P. Ilbert, *op. cit.*, 23-24.

of annuities after a rate of eighty pounds *per* centum *per* annum, and for settling the trade to the East Indies."

This act was primarily a financial act and had as its aim the raising of two million pounds by subscription: and under s. 56 the King could incorporate any person or persons who so subscribed and this body corporate should be known as "The general society intitled to the advantages given by an act of Parliament, for advancing a sum not exceeding two millions, for the service of the Crown of England and by that name shall have perpetual succession and a common seal." S. 67 of this enactment gave the company power to make bye-laws for the government of the East Indies trading including powers of imprisonment, fine and impoundings; and these penalties applied not only to the members of the company but also to the use of "general society." S. 77 made provision for the imposition of a duty of five pounds *per* centum *per* annum on all East India lay goods imported, to be paid and used for the maintaining of any ambassadors, etc. which the King should think fit to appoint in the area whose trade was governed by the Company. This provision was continued by Anne, c. 28. The act of 1698 was to be determined after three years' notice, in 1711, and the repayment of two million pounds, but this was restrained by 10 Anne, c. 28 to three years' notice after 1733, and under s. 81 the company had the sole right to trade in the East Indies. This act also provided for the financial organisation of the company, its basis of membership and government.

In 1707 a further act was passed, 6 Anne, c. 3, providing for "the better securing [of the] duties of East Indian goods." It confirmed 9 & 10 Will. III, c. 44, and by a further act, 6 Anne, c. 17, upon the advancement of a further twelve hundred thousand pounds, the company obtained an enlargement of the term of their exclusive trade for a further fifteen years. This latter act is especially interesting as it provided for the uniting of two bodies, which were distinct though referred to above as "the company": *viz.* the English company trading to the East Indies, and the company of merchants of London trading to the East Indies. The later advance of £ 1,200,000 was made by the English company. S. 12 of c. 17 provided for a union of the two companies under the referenceship of the Earl of Godolphin. The possessions of the old company were transferred to the new one for valuable consideration: and they were principally the island of Bombay, a town and fortress at Madras and another at Calcutta. These three places, of which the property was then in the United Company, were recognised by the Crown in 1726 in Letters Patent of that date, to be British Settlements and under the control of the King.[5]

In 1730 the company was declared in explicit terms, by the statute 3, Geo. II, c. 14, s. 12, to be a perpetual corporation and to be entitled to continue in trade in common with other British subjects if at any time their privilege to exclusive trade should cease. This same section also specifically defined the effect of 9 Will. 3, c. 44 and the Charter given under that act to determine the length and effectiveness of the Company's corporation. (A summary of the internal executive and judicial powers of the Company is given in 3 Geo. II, c. 14 (1730) especially in s. 10).

In 1757 the operation of recovering and protecting the settlement at Calcutta which was undertaken with the assistance of the United Kingdom Government resulted in the cession of Bengal, Behar and Orissa: at the same time the Company found itself involved in the appointment of a new ruler for these areas. By two Charters, 1757 and 1758, the Company, besides having rights to booty and prizes of war, was expressly empowered under the latter Charter to cede, restore or dispose of any territory by way of treaty which had been obtained by the Company during the late hostilities. This latter Charter has been relied upon as one of the foundations of the power of the Government of India to cede territory.[6] It was not until 1765, however, that the Governor and Council at Fort William, on behalf of the Company, decided upon their position *vis-a-vis* political involvement in the districts conquered. In that year, mainly through the initiative of Clive, it was decided to assume *de facto* political and financial control of these provinces. This was accomplished by appointing servants of the Company to positions in the provinces where they could control all public affairs including revenue whilst leaving untouched, at least outwardly, the formality of native rule. The grant of *Diwani* of August 1765 left the responsibility of criminal jurisdiction in the hands of the *Nawab*.

This last event had immediate consequences in England including questions as to the right of a trading company to acquire on its own

[5] See Appendix to the *Report on the Affairs of the East India Company V.* Item 26, Enc. 4, 120. (1830 - House of Commons).

[6] *Lachmi Narayan* v. *Raja Pratap Singh* (1878) *I.L.R.* 2 All. 1 and *Damodar Gordhan* v. *Deoram Kanji* (1876) *I.L.R.* 1, Bom. 367.

account territorial sovereignty. A committee of enquiry set up by the House of Commons in November 1766 led to the passing of a series of acts in 1767 with reference to Indian affairs; *viz.* 7 Geo. III, c. 48, 7 Geo. III, c. 49, 7 Geo. III, c. 56, 7 Geo. III, c. 57. This latter act was apparently the first direct recognition by Parliament of the territorial acquisitions of the Company.[7] The general tenor of these acts and those of 8 Geo. III, c. 1, and 9 Geo. III, c. 24 of 1768 was to guarantee the Company its territorial revenues on condition of the payment of annuities and taxes to the Exchequer. Up until 1768, it is probable that the exact nature of the relationship between the Company and the Crown was never of great moment to either party but in the period 1772 up until the Company's dissolution this became one of the main topics for both parties and of immediate concern to English legal history.

Three events all accruing at closely spaced intervals conspired to bring this about. The first were the reforms of Warren Hastings providing for the civil, criminal and financial government administration of the conquered districts which were adopted in August 1772. These provided for the setting up of Adalats in the Mofussil with rights of appeal in all cases to Sudder Diwani (Civil Appeals) and Nizamar Sudder (Criminal Appeals) Courts.[8] Second, in the south of India, Hyder Ali harried and defeated English forces in the Carnatic and dictated peace on his own terms, and in the north the great famine of 1770 swept away more than one-third of the population of Bengal. Finally, in Juni 1772 it was disclosed to Parliament that the Company was over one million pounds in deficit for current expenditure for the three months following. After a report on the Company by a Parliamentary committee in December 1772, the Company was forced to ask Parliament for assistance and Government took advantage of the situation to introduce extensive alterations into the system of governing the Company's Indian possessions. Under 13 Geo. III, c. 64, money was made available to the Company and severe restrictions were placed upon its future financial actions.

However, it is the passing of the Regulating Act of 1773, 13 Geo. III, c. 63 and the new Charter of the Company in 1774 [9] which make

[7] *Damodar Gordhan* v. *Deoram Kanji* (1876) *I.L.R.* 1, Bom. 367.

[8] See B. B. Misra, *The Judicial Administration of the East India Company in Bengal*, 1765-1782 (1947).

[9] This Charter is described in some detail in Ilbert, *op. cit.* 50 ff. The Charter

it possible at this stage to attempt some answers to the five questions put at the beginning of this note. For reasons which will appear below, the Regulating Act was in many respects unsatisfactory and it was amended in 1781 by 21 Geo. III, c. 70, and its was upon the interpretation of these two acts and the Charter that judicial attention focussed up until Pitt's Act of 1784.

I. The Basis of the Company's Territorial Sovereignty

In this and the following sections the relationship between the Crown and Company is traced through instruments of the legislature, charters and through judicial decisions.

The opinions of Ryan C. J. and Grey J., Judges of the Supreme Court of Calcutta, given is 1830 [10] provide a convenient starting point. The opinion outlines three possible grounds upon which the territorial sovereignty of the Company might rest. First, that the Company was filling, under the Mogul Emperor, the offices of *Diwani* and commander of the army in the conquered provinces. This apparently was considered a possibility because of the formal grant of *Diwani* in 1765; and as holding in perpetuity the conquered districts with such rights annexed as the former ruler had enjoyed. Second, that the Company had become in fact, the sovereign of the ceded districts. Thirdly, that as a British subject it had obtained them by conquest and treaty and held them on behalf of the Crown. The judges concluded that in the light of Hastings' regulations, and the peculiar reliance of the Company on the Crown and Parliament for its continuance in an exclusive trade, respectively, that the first two grounds must fail. They decided therefore in favour of the third.[11]

The judges then went on to conclude that 13 Geo. III, c. 63 seems to have assumed the last of the three possible grounds set out above. It put an end to all questions as to the dependence of the Company on Parliament, and as to the absolute right of the legislature to regulate the territorial powers of the Company. The title of the act itself implied only the establishment of dominion and law over the whole of the

constituted the Supreme Court of Calcutta and remained the foundation of the jurisdiction exercised by the courts until 1861.

[10] In the Appendix to *The Report on the Affairs of the East India Company* 117-138.

[11] It is of course clear that the circumstances of 1765 were not such as had been contemplated by Act 8 & 9 Will. III, c. 44 and its dependent Charter.

newly acquired territory. But there was no formal declaration of the sovereignty of the Crown and the already existing Company and Factory settlements are mentioned distinctly from the provinces at large. However, they went on to point out that the whole civil and military powers of government in the provinces had been in the Company's hands for some time. The Governors, newly nominated and appointed by Parliament (13 Geo. III, c. 63, s. 7) were directed to exercise these same powers (s. 8). In the course of the debates which preceded the act, the House of Commons had resolved, with reference to the revenue and territorial acquisitions, that "all acquisitions made by treaty with foreign princes did of right belong to the state." [12] Under the powers given to the Company by 13 Geo. III, c. 63, s. 8. they thus remained in the Company's hands by will and power of Parliament. In addition there is nothing in the act which can be construed as conferring or even admitting the outright ownership of these assets by the Company.

On the other hand however, four years subsequent to the grant of *Diwani* an agreement was made between the Crown and the Company, to run for a period of five years, and under which the Company was guaranteed the revenue of the conquered territories, upon the condition of paying an annuity. The act of 1773 did nothing to upset these arrangements. It has been suggested however, that British sovereignty did not run over the provinces but that they were held by the Company as servants of the Moghul Emperor by virtue of *Diwani*.[13] This persuasion is unsupported by authority and depends upon a literal interpretation of the grant of *Diwani*.

In support of the third alternative suggested and justified by Grey J. and Ryan C. J. there is overwhelming judicial authority. This authority not only establishes the fact that the Company was *in law* at all material times acting on behalf of the Crown but also illustrates the principles upon which English law was introduced into the Indies generally.

The general principle as to the introduction of English law by conquest into a foreign state was laid down in 1774 in *Campbell* v. *Hall*.[14] In this case the validity of letters patent under the great seal, purporting to impose an excise tax on the inhabitants of recently con-

[12] *op. cit.* p. 22. *Hansard*, May 10, 1773.
[13] M. P. Jain, *Outlines of Indian Legal History* (1952) 84 ff.
[14] 98 *E.R.* 1945.

quered Granada was considered. They were held invalid under later constitutional provisions but in the course of judgment the following principles were established. First, that conquered inhabitants once received under the King's protection become his subjects: and second, that a country conquered by British arms becomes a dominion of the King, and therefore necessarily subject to the legislature. Lord Mansfield cited in support *Calvins Case*,[15] the Statute of Wales, 12, Ed. I, and the statutes of Ed. III, relating to the conquest of parts of France.

Ryan C. J. and Grey J. had no difficulty in deciding that *Campbell* v. *Hall* was relevant authority in the present case on the ground that the three provinces were conquered and ceded through the Company for the Crown.[16] However, a summary of the relevant judicial decisions shows that the position was by no means as clear as the judges thought. This question arose directly in the case of *Commaul al Deen Ali Khan* v. *Goring* [17] decided in 1777.

It was held that on the conquest of Calcutta in 1757 it became subject to the law of England, and that sovereignty of the territory lay in the King. However, Impey, C. J. said that the Company was merely *Diwani* though he admitted that *de facto* territorial government lay in the Company. Hyde J. dissenting, said that the Company cannot be sovereign alone and was also prepared to ignore the formal effect of the *Diwani*. Both judges apparently recognised a distinction in function in the Company as to its respective trading and political roles.

In 1793 in the case of *Nabob of Arcot* v. *East India Company*,[18] it was held that a bill could not be maintained by a sovereign prince of India against the Company to account for monies had and received since the subject was a matter of political treaty between the parties as independent sovereigns and was thus not amenable to municipal regulation. The report does not show what meaning the court here attached to "sovereignty," but in any case the political functions of the Company were clearly distinguished. However, in this last case no mention was made of two earlier cases where the Company seems to have been invested with non-political sovereignty, *viz.*, *Doe dem. Rajah*

[15] Co Rep. 17b.

[16] This was despite the formal grant of *Diwan* in 1765. It seems clear from the general terms of 13 Geo. III, c. 63 that the Company was in fact close to being a "statutory corporation."

[17] 1 *Ind. D.* 64.

[18] 29 *E.R.* 841 and 544 (appeal).

Huzzoree Mull v. *Gossinauth*[19] and *Dutturam Turrufdar* v. *The United Company and Watson*,[20] both decided in 1779. Here a grant of title from the Company was, in certain circumstances (*i.e.* with *pottah*) held to confer a valid title to land.

However, so far as land was concerned it was held in *Doe dem. Savage* v. *Bancharam Tagore*,[21] decided in 1785, that land in Calcutta owned by a British subject is real property and its devise must be as required by the Statute of Frauds. In other words not only was the Statute presumed to apply in India, but matters of real property were made to depend upon it, and this assumption is further borne out in *Re Govindo Lalla*,[22] decided in 1801, where the property of a suicide was handed to the company for administration as "the Company here stood . . . in the place of the King." Further in *Vencata Ruga Pillay* v. *East India Company*,[23] decided in 1803, the Charter of the Company was held possible of construction only within the limits of the enabling act itself. Again in *Murray* v. *East India Company*,[24] decided in 1821, the subjection of the Company to Parliament was apparent in that *assumpsit* was to lie upon a bill of exchange against the Company whose power of drawing and accepting such bills was regulated by statute.

However, there appeared to be a significant change of opinion on the part of the Court in the thirty-three years between the *Nabob of Arcot's Case* in 1793 and *Amerchund Burdeechund* v. *East India Company, Elphinstone & Robertson*,[25] decided in 1826, also known as the *Deccan Prize Money Case*. Here it was held (1) that a proclamation by the Company to a defeated enemy must be considered as stating binding terms between the Company and that enemy and that the Company must observe these terms in good faith. (2) That acts of the government, *i.e.* by the Governor-General in Council, are subject to the jurisdiction of the Court. In the following year, 1827, in *East India Company* v. *Syed Ally Habiboon*,[26] a treaty between the Company and an independent native state was subjected to the scrutiny of the

[19] 1 *Ind. D.* 1035.
[20] 1 *Ind. D.* 1037.
[21] 1 *Ind. D.* 65.
[22] 5 *Ind. D.* 34.
[23] 5 *Ind. D.* 80.
[24] 106 *E.R.* 1167.
[25] 4 *Ind. D.* 547.
[26] 7 *M.I.A.* 334.

Court, but more importantly, the Court held that seizure of territory under such a treaty is not valid until confirmed by the Crown. This clear reliance of the Company as territorial sovereign upon the Crown is even more strikingly illustrated in *Bank of Bengal* v. *The United Company*,[27] decided in 1831. This was an action brought against the Company as Government of India and not as a commercial concern. This decision finally turned in the Company's favour on the ground that it did not, under the relevant empowering statutes, have any power to do the purported revenue acts. It was also said that the Company had no sovereign character such as to prevent an action being brought against it. However, Ryan J. dissented from the majority and held the Company liable; but in 1830 it is clear that the Company's sovereignty was that of the Crown. Thus in 1836, in *Mayor of Lyons* v. *East India Company*,[28] 1 M.I.A. 108 it was held that the extent to which English law is imported into conquered territories is directly dependent upon the acts of Crown and Parliament; these may also show that it was introduced not in all its branches but only *sub-modo*, (this is probably as good a way of describing the introduction of English law as any). Again, in 1843, in *Doe dem. East India Company* v. *Hirabi*,[29] it was held that the Company was the proprietor of waste lands in Bombay.

In *Dhackjee Dadajee* v. *East Indian Company*,[30] decided in 1843, the question for the Court was the interpretation of 21 Geo. III, c. 70, s. 1; it was held that any action might lie against the Company as a corporation, if it is acting in its political capacity, the court citing in support *Mostyn* v. *Fabrigas*. The *Bank of Bengal Case* was distinguished on the ground that it was prior to act 3 & 4 Will. IV, c. 85. On appeal in *Dhackjee's Case*, it was held that after the passing of the Charter Act, 3 & 4 Will. IV, c. 85 in 1833, the Company no longer had the character of a trading company and acted solely as a public trustee vested with the powers of government, and it was therefore not liable for acts done by its servants. This distinction between the various functions of the Company was again adverted to in the following year in *Ramchund Ursamul* v. *Glass*,[31] where some of the difficulties of the legislature having treated the Company merely as a trading corpo-

[27] 1 *Ind. D.* 439.
[28] 1 *M.I.A.* 108.
[29] 4 *Ind. D.* 439.
[30] 4 *Ind. D.* 587 and 313 (appeal).
[31] 4 *Ind. D.* 329.

ration were discussed. Again in *A.G.* v. *Richmond*,[32] decided in 1845, the Court treated the Company's interests and those of the legislature as identical especially in view of 3 & 4 Will. IV, c. 83 and it again drew a distinction between the sovereign powers and trading rights of the Company.

One of the most interesting decisions in this area is *R.* v. *Shaik Boodin*,[33] where the acts of (political and executive) sovereignty on the part of the Company were traced to the Charter of Charles II in 1661. These powers were essentially feudal, said the Court, and it was upon their authority that Clive and Hastings acted in 1769 and 1772. In view of the importance of the Regulations of 1772, this proposition needs to be more firmly based than the report in this case shows but at least the further statement that the Company was given legislative powers by the act 13 Geo. III, c. 63 of 1773 is probably true, especially taken in conjunction with the Charter of 1774. It was also decided that the judges of the Company's Courts in the Mofussil were subject to the judicial regulation of the Crown courts and that 21 Geo. III, c. 70 laid down the principles of judicial responsibility.

The following three cases all illustrate the hitherto hazily expressed effect of the Company's regulations in embodying English law, not only in the Presidencies but also in the Mofussil. In *Storm* v. *Homfrey*,[34] decided in 1850, it was held that the law of the Mofussil is the *lex loci* as modified by the Regulations of the East India Company, the only exception being that if real property is in litigation, even if situated in the Mofussil, then English law must apply insofar as it has been introduced. In *Doe dem. Sibchunder Doss* v. *Sibkissen Bonnerjee*,[35] decided in 1854, the Court specifically approved Regulations III, 1793, and II of 1805 as being in accordance with English law. Again, in *Varden Seth Sam* v. *Luckpathy Royajee*,[36] the same approval was given to Regulation II of 1802, which provided that where no local law applied then English law must apply (s. 17). In *Musleah* v. *Musleah*,[37] decided in 1856, it was held (1) that the law of England had been introduced into Calcutta with such modifications as attend

[32] 4 *Ind. D.* 516.

[33] 4 *Ind. D.* 397: decided in 1846. See also *Doe Dem. De Silveira* v. *Texeira*, 4 *Ind. D.* 529 (1845).

[34] 2 *Ind. D.* 466.

[35] 3 *Ind. D.* 42.

[36] 9 *M.I.A.* 185.

[37] 3 *Ind. D.* 140.

its introduction into any new settlement and in particular the modifications imposed by 21 Geo. III, c. 70, s. 21. (2) The descent of real property in Calcutta from any person other than a Hindu or Muslim is governed by the English law of inheritance as the *lex loci situs* and (3) where English law is administered in the Mofussil in relation to land, it is subject to variations as to local law and custom. In *Ousley* v. *Plowden*,[38] decided in 1857, a general statement was made to the effect that the territory governed by the Company is, and has always been, subject to the legislature. In *Lachmi Narayan* v. *Raja Pratap Singh*,[39] it was held (1878), first, that the Court has power to cede territory in British India to a foreign prince and second, that an act of the Company to this effect is an act of the Crown, since it is from the Crown that the Company gets its authority.[40]

II. The Definition of "British Subject"

The case of *A.G. of Bengal* v. *R.S. Dossee*,[41] decided in 1863, provides a useful link between the history of the introduction of English law into India, and the territorial sovereignty of the Company on the one hand, and the closely related problem of who were in fact the subjects of common law. That is, was it confined to British subjects and if so, how was this phrase to be interpreted? *Dossee's Case* gives a statement of general principle that English law travels with all colonists, and applies to all members of their own community. The history and refinements of this principle in India, as shown by the cases, runs as follows.

The first point to note, is that in the Charter of 1774 writs in the King's name were directed to be issued in every part of the provinces of Bengal, Behar and Orissa. In addition, the act of 1773, in conjunction with the Charter, created some difficulty between the Company and the Supreme Court, the main source of friction being the claim of the latter to exercise complete jurisdiction over the whole of the native population to the extent of making them plead jurisdiction if a writ was served on them. S. 14 of the statute provides for the extension of jurisdiction to "British subjects," and in defining this term

[38] 3 *Ind. D.* 87.
[39] *I.L.R.* 2 All. 1.
[40] See also, *Damodar Gordhan* v. *Deoram Kanji, I.L.R.* 1, Bom. 367.
[41] 9 *M.I.A.* 235.

the Courts of the King and the executive of the Company by no means always saw eye to eye. So far as writs were concerned, it was held in 1775, in *R.* v. *Warren Hastings*,[42] that the court had no general power to issue writs of *mandamus* though the court was evenly divided in this question. Hyde and Lemaistre JJ. thought that this power was conferred by Clause 38 of the Charter of 1774 and also by 13 Geo. III, c. 63, s. 13, but Impey C. J. and Chambers J. were of opposite opinion.

So far as the definition of "British subject" is concerned it is unnecessary and tiresome to consider in detail all the reported cases from 1774 up until 1850 on this topic as an adequate historical summary will be found in *Re Ameer Khan*,[43] decided in 1870. Before going on to consider this case however, the position of non-English Christians should be examined. This class of persons comprised mainly Armenian traders.[44] Under a deed poll, or rather a series of deed polls dated June 1688, Armenians were specifically given the same rights and privileges in trade and residence for India as any other [English] "freeman." In *The Goods of Phanus Johannes*,[45] decided in 1790, the court was called upon to administer an Armenian estate situated out of the jurisdiction, the late owner of which had also died out of jurisdiction. The court found itself able to order administration on three grounds. First, that the deceased Armenian belonged to a body of Christians who considered themselves "as residing under the protection of the British Government." Second, that this construction of the Charter of 1774 so as to include Armenians within the jurisdiction is one admitted in practice. Third, that these men must be considered British subjects under the terms of the deed poll alluded to above. In the following year, this decision was followed in *Re Cachick*,[46] and in 1796 in *Padre Stephanus Aratoon* v. *Sarkies Johannes and the Cross Libel*.[47] The court found itself able to exercise jurisdiction on the further ground of the necessity for ecclesiastical jurisdiction to be extended so far as possible even in relation to matters of jurisdiction not specifically mentioned in the enabling statutes or charters.

[42] 1 *Ind. D.* 1005.

[43] 6 *Bengal L.R.* 392 at 442 ff.

[44] These people were independent traders separate from the Company. Their rights to trade and reside in India at this time provide the only example of non-Company activity.

[45] 1 *Ind. D.* 10.

[46] 1 *Ind. D.* 960.

[47] 1 *Ind. D.* 12.

Ameer Khan's Case, in respect of "British subjects" turned upon s. 36 of 13 Geo. III, c. 63. The point at issue concerned the applicability of *habeas corpus* proceedings to a native of Calcutta, and the court said that within the area of the Presidency, Fort William, the provisions of the statute and the charter apply to native inhabitants as well as to Englishmen given the fact of residence.[48]

However, there appear to have been some limits to the scope of the term "British subject," the main one involving the status of foreigners, which did not include Armenians. In *Prinsep* v. *Fairie*,[49] decided in 1783, a French subject taken prisoner of war by the British was held not to be a "British subject"; similarly in *Mandeville* v. *Da Costa*,[50] decided in 1802, and *Walter* v. *Desanto*,[51] these persons, even though born in the territories of the Company, were held not to fall within 13 Geo. III, c. 63, s. 30. The courts also had some reservations as to inhabitancy alone constituting a "British subject" within the meaning of 13 Geo. III, c. 63 and 21 Geo. III, c. 70. In *Manickram Chattopadhia* v. *Meer Conjeer Ali Khan*,[52] decided in 1782, Impey C. J. was disposed to draw a distinction between two sorts of British subjects, those indictable for taking more than twelve per cent interest on loans and those not. It should also be noted that in 21 Geo. III, c. 70, s. 24 the terms "native" and "British subject" are expressly contrasted. In

[48] See further: *Anonymous Case* (1777) 1 *Ind. D.* 947: *Killican* v. *Juggernauth Dutt* (1777) 1 *Ind. D.* 946 where jurisdiction arises *inter alia* (1) if a party is born in Calcutta, (2) is a settled inhabitant: *Bux* v. *Alley Gawny* (1782) 1 *Ind. D.* 64: *Manickchund Tagore* v. *Johnson* (1785) 1 *Ind. D.* 954: *Wyatt* v. *Grant* (1789) 1 *Ind. D.* 960: *Chalunnal* v. *Garrow*, 1 *Ind. D.* 20: *Punchanund Bose* v. *Davision* (1812), 1 *Ind. D.* 968: *Ramalingum* v. *Sashian* (1813) 5 *Ind. D.* 274 where it was held that inhabitancy in regard to natives subject to the jurisdiction is a question of law: *Ram Narrain Tauker* v. *Chederaula Nursiah* (1815) 5 *Ind. D.* 297 where inhabitancy was equated with residence: *Madoo Wissenauth* v. *Baloo Gunnasett* (1818) 1 *Ind. D.* 968: *Jannokee Doss* v. *R.* (1837) 1 *M.I.A.* 42 where though residence was out of the jurisdiction, it was held that the commission of an act within the jurisdiction was sufficient to attract liability: *Akeenah Banoo* v. *Moonshee Boo Alley* (1840) 1 *Ind. D.* 1031: *Tucket Roy* (1858) 3 *Ind. D.* 217. The court approved Lord Brougham's *dictum* in *Warrender* v. *Warrender*, 9 *Bligh's N.S.* 119 and the decisions in *Somerset* v. *Stewart*, *Lofft's Rep.* 1 and *Campbell* v. *Hall* 98 *E.R.* 1045. It is also interesting to note that the *Habeas Corpus* Act, 31 *Car.* II, c. 2, was extended, at least in its general part, to the Fort William Presidency.

[49] 1 *Ind. D.* 953.

[50] 5 *Ind. D.* 73.

[51] 2 *Ind. D.* 870.

[52] 1 *Ind. D.* 957.

a later case, *De Rozio* v. *Chatgeer Gosain* [53] it was held that birth in Calcutta before 1757 did not bring the person involved within the term "H.M. subjects" used in 13 Geo. III, c. 63, s. 16 and clause XIII of the Charter of 1774. Further, the son of a native woman and a British born father, born out of wedlock, is not a "British subject" in terms 13 Geo. III, c. 63.[54]

The question as to the extent of writs running, adverted to briefly above, is one of the keys to the definition of "British subject," especially in its relevance to executive acts of the Company in the provinces. Under 13 Geo. III, c. 63, s. 14 and clause XIII of the Charter the jurisdiction of the Court in civil cases is defined as extending to all British subjects residing in the provinces and persons employed in the service of the Company. Criminal jurisdiction extended to the same classes of persons.[55] Thus in *R.* v. *Clark*,[56] verbal evidence of being in the service or employ of the Company was sufficient to establish jurisdiction. There is some doubt as to whether a foreigner in the Company's service was also similarly affected. In *R.* v. *Francisco Jose* [57] it was held that such a person indicted for an offence committed beyond the provinces was not subject to the jurisdiction but Dunkin J. dissented, citing 13 Geo. III, c. 63, s. 14, and clause XIII of the Charter. However, in *Janardanah Roy* v. *East India Company and Munro* [58] it was held that the jurisdiction will run outside the provinces to compel a British subject, the servant of the Company, to answer a claim against him in his capacity as Company's servant.

Act 21, Geo. III, c. 70, s. 19 empowers the court to frame process against the natives of the provinces, and by s. 3 of this act, the court retains full and competent jurisdiction in its powers as a court of record, so notwithstanding the decision in *R.* v. *Warren Hastings* [59] which was a case in which the judges were equally divided, the right to issue writs, especially of *habeas corpus* remained in the court.[60] In addition in clause IV of the Charter the judges were to have the powers of judges of the court of King's Bench.[61]

[53] 1 *Ind. D.* 958; decided in 1789.
[54] *Byenaut* v. *Reed*, 3 *Ind. D.* 792, desided in 1821.
[55] Clause XIX of the Charter (1774) and 13 *Geo.* III, c. 63, s. 17.
[56] 1 *Ind. D.* 1012, decided in 1791.
[57] 1 *Ind. D.* 1013, decided in 1797.
[58] 5 *Ind. D.* 336, decided in 1816.
[59] 1*Ind. D.* 1005.
[60] See also *Re Ameer Khan*, 6 *Bengal L.R.* (1870) 392.
[61] See also *Re Coza Zacharia Khan*, 1 *Ind. D.* 1043. It should be noted that so

A final difficulty occurs however in the construction and effect of 21 Geo. III, c. 70, s. 1, which provides that the Governor-General and Council shall not be subject to the jurisdiction of the Supreme Court for acts done in their public capacity. This raises the question of the status of the Company itself, as a British subject, especially in view of the provisions of clauses XIII and XV of the Charter. Macnaughton J. in *Jacob Joseph* v. *Rowand Roland* [62] considered this question at p. 83 and he came to the conclusion that the Company is distinguished from other British subjects in that it is open to much higher penalties in execution against its goods, and further, that from clause XXXIV of the Charter, this distinction is quite clear.

Finally, there was the *Cossijurah Incident* (1779-80) which shortly preceded the amending act 21 Geo. III, c. 70 in 1781. This case arose out of an attempt by a sheriff of Calcutta to arrest the Zemindar of Cossijurah for non-payment of a debt due for payment through the Calcutta Board of Revenue. The sheriff, who was acting under process of Court, was prevented from so doing by armed troops dispatched for this purpose to Cossijurah by the Governor-General and Council. Stephen suggests that the net result of the whole affair was that the jurisdiction of the Court outside Calcutta was destroyed by military force in the face of the Regulating Act (13 Geo. III, c. 63).[63] Whatever the motive, it is probably true to say that the exercise of a purported jurisdiction was made inapplicable by the Company's action. It should also be noted that in *R.* v. *Monisse* [64] a writ of *Habeas Corpus* was granted against the Nabob to release persons (natives) improperly imprisoned by him. Further, it was held in *Ousley* v. *Plowden* [65] that any person who at the time of committing a trespass was in the employ of the Company and who had been resident in Bengal was subject to the jurisdiction of the court.

III. Jurisdiction

The third question outlined at the beginning of this Note – the

far as prerogative units were concerned the term "British subject" included persons autside the categories of resident or British born, see *Rajah Mohinder De Rai* v. *Ramcanai Cur* (1794) *Smoult's Orders* 148.

[62] 1 *Ind. D.* 69, decided in 1818.

[63] Sir James Stephen, *Nuncomar and Impey* (1885) ii, 217.

[64] 5 *Ind. D.* 216.

[65] 3 *Ind. D.* 87.

conflict between the Courts and the Company as to the latter's jurisdiction in executive – mainly revenue – fields and the territorial extension of this jurisdiction, has been mentioned at least by implication in the discussion of the two questions which have gone before. The main heads of difference were:

(i) The claim of the court to subject the native population to the jurisdiction of its writs (see above);

(ii) The claims to jurisdiction by the Court over English and native officers of the Company employed in the collection of revenues, for corrupt or oppressive acts done by them in their official capacity;

(iii) Claims by the Court to try judicial officers of the Company for acts done in the supposed execution of their duty.

As to (ii) above, the Company was compelled to admit the jurisdiction of the Court [66] but under the act of 1781, 21 Geo. III, c. 70, s. 8, the Court was to have no jurisdiction concerning matters of revenue or any act done in the collection thereof. Further the Governor-General in Council was empowered "from time to time to frame regulations for the provincial courts and councils." These regulations might be disallowed by the King in Council but were otherwise to remain in force for two years.[67] The act of 1773 made such regulations registerable in the Supreme Court, and thus effective only with the consent and approbation of the Court, 13 Geo. III, c. 63, s. 36. The extent of the jurisdiction of the Court as to revenue matters remained for some considerable length of time uncertain. In *Doe Dem. Rada Govind Sing* v. *Juggessore Mustabee* [68] it was held that the act of 1781 clearly ousted the jurisdiction of the Court. The case involved an action by the lessor of the plaintiff who had been turned out of his land on the pretence of being in arrear in the payment of revenue to the Government. However, the Court was not always so compliant and in 1791, in *Ramcaunt Mundil* v. *Colebrook*,[69] the Court stated that in an action against the Collector of the Company, it would issue process as of course without inquiry as to whether the act done was in fact a revenue matter. In *Vencata Runga Pillay* v. *East India Company*,[70] it was said that for jurisdiction to be excluded in revenue matters, the cause of action must relate immediately to revenue and not be

[66] 13 *Geo.* III, c. 63, ss. 1-6.
[67] 21 *Geo.* III, c. 70, s. 23.
[68] 1 *Ind. D.* 950, decided in 1782.
[69] 1 *Ind. D.* 961.
[70] 5 *Ind. D.* 80.

consequent or argumentative. In *Budden Soorye* v. *D'Oyley*[71] the Court said that notwithstanding that 21 Geo. III, c. 70, s. 8 and 37 Geo. III, c. 142, s. 11 deny the jurisdiction of the Court in revenue matters, it could still look to the revenue laws of the presidency and inquire whether property was rightfully withheld from a plaintiff on the basis of those laws. However, in *Doe dem. Peareemony Dosse* v. *Bonnerjee*,[72] the Court refused to accept want of jurisdiction under s. 8 though, since in this case the land in question was not sold for arrears of revenue, the Court's action seems justified. However, a sale by the Collector of Revenue on a written authority from the Board of Revenue and a conveyance to the purchaser by the Collector was held to be no defence against the title of the lessors of the plantiff in ejectment. Finally, in a later case in 1850, *Spooner* v. *Hurkissondass*[73] the Privy Council stated the effect of s. 8 to be exclusive, if the Collector had acted in good faith.

As to (iii) above, the claim by the Court to try judicial officers of the Company for acts done in the supposed execution of their duty, this may be considered together with the fourth question, the conflicting claims as to jurisdiction between the Crown Courts and the Company Courts, the latter being the results of Hastings' recommendations of 1772. The conflict here was almost immediate following the act of 1773, and appeared first in the celebrated *Patna Incident* (1777-1779).[74] Here the Court awarded damages to a native plaintiff in an action against the Patna Provincial Council acting in its judicial capacity. Impey's judgment in this case was one of the grounds of impeachment against him.[75]

The remarks of Impey C. J. in *Grand* v. *Philip Francis*,[76] decided in 1779, provide in a very summary form some idea of the relations between the Court and the Company at that time. This action arose to enforce the attendance of witnesses and Impey C. J., in stating the power to enforce attendance under the Charter, said that the powers he had were greater than those of a Court in England because in Bengal the patronage and influence of the Governor-General and members of the Council was of such a nature as to necessitate these

[71] 3 *Ind. D.* 889, decided in 1819.
[72] 1 *Ind. D.* 403.
[73] 4 *Ind. D.* 351, and 358 (appeal).
[74] See Ilbert, *op. cit.* 54-55.
[75] *ibid.*
[76] 1 *Ind. D.* 1043.

powers. The defendant in this case was a member of the Council. The *Cossijurah* and *Patna Incidents* already mentioned provide early illustrations of this conflict, and of the later cases, two only need be mentioned here. First, *Dhackjee Dadajee* v. *East India Company*,[77] decided in 1843. At first instance the Court held that, since the Charter Act of 1833, 3 & 4 Will. IV, c. 85, the Company existed only as a public trustee vested with powers of government and that therefore no liability would lie against it, for personal acts done by its servants. However, in the later proceedings which involved the interpretation of 21 Geo. III, c. 70, s. 1 conferring immunity from jurisdiction on the Governor-General and Council for any act done in their official capacity, including powers of appeal, the Court held that this immunity was not absolute, and that an unjustified act of trespass by these bodies would lay the Company open to proceedings. *Bank of Bengal* v. *United Company*[78] which had earlier decided that the Company was not liable as a corporation was distinguished on the ground that since the act 3 & 4 Will. IV, c. 85, a writ to levy execution on the Company's assets as a trading corporation would not run, since there was no trading corporation then in existence. This distinction appears however, not to be wholly satisfactory since in the *Bank of Bengal Case* the Court acquitted the Company of liability, citing as in *Dhackjee's Case*, the decision in *Fabrigas* v. *Mostyn*. This present decision can only be explained as an attempt by the Court, even at this late date, to impose its jurisdiction on the Company's government. However under the Regulations made by the Governor-General in Council, which the Court was bound to notice and act upon, its jurisdiction, especially in the exercise by the Company of prerogative rights in the judicial field, was successfully excluded.

In *Re Tuckut Roy*,[79] decided in 1858 it was held, that under Regulation III of 1818, the Governor-General in Council might issue his warrant to arrest and detain any British subject without trial within and without the limits of territorial jurisdiction of the Court, and that such a warrant was a good answer to a writ of *Habeas Corpus*.

[77] 4 *Ind. D.* 313 and 527.
[78] 1 *Ind. D.* 439.
[79] 3 *Ind. D.* 217.

IV. The Respective Jurisdiction of the Supreme Court and the Mofussil Courts

As to the fourth question, that is the relevant spheres of jurisdiction of the Supreme Court and Mofussil Courts, the matter appeared not to have come up for decision since the *Patna Incident* of 1780 and the subsequent act of 1781, 21 Geo. III, c. 70, for a period of forty-five years. However, in 1825, the Court decided that under 21 Geo. III, c. 70, s. 24 it had no jurisdiction to entertain a civil action for false imprisonment against a provincial magistrate acting in his judicial capacity.[80] An action must be *bona fide*, but trespass will lie if the judge knew or had means of knowing of the defect of jurisdiction and the plaintiff must prove this. In *R. on the prosecution, Shaw* v. *Ogilvy*,[81] the Court held that it had jurisdiction on a criminal prosecution for false imprisonment against a provincial magistrate, and it appears that the magistrate's action was clearly illegal thus bringing it within the conditions set out above. In *Kerry* v. *Duff*,[82] decided in 1841, the Court allowed itself the luxury of a statement of principle in stating that a judgment of one of the Company's courts is on the same footing as those of the Supreme Court of Bengal.

However, the following cases show that this statement was not always adhered to. In *Khursetjee Manockjee* v. *Dadabhai Khursetjee*,[83] the Court found that it was discretionary for judges to endorse a Mofussil process and that they ought not to do so unless the parties were liable to the jurisdiction of the Mofussil Courts, *i.e.* that they were resident within that jurisdiction.

Even more to the point is the decision in *Age Mahomed Jaffer* v. *Mahomed Saduck*,[84] decided in 1847. It was held to be a contempt of the Supreme Court to arrest its officer while in execution of its process and the officers of the Mofussil Court who effect the arrest were themselves liable to be committed. The decision in *Calder* v. *Halkett* and *Shaw* v. *Ogilvy*, were somewhat varied by the decision in *Fewson* v. *Phayre*,[85] in 1848. In considering the interpretation of 21 Geo. III, c. 70, s. 24, in an action for false imprisonment against a provincial

[80] *Calder* v. *Halkett*, 1 *Ind. D*. 988, 13 *E.R*. 12, 18 *E.R*. 311.
[81] 1 *Ind. D*. 989 (note only; decided in 1839).
[82] 1 *Ind. D*. 711.
[83] 4 *Ind. D*. 367.
[84] 4 *Ind. D*. 363.
[85] 2 *Ind. D*. 242.

judge, the Court held that the onus of proving jurisdiction falls upon the judge and not, as in the two earlier cases, upon the plaintiff. This clearly amounts to a grave weakening of *Calder* v. *Halkett*. In the case of the *Dharwar Process*,[86] in 1849, the judges of the Supreme Court took it upon themselves to decide upon the principles of endorsement of process and in 1850, the last blow was delivered at the independence of the Company's courts in *Re Samuel Valentine Roy*.[87] It was held (1) that the Supreme Court of Bengal has, in general, no power to bring up by *certiorari* the proceedings of the Company's courts. (2) but the Court has the power to interfere in criminal matters, and (3) as this involves a question of jurisdiction the Supreme Court will issue *Habeas Corpus*. In the same year the Court decided in *Mohar Ranee* v. *East India Company*,[88] that the Company could not deny its (the Supreme Court's) ecclesiastical jurisdiction in demanding an account for the property of a deceased person which the Company had dealt with as sovereign.

V. The Sovereignty of the Native States

The fifth and final question, the sovereignty of the native states and their relationship which the Company and the Supreme Courts may be briefly illustrated in the following cases. The case, *Nabob of Arcot* v. *East India Company*,[89] illustrates the restrictions placed upon the court process and its jurisdiction in relation to the political sovereignty of the Company. Here it was held that a Sovereign of India could not maintain a bill against the Company for monies had and received since the subject was a matter of political treaty between the parties as independent sovereign powers and was thus not amenable to municipal regulation. However, in *Amerchund Burdeechund* v. *East India Company & two others*,[90] the Court took it upon itself to state the effect of a treaty between the Company and an independent sovereign. In the year following this case, 1827, the Court held that seizure of territory by the Company under treaty was subject to confirmation by the Crown as to its validity.[91] It is thus possible to notice a progression

[86] 4 *Ind. D.* 371.
[87] 2 *Ind. D.* 396.
[88] 2 *Ind. D.* 441.
[89] 29 *E.R.* 841 and 544.
[90] 4 *Ind. D.* 547; decided in 1826.
[91] *East India Company* v. *Syed Ally Habiboon*, 7 *M.I.A.* 334.

from the late seventeenth century up to the nineteenth century in the court's attitude from one of non-interference to one whereby the Court arrogated to itself the right to pronounce upon treaties made by the Company. This is perhaps further evidence that the Company was not regarded either as an independent sovereign or as a servant of the Moghul Emperor.

In one other field only is there any interest for the present purpose and that is the relation of the Court to the independent sovereign princes of India. Generally, the Court would not entertain any actions by or against these sovereigns, or members of their family or servants, on the ground of privilege.[92] However, two decisions both in 1799, are of some extra relevance to what has been discussed earlier. The first, in relation to "British subject," *Frank* v. *Barrett*,[93] decided that an Englishman in the service of the Nabob is entitled to privilege in respect of an action of covenant, as being a public minister of a foreign prince. The second, *Johnston* v. *East India Company*,[94] in relation to the Court's purported lack of revenue jurisdiction under 21 Geo. III, c. 70, s. 8, decided that grain delivered by the Nabob of the Carnatic in discharge of a war subsidy was not revenue in the hands of the government so as to exclude the jurisdiction of the Court. Finally, it must be noted that the generality of privilege was held not to apply to the issue of a writ of *Habeas Corpus* to run so as to release persons (natives) improperly imprisoned by the Nabob.[95]

VI. Later Constitutional History of the Company and the Straits Settlements

In this survey of cases and statutes, some of the important constitutional history of the Company has been omitted and this must now be supplied. Even as late as 1780 the relation between the Crown and Legislature, and the Company, was by no means stabilised and this led, in 1783, to the introduction of the East India Bill of Fox and the act of that name of 1794 passed during the Pitt ministry, 24 Geo. III, session 2, c. 25. This act provided for a board of six commissioners, popularly known as the Board of Control, one to be the Chancellor of

[92] See *Doe dem, Lantour*, 5 *Ind. D.* 38 (1801), *Zeib un Nissa Begum* v. *Nabob Azeem*, 5 *Ind. D.* 220 (1810).

[93] 5 *Ind. D.* 6.

[94] 5 *Ind. D.* 10.

[95] *R.* v. *Monisse*, 5 *Ind. D.* 216 (1810).

the Exchequer, one, a Secrtary of State and the other four Privy Councillors. They were unpaid and had no patronage but had the complete control of civil and military government and revenues both in England and in India. The Governor-General, Governors, Commander-in-Chief and Council might be removed by the Board of Control. This enactment though later repealed, was substantially reproduced in 33 Geo. III, c. 52, s. 42. All British subjects were deemed to be subject to all courts of competent jurisdiction in India or England for acts done in native states.

That all was not well between the Company and the Crown was evidenced by the investigations of a Committee of the House of Commons into the affairs of the Company which began its sittings in 1808. These finally resulted in the Charter Act of 1813, 55 Geo. III, c. 155, the language to the preamble of which is significant: it recites the expediency of continuing the Company for a further term in the possession of territories and revenues in the East Indies, "without prejudice to the undoubted sovereignty of the Crown of the United Kingdom of Great Britain and Ireland in and over the same."

This claim of sovereignty was demonstrated in fact, in regard to the Anglo-Dutch Treaty of 1824 and the subsequent (Straits Settlements) Charter of Justice in 1826. Under this treaty Malacca was ceded to the British Government (Art. X) and the Dutch withdrew their objections to the British possession and settlement of Singapore Island (Art. XII). This treaty was followed in 1824 by act 5 Geo. IV, c. 108 which transferred Singapore and Malacca to the Company to be held by it subject to the restrictions and rights already set out. By act 6 Geo. IV, c. 85 the act pronounced that it would be lawful for the Crown under letters patent to provide for the administration of justice in Singapore and Malacca, s. 19, and under s. 21 Singapore and Malacca were annexed to the settlement of Prince of Wales Island and subject to such government as the Company might think fit to establish. After 1830, the three Settlements ceased to form a separate Presidency and became subordinate to Fort William in Bengal. This action was prompted by the fact that the Company's charter was due to come up for renewal in 1833, and the Company's Indian administration was already the target for considerable adverse criticism in England. Lord Ellenborough, the President of the Board of Control, had warned the Directors at the end of 1828 that the Government would not renew the Company's privileges unless their expenses were considerably reduced.

Retrenchment was thus an urgent political necessity. The offices of Governor (then held by Fullerton) and Resident ceased, and the Court, sitting in 1830, declared itself *functus officio* and adjourned *sine die*. However, as a result of dispatch to the Court of Directors in July 1831 the original position was restored and the Court re-opened in June 1832. It was later held that the legality of this adjoinment was questionable; see *Caunter* v. *East India Co.*[96] There it was said that this suspension was wrongful, for under the Charter of 1826 the principal officer of the Company, by whatever name he is called, is impliedly at liberty to act as head of the Court. Thus the abolition of the government of the Straits Settlements was an act, and a wrongful act, of the local authorities only.[97]

The final legislation of which note has to be taken is the Charter Act of 1833, 3 & 4 Will. IV, c. 85 which came into operation in April 1834 (s. 117). The territorial possessions of the Company were allowed to remain in its possession for another twenty years but were to be held "in trust for" the Crown. The Company was required to close its commercial business and wind up all its affairs, and its debts were charged upon the revenues of India. However, the Company retained some administrative and political powers especially that of patronage.

The last Straits Settlements Charter, that of 1855, was concerned mainly with a re-organisation of the courts into two divisions and by the addition of a second recorder. Its substantive law content is much the same as that contained in the Charter of 1826. The latter Charter was granted by letters patent issued under the authority of 18 & 19 Vic. c. 93. The East India Company was finally abolished in 21 & 22 Vic. c. 106 in 1858 and the Straits Settlements came under the government of the India Office.

VII. Company and Common Law in the Straits Settlements – Bases of Sovereignty

This section is concerned with the expansion of common law into Penang and its later extension to Malacca and Singapore. The period under consideration runs from 1786 when Penang was taken possession of [98] up until 1856 when the Company was dissolved. Some of the

[96] 1 *Kyshe's Report* 12 - hereafter cited as Ky.

[97] See also 1 *Ky*, lxviii-lxxii.

[98] . . . "in the name of His Britannic Majesty, and for the use of the Honourable East India Company."

important grounds of conflict between the Company and the judicial administration which had bedeviled India for a hundred and thirty odd years were no longer in existence. There is no series of revenue cases to be found in the Straits Settlements and, in general, disputes about finance were mainly of a personal nature, involving salary and emoluments due to various judical functionaries in Company employ.

Two questions, similar to those in India, did however, arise and these were:

1. The date upon which the common law became applicable in Penang. The exact date itself is not of great moment, but the implications arising out of the dating are of some importance and may be summarised as follows:

(a) Did the common law become applicable in 1807 by virtue of the first Charter;

(b) Did it become applicable earlier, either because Penang was an "English settlement" or because Penang was under the legal, political and executive suzerainty of the Bengal presidency?

In other words what were the relations between the Company and the Crown in respect of the three settlements, Penang, Malacca and Singapore?

2. The scope of the term "British subject."

Proposition 1(a) is the generally accepted one but an analysis of the Company – Crown relationship does show the possibility of making a case to support proposition 1(b). This is our present concern and each of the three settlements will be examined in turn.

(a) Penang

Captain Light took possession of Penang on 12 August 1786.[99] Occupation was established by virtue of an "agreement" with the King of Kedah for the use of the island. This agreement is set out in the form of a series of conditions on the part of the King of Kedah together with the appropriate replies on the part of the Company. The agreement provided for trading conditions and some protection for the King of Kedah by the Company. There was however, no formal recital of cession and this cannot even be inferred from the terms of the

[99] The island at this time was inhabited though sparsely: see T. Braddell, "Notice of Penang," 4 *Journal of the Indian Archipelago and East Asia* (1850) 629-663 at 630 (hereafter cited as *J.I.A.E.A.*). There was certainly no large scale political or executive organisation in Penang as there was in India.

agreement. The most that could be inferred is a right to occupation subject to certain conditions.

The subsequent treaty with the King of Kedah, 1 May 1791, again makes no formal recital of cession though Art. 1 makes provision for Company possession of Penang upon condition of payment of six thousand Spanish dollars *per annum*. Arts 2-8 make provision for respective trading rights and for the apprehension and return of slaves, forgers and insurgents to the King of Kedah if they happen to fall into Company hands. Art. 9 has a statement that "Quedah and Pulo Penang shall be as one country," but whether or not this has any more meaning than symbolic is doubtful. From the terms of the treaty itself, there do not seem to be any grounds for implying the cession of the island.[100]

There is however one difficulty arising out of the use of the term "cession" in the sense of transfer of sovereignty from one state to another as it is by no means clear that Kedah was at this time an independent sovereign state. The question of the Company's relations with Kedah from 1786-1821 provided much controversy in the later Straits Settlements, revolving around the interpretation of the agreement of 1786 and the treaty of 1791, and Kedah's claim for protection by the Company against Siam. It is clear that there was some dependence by Kedah upon Siam and that the latter regularly obtained money, men, and tribute, from Kedah. All the writers on the subject however seem to concur that the treaty and agreement acted so as to cede Penang to the Company though the clear evidence of vassalage on the part of Kedah which they produce seems to involve them in some contradiction.[101] However, British sovereignty over Penang was expressly recognised by the Siamese in the Treaty of Bangkok, 20th June 1826.[102]

Whatever might be the correct answer to the question of cession it is clear that from 1786 the island was in the occupation of the Company and from 1791 in its possession. The Company certainly regarded itself as having sovereign rights in the area as did the King of Kedah

[100] See further R. St. J. Braddell, *The Law of the Straits Settlements* (1931) i, 2-4

[101] On this point see the following sources: Sir Frank Swettenham, *British Malaya* (1948) pp. 36-54. John Crawfurd, *History of the Indian Archipelago* (1820) ii, p. 404. P. J. Begbie, *The Malayan Peninsula* (1834) pp. 24-29.

[102] W. G. Maxwell & W. S. Gibson. *Treaties and Engagements affecting the Malay States and Borneo* (1924) 77.

and the Siamese government.[103] The early journals are full of references to the fact that no provision had been made on the subject of laws for Penang for several years after its acquisition; the Regulations of 1794 (Lord Teignmouth's Regulations) being the only ones in existence and even these were considered not able to be delegated from the Governor of the island to the Magistrate and Judge.[104]

Within four years Light was complaining of the difficulties which he encountered in keeping a rapidly rising population in some semblance of order. He evidenced the claims of certain Malays, members of the Syid family of Perak, who wished for a written declaration of their own personal law and for a licence to govern themselves, their families, slaves and dependents. He also mentions crimes among the natives. In 1793 two further matters took place supporting his representations for the establishment of some sort of judicial regulation. First, there was the possibility of a civil action against Light in the matter of the administration of the estate of one Wright deceased. The matter was eventually dropped but not before the Company's Advocate-General had been instructed, with the approval of the Court of Directors, to defend Light in the Supreme Court of Calcutta. The second matter involved the murder of one European by another which took place in the Nicobar Islands. Light held a Court of Enquiry in June 1793 and forwarded the offender to Calcutta. In the event nothing was done with the offender as the Advocate-General was of the opinion that 26 Geo. III, c. 57, s. 29 did not authorise the trial of offences committed at sea.[?] The only ground of jurisdiction which the courts might possess was the fact that the offender was a subject of the King in terms of 26 Geo. III, c. 57. Light died in October 1794.

Light was succeeded in 1796 as Superintendent by Macdonald, and during this time (1796) a request was made by him to the European inhabitants to show their authority or permission to reside in the island, which, (still being part of the Presidency of Fort William) it was necessary to obtain or have obtained from the East India Company. A sample of the replies for this information discloses the following "authorities": [105]

[103] L. A. Mills, A History of British Malaya. 33 *Journal of the Royal Asiatic Society - Malayan Branch* (1960) Part III at p. 49 and p. 155: see also the *Straits Settlements Records*, December 1821, p. 83.

[104] See the complaints of Mr. Dickens, Judge and Magistrate of Prince of Wales Island in 1 *Ky*. lxviii.

[105] T. Braddell, Notices of Penang, 5 *J.I.A.E.A.* (1851) pp. 114-117.

(a) "under the protection of Mr. Light";

(b) "Covenant as Free Merchant for Prince of Wales Island";

(c) "my Commanding Officer was induced to recommend me to Lord Cornwallis, who was pleased not only to give me my discharge (from one of His Majesty's Regiments) but to permit me to reside in any part of India . . .";

(d) ". . . from his Majesty King George the Third, . . . also from Superintendent Francis Light, Esq., . . . the public faith being pledged for that purpose continued, . . ."

This last class (d), was queried by Macdonald and elicited the further information; that the resident, one Nason, came to the island in 1786 at the request of T. H. Davis, Advocate-General to the Company at that time and lived with Light, assisting him on the island. Further, Nason had cultivated and finally sold the first estate to the Company.

From the two judicial matters mentioned above, and from the replies to the respective licenses to reside on the island, it is obvious that relations between the Company and the Crown at this time were by no means clear. Respective spheres of authority, especially in day to day administration still remained obscure.

Sir George Leith was appointed Lt.-Governor in 1800 and his instructions included some vague provisions for the administration of civil and criminal law: [106] these regulations provided for the setting up of a court, appeal from which should be to the Lt.-Governor in the first instance, and to the Governor-General in Council. It was to apply native law and usage to the inhabitants of the island, and the Europeans "should be required to render themselves amenable to the same courts as the natives." The Governor-General in Council had of course power to make such regulation.[107] It is clear that the content of these regulations was not English law strictly so-called, but was rather a set of instructions allowing full play to martial law and the individual propensities of the authorities so far as the English inhabitants were concerned. It was the early history of the Company in India repeated.

The arrival of Mr. Dickens, Judge and Magistrate on the island, in 1801, underlined the state of affairs referred to above. He was of the opinion and said so repeatedly, that he had no authority to deal with offences committed by Europeans on the island, and further that the

[106] T. Braddell, *op. cit.* pp. 157-158.

[107] 13 *Geo.* III, c. 63, s. 36 and 39 & 40 *Geo.* III, c. 79, s. 20.

powers given to Light in 1794 by the Governor-General in Council, and which were now vested in the present Lt.-Governor as to the summoning of British subjects, were not such that could be delegated to the Judge and Magistrate.[108] Even as late as 1823 Mr. Phillips, the Governor of the settlement said, "the rules which, according to British law, govern the disposition and inheritance of real property have never been applicable to our lands." [109] Again slaves were bought and sold with the sanction of the local government who registered these transactions. Further, taxes were imposed by the sole authority of the Governor-General in Council, *viz.*, a two per cent duty on all sales of land, and on the estate and effects of deceased persons. As a final comment a statement of Dickens may be quoted; this runs as follows: "The law of nature is the only law declaring crimes and respecting property, which, to my knowledge, at this day exists at Prince of Wales Island . . ." [110]

This then was the situation up to the grant of the First Charter of Justice on 25 March 1807. The Charter was the result of a petition by the Company in March 1805 to the King. The Company was not applying the law of England to its own subjects, and it was in fact, a *quasi-sovereign* power in regard to Prince of Wales Island. In the political and financial spheres it was clearly under the control of the home legislature, but so far as the law was concerned the relation was in general, not one of principal and agent. It must be presumed that the Charter was granted with some knowledge at least of this state of affairs, and was adapted to it. It was competent for the Crown to introduce the law of England into this settlement by such an instrument,[111] and the provisions of the Charter may be usefully compared to the provisions of 13 Geo. III, c. 63 and its subsequent Charter.

However, the possibilities of act 13 Geo. III, c. 63 (1773) which established the Supreme Court of Judicature in Bengal, Behar and Orissa, having applicability to Penang were never seriously considered. S. 36 of this act gave the Governor-General in Council powers to make laws for the good order and civil government of the settlements at Fort William and the factories and places subordinate thereto. Act 21 Geo. III, c. 70 (1781) which confirmed and added to the act of 1773

[108] T. Braddell, *op. cit.* pp. 191 ff.

[109] Minute on the Landed Tenures of Prince of Wales Island (1823) 8.

[110] Quoted by Sir Peter Benson Maxwell in The Law of England in Penang, Malacca and Singapore. 3 *J.I.A.E.A.* (1859) N.S. 33.

[111] *Campbell* v. *Hall*, 98 *E.R.* 1045.

made no alteration to this provision. It is of course admitted that Penang was well outside the territorial areas of Bengal, Behar and Orissa. Maxwell [112] seems to have approved of the opinion of Sir W. Burrows, the Advocate-General of Bengal, who interpreted 13 Geo. III, c. 63, s. 14 so as to confine jurisdiction to the provinces of Bengal, Behar and Orissa. The Supreme Court in some circumstances however, recognised its jurisdiction as running outside of these areas. This occurred in two cases, the first being the extent to which the prerogative writs ran, and the second, for the determination of jurisdiction in revenue cases. Only the first is relevant here. Under s. 14 of the act of 1773 and clause XIII of the Charter of 1774 the jurisdiction of the Court in civil cases is defined as extending to all British subjects residing in the provinces *and persons employed in the service of the Company.* Criminal jurisdiction extends to the same two classes of persons, the second of which at least is applicable to the garrison of Penang in 1786-1800.[113] The relevance of this act to the situation in Penang is made even more striking by a consideration of the answers given to Superintendent Macdonald in 1796 by the inhabitants of Penang in answer to the question as to what authority they could show for being in the island. In essence, the various licences to remain in the island depended upon the goodwill and permission of the Company's authorities in India. If these propositions are regarded as tenable then the decision of the A.G. of Calcutta regarding the case of Sudds who was arrested and indicted for murder committed in the Nicobar Islands shows a want of consideration of the terms of the statute of 1773.

In 1800, act 39 and 40 Geo. III, c. 79 was passed, s. 20 of which extended, in general terms, the jurisdiction of the Supreme Court. Under s. 2, the act specifically makes provision for the applicability of 13 Geo. III, c. 63 and divers subsequent statutes *i.e.* 21 Geo. III, c. 70. There can be no doubt of the intention of the legislature to include Penang within the scope of 39-40 Geo. III, c. 79. If this is admitted, then the agreement basing the introduction of English law upon cession, which is, as has been seen, not a wholly satisfactory ground, may be dispensed with, and instead that line of Indian cases dealing with

[112] Sir Peter Benson Maxwell, *op. cit. R.* v. *Willans*, 3 *Ky.* (1858) 16.

[113] 13 *Geo.* III, c. 63, s. 17, Clause XIX of the Charter of 1774: see also *R.* v. *Clark* (1791) 1 *Ind. D.* 1012 and *Janardanah Roy* v. *East India Company and Munro* (1816) 5 *Ind. D.* 336.

the interpretation of the scope and jurisdiction of the acts of 1773 and 1781 and the Charter of 1774 becomes germane.

More important however, is the case of *Freeman* v. *Fairlie*,[114] which in approving *Gardiner* v. *Fell*,[115] laid down that English law may be assumed to exist by virtue of English settlement only, that is, its introduction does not have to be specifically located in point of time. This is especially relevant in view of 21 Geo. III, c. 70, ss. 19-23. There is thus the possibility of a case to show that the legal chaos of 1786-1807 in Penang was not due so much to want of jurisdiction as lack of administration to exercise the jurisdiction.

(b) Singapore

What of the position in Singapore? The condition of Singapore when occupied by Raffles in February 1819 seems almost precisely similar to that of Penang thirty odd years earlier. The island was inhabited by a very small number of people and its areas of cultivation amounted to a few acres only. The island was actually under the control of the Temenggong of Johore and some of his followers. The Temenggong was nominally subject to the Sultan of Johore who was himself subject to the governors of Rhio.

Raffles entered into a series of agreements and treaties with the local rulers, *viz*:

(i) "Preliminary Agreement with the Dato Temenggong of Johore," January 1819;

(ii) "Treaty of Friendship and Alliance between the East India Company and the Sultan of Johore," February 1819;

(iii) "Arrangements made for the Government of Singapore" between Raffles and Farquhar, and the Sultan of Johore, June 1819;

(iv) "A Treaty of Friendship and Alliance between the Company and the Sultan and Temenggong of Johore," November 1824;

(v) There was also a "Memorandum" by Raffles on sovereignty of the Company over Singapore, (presumed June 1823).[116]

Numbers (i) and (ii) above show nothing in the way of a transference of sovereignty except perhaps Art. 6 of (ii) which recites that all persons belonging to the English factory "or who shall desire to place themselves under the protection of its flag shall be duly registered and considered as subject to the British authority." What effect if any, this

[114] 1 *M.I.A.* 306, 18 *E.R.* 117, decided in 1828.
[115] 18 *E.R.* 113.
[116] See R. St. J. Braddell, *op. cit.* i, pp. 150-167.

Article had is unknown. The rest of the provisions of instruments (i) and (ii) deal mainly with trade and payments to be made to the Sultan and Temenggong of Johore. Instrument (iii) makes provision for residence and control of the population, Chinese and Malay. This instrument was sealed by both Sultan and Temenggong, and signed by Raffles and Farquhar and is interesting as illustrating a state of joint government on analogy to a *condominium*. It was not until the issue of instrument (iv) that the island was actually ceded to the Company (Art. 2) but instrument (v) which was issued over a year before instrument (iv) is interesting for the following reasons. First, the rules forming the subject matter of the instrument, although laid down by Raffles, are concurred in by their Highnesses and are intended to define the rights of all the parties. Second, Singapore and the islands immediately adjacent, are stated to be at the "entire disposal of the British Government." Third, the memorandum refers to their Highnesses sitting on the bench (Art. 5) and that the laws of the Malays shall be respected where not contrary to reason, justice or humanity, but in other cases English law will be applied with "due consideration to the habits and usages of the people" (Art. 6).

In 1823, under Regulations III and IV of that year, (*i.e.* one year before formal cession under (iv) above) Raffles had appointed twelve magistrates to be nominated yearly by the Residents from among the principal British merchants. They were to try minor civil and criminal cases under the general supervision of the Resident. Raffles drew up a set of laws based to some extent on the forms and principles of English law but directing that regard be had to native customs especially in matters of marriage, inheritance and religion. These regulations were very general and left large powers of discretion to the magistrates.[117]

Raffles' "Memorandum" (v above) did not give an absolute cession of the right of sovereignty though in the opinion of the Advocate-General of Bengal it was a "near approach to it." The Advocate-General went on to say that henceforth English law could "... operate with effect and without injustice." However, the Treaty of 1824 (iv) above was not ratified until March 1825 on the part of the Company, and not ratified by Parliament until 1826 and it was thus that the Directors were unable to establish Courts in the Settlement.

From the time of the first agreement with the Temenggong of

[117] H. A. O'Brien (ed.). An Old Minute by Sir Stamford Raffles, 24 *Journal of the Royal Asiatic Society - Straits Branch* (1891) pp. 1-12.

Jobore, (i) above, until Raffles departure in June 1823, Singapore was under the control of the government of Bencoolen. During this period, Bencoolen, if not a separate Presidency as provided by 42 Geo. III, c. 29 was at least a Lt.-Governorship under powers given to Raffles, though it was subject to the general control of the Governor-General in Council. Raffles was succeeded in Singapore by Crawfurd and the island was removed from the control of Bencoolen and made a dependency of the Indian Government (in 1823). Crawfurd continued Raffles' judicial scheme, with some alterations until the arrival of the Charter in March 1827, which extended the jurisdiction of the Penang Recorder's Court to Malacca and Singapore.

Thus from the date of the ratification of the treaty with the Sultan and Temenggong of Johore, Singapore must be considered a place acquired by cession and on the same footing as Malacca though varying in its antecedents. It should also be noted that under 13 Geo. III, c. 63, s. 9, Bencoolen was subject to the jurisdiction of the Supreme Court in Calcutta. Singapore may therefore be considered as being a recipient of common law before its formal cession.

(c) Malacca

Malacca was ceded to the Crown in 1824 under the terms of the Anglo-Dutch Treaty of that date. This treaty and the peaceful occupation of Singapore were ratified by 5 Geo. IV, c. 108. In 1825, by virtue of 6 Geo. IV, c. 85, s. 19, Malacca was transferred to the control of the East India Company. The same Act made arrangement for reducing Bencoolen from the rank of Presidency to that of a factory subordinate to Fort William in Bengal and so by virtue of 39 & 40 Geo. III, c. 79 the places ceded, Malacca and Singapore, became subject to the jurisdiction of Fort William (s. 20). The act of 1825 [6 Geo. IV, c. 85] also gave power to the Crown to make arrangements by letters patent for the administration of the law in Singapore and Malacca, S. 21 authorized the Company to annex Singapore and Malacca to Penang, and in October 1825 the Company issued an order to this effect, and at the same time presented a petition to the Crown for a new Charter of Justice. This Charter for the incorporated settlements was issued in 1826. Malacca, unlike Penang and Singapore, was before its cession a province under the control of the Dutch authorities and had been so from 1641. There is thus no doubt as to the effect of the cession on its laws. Those laws must continue as before until altered by competent authority – in this case Crown and Parliament. These laws were so altered in the absence of any stipulation to the contrary by the treaty of March 1824 and from that date Malacca is placed on a par with Penang and Singapore. As has been noted above, Penang became subject to the jurisdiction of the Supreme Court at Fort William by virtue of 39 & 40 Geo. III, c. 79, s. 20 in 1800, and the same act was also applicable to Malacca and Singapore from at least 17 March 1824 by virtue of 6 Geo. IV, c. 85, ss. 19-20. It therefore appears that the law of the Supreme Court of Calcutta might have been in force in each of the three stations before the publication of their respective first Charters.

Further support for proposition 1(b) may be adduced from a consideration of the effect of the charters on pre-existing laws. It is clear that if the Charters operate *ipso facto* on existing law then the validity of 1(b) will be very doubtful. Conversely, if the Charters can alter existing law only by virtue of a specific discretion contained within a Charter, then the proposition will gain in probability. This question may be answered in part, by analogy with the practice of the Indian Supreme Courts, and in part by the later practice in the Straits Settlements.

(i) Indian Practice. Many of the Indian cases having a bearing on this topic have already been considered.[118]

There is however, one Indian opinion and four cases which must be considered in little more detail. The opinion, which was given in 1818-23 by Mr. Serjeant Bosanquet, Mr. Spankie, A.-G. of Calcutta, and Mr. Mallin, A.-G. of Bombay,[119] concerns the extent of the Court's jurisdiction, respect of executive acts, and arose out of the

[118] But see especially the following: *Freeman* v. *Fairlie* (1828) 18 *E.R.* 117, *Vencata Runga Pillay* v. *E.I. Company* (1803) 5 *Ind. D.* 80, *Doe dem. Rada Govind Singh* v. *Juggessore Mustabee* (1782) 1 *Ind. D.* 950, *Budden Soorye* v. *D'Oyley* (1819) 3 *Ind. D.* 889, *Doe dem. Peareemony Dosse* v. *Bissonauth Bonnerjee* (1830) 1 *Ind. D.* 403, *Spooner* v. *Hurkissondass* (1850) 4 *Ind. D.* 351, 358, *R.* v. *Cock* (1791) 3 *Ind. D.* 925, *Maclean* v. *Christall* (1849) 4 *Ind. D.* 69, *A. G. of Bengal* v. *R.S. Dossee* (1863) 9 *M.I.A.* 235, *Dutturam Turrufdar* v. *The United Company & Watson* (1779) 1 *Ind. D.* 1037, *Doe dem. Savage* v. *Bancharam Tagore* (1785) 1 *Ind. D.* 65, *Re Govindo Lalla* (1801) 5 *Ind. D.* 34, *Murray* v. *E.I. Company* (1821) 106 *E.R.* 1167, *Doe dem. Sibchunder Doss* v. *Sibkissen Bonnerjee* (1854) 3 *Ind. D.* 42, *Mayor of Lyons* v. *E.I. Company* (1836) 1 *M.I.A.* 108, *Varden Seth Sam* v. *Luckpathy Royajee* (1862) 9 *M.I.A.* 185, *Musleah* v. *Musleah* (1856) 3 *Ind. D.* 140, *Padre Stephanus Aratoon* v. *Sarkies Johannes* (1796) 1 *Ind. D.* 12, *Re Cachik* (1791) 1 *Ind. D.* 960, *Re Phanus Johannes* (1790) 1 *Ind. D.* 10, *R.* v. *Eduljee Byramjee* (1846) 3 *M.I.A.* 294.

[119] 1 *Ind. D.* pp. 1119-1132.

decision in *Madow Wissenath* v. *Balloo Gunnasett* [120] judgment in which was delivered by Sir Alexander Anstruther. All the opinions given assumed that the Charters: (i) Define the outer limits of jurisdiction; (ii) Define the depth of jurisdiction and in this sense they are analogous to legislation. There is therefore an assumption as to an existing body of law dealing with matters outside the scope and jurisdiction of the Charters proper.

In *Jebb* v. *Lefevre* [121] the judge considered the effect of the Charters commencing with the letters patent of Charles II and James II. The Charters under these two monarchs make quite plain the extent of the Court's jurisdiction, and where causes are specified, then matters not falling within the specification do not admit of jurisdiction. This, and the effect of the Charters on matters of real and personal tenure in this case appear as follows. The Charters of Charles II and James II gave no jurisdiction though it appears, both in theory and in fact, that the law of England was introduced into India, at least from the cession of Bombay in 1669. The problem which arose for determination was the nature of tenure in India, more specifically the rights of an executor or administrator as against an heir in relation to real proporty. The practice had grown up of vesting land in the former, the only authority for which, and this was but partial, being given by 29 Car. III, c. 3 and 14 Geo. II, c. 20, both relating to estates *per autre vie*. Grey, C. J., who gave a dissenting judgment in this case, held that in the absence of express provisions the law relating to real property in India must remain that of England. In other words Grey C. J. regarded the Charters as containing within themselves the exact content of English law and he presupposes no existing body of law. In this respect the assumptions given in the opinion earlier differ from those of this judge.

However, Lord Lyndhurst in 1828, has decided in *Freeman* v. *Fairlie*,[122] that English law had been the law of Calcutta from the earliest period of settlement and that therefore variations of it were matters for the Charters. Further, Buller J. in *Joseph* v. *Ronald*,[123] whilst admitting the possibility of the English law of inheritance being in force before either act or Charter specifically mentioned it, held that there were in fact variations of English law which appeared to have arisen

[120] 1 *Ind. D.* 968, decided in 1818.
[121] 1 *Ind. D.* 92 at pp. 101 ff. decided in 1824.
[122] 1 *M.I.A.* 306.
[123] 1 *Ind. D.* 68.

out of practice and which he was not prepared to upset. Franks, J. in *Jebb's Case* found no difficulty in deciding that matters of tenure were matters, in India at least, which were established by imported English law, Charter and Act of Parliament. He also held that the rules established by the previous Charters stood until expressly altered by the new Charter, in this case that of 1774.[124]

The other three cases may be shortly dealt with as they all establish that each successive Charter does not of itself alter the pre-existing law unless specifically so directed. In *Perozeboye* v. *Ardaseer Cursetjee*,[125] where, in defining "British subjects," the effect of the successive Charters from Charles II in 1661 was held to be restricted to the actual terms of the Charters themselves. Similarly in *Doe dem. De Silveira* v.*Texeira* [126] and *R.* v. *Shaik Boodin*.[127]

(ii) Straits Settlements Practice. Turning now to the practice in the Straits Settlements the position is slightly different. It has been noted above, that a case may be made out to show that English law was in existence in each of the three settlements before the date of their respective first Charters. In all three cases this was the law as practised in Fort William, that is, as administered by the Supreme Court of Bengal. The cases which follow are closely analogous to the general tenor of Indian decisions on the point and show that Charters subsequent to the first do not necessarily abrogate all existing law except where specifically mentioned. In the only case on this question involving the first Charter of 1807 the Privy Council based their judgment upon the ground that English law became the *lex loci* upon occupation of the island but expressed no opinion on the effect of the Charter, *Ong Cheng Neo* v. *Yeap Cheah Neo*.[128]

There are however local cases on the point. *Kamoo* v. *Thomas T. Bassett* [129] extended English criminal law to Penang and this extension was applicable to offences committed before the coming into force of the Charter. However, in *Rodyk* v. *Williamson* [130] Sir Benjamin Malkin regarded the Charter as abrogating any previously existing law. Further cases do not throw much light on this question since they are

[124] 1 *Ind. D.* at pp. 108 ff.
[125] 4 *Ind. D.* 53 and 614.
[126] 4 *Ind. D.* 529.
[127] 4 *Ind. D.* 397.
[128] *L.R.* 6 *P.D.* 381.
[129] (1808) 1 *Ky.* 1, see also 13 *Geo.* III, c. 63, s. 34.
[130] Unreported but mentioned in R. St. J. Braddell, *op. cit.* i, 14.

mainly concerned with repeating the statement that English law became the *lex loci* in Penang in 1807, and of Malacca and Singapore in 1824.[131]

However, cases arising out of the Indian Acts provide some grounds for supposing that the Charters did not alter an existing law. Act 3 & 4 Will. IV, c. 85 (1833) which was passed to provide for the "better government of His Majesty's *Indian* Territories" set up an Indian Legislature (s. 39) which included Penang, Malacca and Singapore, ss. 1-2. Acts made by the Indian Legislature therefore applied to the territories of Penang, Malacca and Singapore, and the question therefore arose as to the effect of the Charters of 1826 and 1855 as importing English statute law into these territories, *i.e.* did the Charters introduce statutes abrogating local law? (It should be noted at this stage that the Imperial Parliament reserved the right to legislate on certain matters for itself; see 16 & 17 Vic. c. 95).

The first Straits Settlements case on the point would seem to suggest that this was so. In *Jemalah* v. *Mohd. Ali*,[132] decided in 1875, Ford J. held that English statute law from 1826 up until the passing of 3 & 4 Will. IV, c. 85 (1833) became law in the Colony. The ground for this proposition was that the Charter of 1826 had the effect of carrying into the Colony all English statutes subsequent to 1826. This was the case at least up until the creation of a special legislative body having authority in the Colony. However, this decision was overruled by a full bench on appeal in *Ismail bin Savoosah* v. *Madinasah Merican*,[133] decided in 1887. The law of the Colony was given by Wood J. as being (a) the law of England as at 1826; (b) Indian Acts having reference to the Colony; (c) Ordinances of the Colony and (d) English statutes in terms applicable to the Colony. As to (d) it is clear from the judgment that these statutes were not automatically applicable to the Colony. Braddell [134] remarks that the decision in *Jemalah's Case* is quite inapplicable to the Straits Settlements as the Governor-General in Council had power to legislate for the Colony by virtue of 13 Geo. III, c. 63, s. 36. Presumably he is referring to the effect of 39 & 40 Geo. III, c. 79, s. 20 (1800) which extends the former statute. However, if this is so the applicability of that act should have run from 1800-1805 when

[131] See: *In the goods of Abdullah*, 2 *Ky. Ecc. Rs.* 8. *Moraiss* v. *De Souza*, 1 *Ky*. 27. *Ismail bin Saroosah* v. *Madinasah Marican*, 4 *Ky*. 311.

[132] 1 *Ky*. 386.

[133] 4 *Ky*. 311.

[134] R. St. J. Braddell, *op. cit.* i, 30.

Penang became a separate Presidency though neither Braddell nor any of the judiciary had proceeded upon this assumption.

The applicability of Indian Acts to the Settlements was confirmed in *R.* v. *Rodriguez* [135] and in *Mahomed Meera Nachair* v. *Inche Khatijah*.[136] The latter case is interesting because it points out, first of all, that land in the colony is not on the same footing as land in England so far as heirs-at-law are concerned because the English rules have been replaced by Indian acts – at this date by Act XX of 1837. On the other hand the point is made that the law relating to wills in the Colony is the same as English law the reason being that the English (Statute – 7 Will. IV & I, Vic. c. 26) rules are embodied in an Indian act, *i.e.* Act XXV 1830.

Further evidence relating to Charters and the introduction of English statutes may be gathered from the following cases. In *R.* v. *Till* [137] it was held that the "Black Act," 9 Geo. I, c. 22, is applicable in India and Penang because of its general applicability. In *R.* v. *Adam Singh* [138] it was held that statute 43 Geo. III, c. 58 does not extend to this Colony. Far from having the Charter of 1807 introduce this automatically, a letter from the Court of Directors of the Company quoted in the report directs the Court in Penang to establish the applicability of an Imperial Act either by an appeal to His Majesty in Council against a conviction or by considering the clause of the Charter 1807 by which the judge may recommend a reprieve to the Court of Directors. *Moraiss* v. *De Souza*,[139] decided in 1838 showed that from 1807 to Indian Act XX of 1837 the English law of inheritance was the law in Penang. In *Mohammed Ally* v. *Scully*,[140] it was decided that the Charter of 1826 did not introduce English statute law into the settlements between 1826-1855. The full judgment in this case is unfortunately not reported. In *Re Khoo Chow Sew*,[141] it was held (a) that the statutes 31 Ed. III, c. 2 and 21 Hen. VIII, c. 5 extend to the Colony; (b) the words "next-of-kin" in the Charters of 1807, 1826, 1855 must be construed liberally in connection with these acts. In other words the provisions of the Charters were apparently taken as pro-

[135] 4 *Ky*. 323.
[136] 4 *Ky*. 608.
[137] 2 *Ky*. *Crim*. *Rs*. 1, decided in 1809.
[138] 2 *Ky*. *Crim*. *Rs*. 12, decided in 1822.
[139] 1 *Ky*. 27.
[140] 1 *Ky*. 254, discussed in R. St. J. Braddell, *op. cit.* i, 33.
[141] 2 *Ky*. *Ecc*. *Rs*. 22.

viding standards of applicability for the introduction of English acts. Finally, in *Tengah Chee Nachiar* v. *Nacodah Merican* [142] it was decided that the Statute of Distributions was applicable only when its provisions were taken in conjunction with the Indian Wills Act, XXV of 1838, and the Mohammedan Marriage Ordinance V of 1880. To the question, did the Charters introduce English statutes abrogating local law? – an answer firmly in the negative may be returned.

It seems, in conclusion, that a case may be made out to support proposition 1(b) outlined at the beginning of this Note. Although it is doubtful if Penang was a "settlement" in the sense demanded by *Campbell's* case, its European inhabitants were either Company servants or resided on the island with Company permission. Although *Campbell's* case does not contemplate the peculiar situation in Penang, where, as has already been suggested, cession may not in fact have taken place, there seems to be no reason why the principles of *Campbell's* case should not be extended: and this extension may plausibly be based upon residence and licence to reside. It also seems that the mechanics of the introduction especially in regard to the agreements and treaties with Kedah and Johore are a good deal more complex that was imagined at the time; a cautionary word must be said about the value and effect of treaties entered into with native rulers at that period. There is no doubt that these documents were treated at the time as setting out binding conditions as between contracting parties. However, this should not be allowed to obscure the fact that these treaties and agreements are not the same documents which *mutatis mutandis* bear these names today. Given that the treaties and engagements do not show a formal cession the alternative grounds for the introduction of common law may be summarised as follows:

(1) An extension of the principle in *Campbell* v. *Hall* to include residence and residence by licence.

(2) The competency of the Supreme Court at Fort William in issuing writs out of the jurisdiction in respect of servants of the Company, and possibly also licencees of the Company;

(3) The jurisdiction of the Court under 13 Geo. III, c. 63, 21 Geo. III, c. 70, 39 & 40 Geo. III, c. 79.

[142] 4 *Ky.* 265: see also *Re Native Witnesses*, 2 *Ky. Crim. Rs.* 15 on the extension of Indian Acts and *R.* v. *Overee*, 2 *Ky. Crim. Rs.* 88 on the limitation of Indian Acts in the Colony.

(4) The fact that the Charters all assumed a *preexisting* body of law, and did not affect this law unless specific provisions were contained in the Charter.

(5) Following from (4) Straits Settlements and Indian practice in respect of Charters and Statutes;

(6) The political and commercial *de facto* control of the Company in the Straits Settlements at least up until the Charter Act of 1833, 3 & 4 Will. IV, c. 85.

VIII. Company and Common Law in the Straits Settlements – "British Subject"

A full consideration of this topic involves questions as to the modifications of substantive common law. This is outside the scope of this essay.[143] In general the courts in the three settlements were more concerned with applying common law to all the inhabitants [144] than with discussing whether or not it should be applied.

Problems as to residence and the validity of writs issued out of Court, which were the forms in which "British subject" was considered in India, never arose to any great extent in the Straits Settlements. The reasons for this appear to be four in number.

First, the terms of the initial Charter of 1807 were quite clear in purporting to apply common law to all people in the territories under the Company's control. Though the substance of the law to be administered might be subject to dispute, the subjection of all the inhabitants, whatever their race and religion, to the formal processes of the Court was not in question. At the same time, the native inhabitants had no legal structure or system comparable in its formal organisation to that possessed by some sections of the population in India. Written codes and *pandits* on the Indian model were conspicuous by their absence.

Second, the areas in the Straits Settlements under the political control of the Company, and those under its trading and financial control, were for the most part identical. There was not the Indian situation of a Company controlled town or factory together with the financial

[143] For a brief summary see M. B. Hooker, Private International Law and Personal Laws: The Malaysian Experience, 10 *Malaya Law Review* (1968) 55-67. A full description of modification is in preparation.

[144] With due regard to local customs, religions, etc.

control of large outside areas. At the same time there were no great territorial expansions at the expense of local governments tending to raise questions of the Company's status as sovereign.

Third, from the period of the Charter Act of 1813, 55 Geo. III, c. 155, the competency of the Company in political, executive and financial fields was steadily reduced. The Crown was by now the *de facto* as well as *de jure* sovereign so far as the administration of law was concerned. The act of 1813 contained special provisions relating to civil, military and judicial government, the Company was required to keep accounts in such a way as to distinguish between territorial and political revenue and commercial revenue. The language ot the preamble recites "the undoubted sovereignty of the Crown . . ." Between 1813 and 1833 there were a series of rather unimportant acts, noteworthy only because the Company's power to resist the exercise of control by parliament either by lobbying or outright defiance was now almost at an end: these acts were; 54 Geo. III, c. 105; 55 Geo. III, c. 84; 58 Geo. III, c. 84 which act related to the validity of certain Indian marriages and is important in the history of Indian marriage regulation; 4 Geo. IV, c. 71 which authorised a grant of Charter for a supreme court at Bombay in substitution for the recorder's court, and made some revenue provisions relating to the payment of troops in India; restrictions on the Indian trade were gradually reduced, 4 Geo. IV, c. 80; an act of 1828, 9 Geo. IV, c. 33 declared the real estates of British subjects dying within the jurisdiction of the Supreme Court to be liable for payment of debts.

This unity of legal administration was further consolidated in the period 1830 onwards when the settlements came under the administration of Fort William (1830-1851) and the Government of India (1851-67).

In any case, 1833 saw the passing of the Charter Act 3 & 4 Will. IV, c. 85 which removed all commercial activity and privilege from the Company and stated that the Company held all its territories "in trust for" the Crown. In addition it should be noted that acts 13 Geo. III, c. 63 and 39 & 40 Geo. III, c. 70 tend to emphasise this unity of government.

Finally, there did not appear to have been very much confusion between the executive and commercial functions of the Company. This is probably due to the fact that the volume of trade through Penang, though quite considerable was not of first importance compared with the intention of making full use of the strategic importance of Penang as a naval base to control the Eastern seas.

However, some difficulty did arise as to the relevant spheres of jurisdiction between the executive and the judiciary in the early years in Penang. Though these were not on such a scale as to repeat the *Patna* or *Cossijurah* incidents, there was confusion especially in the period 1801-1805. This was the period of Mr. Dickens's appointment as judge and magistrate and the disputes arose because of the supposed lack of any law applicable and the subsequent impossibility of controlling a turbulent European population. This position was thought remedied by the Charter of 1807 and subsequent Charters. It is noteworthy that the cases requiring the interpretation of the Charter, never repeated those lines of cases dealing with conflicts of jurisdiction which were so characteristic of India in 1773-1820. A constitutional distinction seems to have been assumed by both sides after the initial five-year period of difficulty.

IX. Summary

It is now time to attempt a summary of the part played by the Company as a propagator or agent of the common law.

In the first place it may be said that the place of law in the Company's scheme of things was incidental rather than purposeful. Its main ambitions were financial, and only territorial insofar as the commerce of the Company remained unimpaired and in good order. Politically, the Company had found itself *de facto* master of extensive territories containing a large number of people and its handling of this situation, was dictated by the attempted steering of a course between the effect of restrictive financial regulations on the one hand, and by the avoidance of outright and probably costly executive control of native states on the other. In course of time, however, this latter did take place but always in opposition to the views of many M.P.'s in England and always with power struggles between the Court of Directors and the later Boards of Control.

So far as any of the courts were concerned, it is evident that the legislature also was not confident of its abilities in these territorial acquisitions, and for many years avoided important questions of constitutional law and procedure. This avoidance is mirrored in the vague and woolly language of many enactments, and more especially in many of the Charters, especially that of 1807 (Penang Charter).

Common to all facets of this narrative is the obscurity which has hung about the relations between the Indian territories on the one hand, and Crown and Parliament on the other. By 1830, or at least by the slightly earlier statute of 9 Geo. IV, c. 74 (ss. 7, 8, 57, 70) the bulk of the Indian territories were considered as having been annexed by conquest or cession to the Crown of the United Kingdom: 9 Geo. IV, c. 74, s. 7 etc. provided for trial by the Supreme Courts of offences committed by native or British persons without distinction, whether or not the offence was committed outside the jurisdiction. Further 26 Geo. III, c. 57 contemplates cases in which the Court would have to enforce in any part of the Presidency, by exchequer process, the execution of judgments obtained in England. Similarly, there are other statutes which have created occasion for the exercise of powers of the Court in the provinces, as for example, in taking evidence on divorce bills in the House of Lords.

If the sovereignty of the Crown is held to have been established throughout the provinces, as it must be, especially in view of the right of the King in Council to decide appeals in the period under discussion, then it must also be admitted that the Company, mainly from the force of historical circumstances, was the only despository and organ of the powers which it was necessary to exercise *in situ*. It had the functions of government and replaced in part the old native governments, especially in the administration of justice. However, its functions in regard to the judicial administration were not derived wholly from the Crown, but in part from local law, at least as to its rules and content, if not to its formal procedure. This latter position, was perhaps overstated on behalf of the Company, subsequent to Clive's conquests, when it was suggested that the Company had delegated sovereignty from the Mogul Emperor, who himself retained a formal and nominal sovereignty. This contention was however disposed of by *Campbell* v. *Hall*. This question is especially important in determining the validity of treaties entered into by the Company with foreign states in India which involved both judicial administration and the presence or action of the Crown. This is illustrated in the case of *The Sec. of State in Council of India* v. *Kamachee Boye Sahaba*.[145] Here a Rajah had entered into three treaties with the Company, the

[145] 7 *M.I.A.* (1859) 287.

most important of which was the third treaty of October 1799; by Art. 4 of that treaty the Company was to set up a system of civil and criminal judicial administration, the laws for which were to be framed by the Company. Officials in this administration were the Company's officials and the laws were to apply to all the inhabitants of the state, having due regard to existing laws and customs. The Rajah was to have no control whatsoever over this administration. Upon the death of the Rajah, leaving no male heirs, the Company seized the whole of the state as an escheat on the ground that the dignity of the *Raj* lapsed for want of a male heir and that the property lapsed to the British Government for whom the Company was acting as a delegated authority. This act was ratified and adopted by the Crown, though the act of seizure was in itself *ultra vires* the Company. This decision was approved in *In Re Ameer Khan.*[146] It should be noted that no question was raised as to the validity of the Company's power to enter into treaties, including provisions to set up a judicial administration.

Arising out of the question of sovereignty was the uncertainty as to content of the term "British subjects" in those areas not being settlements or factories of the Company. It seems clear that the term includes those who were either British born or descendants of British born on the one hand and those who were inhabitants of British settlements or factories. But the activities of the Company involved people not in these two classes and therefore the applicability of the Company's regulations to them by statute and charter might very well have been ultra vires their competency. Despite *Campbell* v. *Hall* and the cases cited earlier, this question remained unsettled. The legislative and judicial powers of government were never under one control: thus the regulations for government in the provinces, and civil cases tried in the provincial courts above a certain value, were nominally subject to the control of the King in Council, as much as were the regulations registered in the Supreme Court of any Presidency. But this was effective more in name than in fact, and the legislative and judicial functions of the Indian governments in the provinces were exercised under no other control than that of the Directors and Commissioners for the Affairs of India, whilst the administration of law for British persons was, in theory, independent of both the Indian Governments, and the Directors and the Board of Control. Those who resided within the

[146] 6 *Bengal L.R.* (1870) 392.

areas of any Presidency were subject only to "judicial legislation" or to regulation registered in the Supreme Courts.

This state of affairs is probably traceable to the imperfections of the statutes and letters patent under which judicial administration was established. Thus, nothing could be more vague in some respects than 21 Geo. III, c. 70 which did nothing to settle the argument as to who were the subjects of His Majesty. It left to the Supreme Court the determination of suits respecting land, but forbade it to deal with revenue. But these topics were so closely related that it was not possible to separate them.

In the Straits Settlements, on the other hand, the position was relatively clearer through the relation between the executive and the judiciary characterised by a conflict as to their respective spheres of authority. As in India much of the difficulty was caused by the *ad hoc* approach to judicial regulation adopted by the Company.*

* As to international legal aspects of problems discussed in the above article, see "The Evolution of British Sovereignty in India" by Dr. R. Kemal in *Indian Year Book of International Affairs* 1957, pp. 143-171 (Editor's Note).

DR. PAUL O'HIGGINS

Fellow of Christ's College, Cambridge

The Treaty of Limerick 1691

On the third of October 1691 the war in Ireland between William III and the Irish followers of James II and their French allies came finally to an end with the conclusion of the Civil Articles of Limerick [1] which, together with the Military Articles, are known collectively as the Treaty of Limerick.[2] The Civil Articles were signed on the English side by Baron De Ginckel, William's Commander in Chief in Ireland and the two Irish Lords Justices representing the English Crown in Ireland, and on the Irish side, by the leaders of the Irish forces. The Military Articles [3] were signed by De Ginckel for the English and on the other side by the two French generals who were commanders in chief of the Irish army, together with a number of general officers.

The war thereby ended was the consequence of the Irish catholics giving their support to James II who after his overthrow in England, planned to use Ireland as a base from which to recover the English throne. William III invaded Ireland to protect his rear from James

[1] For text of the Civil Articles see the Appendix.

[2] There exist several printed versions of the Treaty, e.g. i. *Articles of Limerick, Ratified under the Great Seal of England* (no place, no date; English text only); ii. *The Civil and Military Articles of Limerick. Agreed upon the 3d Day of October, 1691* (London, 1691?; English, French and Latin texts in parallel columns); iii. *The Civil Articles of Limerick, Exactly Printed from the Letters Patent. Wherein they are Ratified and Exemplified by their Majesties, under the Great Seal of England. Les Articles Civiles de Limerick, tirez des Lettres Patentes. Par lequelles ils sont Ratifiez & Prouvés par leurs Majestez sous le Grand Seau d'Angleterre* (London? 1691? English and French versions); iv. *The Civil Articles of Lymerick Exactly Printed from the Letters Patents: Wherein they are Ratified and Exemplified by Their Majesties under the Great Seal of England* (Dublin, 1692; English text only); v. *The Civil and Military Articles of Limerick, Exactly printed from the Letters Patents. Wherein They are Ratified and Exemplified by Their Majesties, under the Great Seal of England* (Dublin, 1731; English text only).

[3] For a modern reprint of the Military Articles, see T. Dunbar Ingram, *Two Chapters in Irish History* (London, 1888), pp. 149-54.

and his ally France, and was supported by the protestant community in Ireland.[4] The Treaty was vital to the Irish Catholics because they hoped that it would ensure that, notwithstanding having backed the loser, they would still enjoy civil liberty. The laws passed by the Irish Parliament after the Treaty depriving the Irish Catholics of all civil status were seen by the Irish as a violation of the Treaty. The allegation of a violated treaty was not only a major issue in the campaign for the restoration of civil liberty to Catholics,[5] which culminated in the grant of Catholic Emancipation in 1829, but even became a battle cry for Irish soldiers belonging to the Irish regiments in the service of France. In 1745 at Fontenoy, the Irish Brigade charged the English lines to the cry "Cumhnigidh ar Luimneach agus feall na Sassanach" – "Remember Limerick and the treachery of the English." [6]

To the historian of international law the Treaty is of special interest because it marks an important stage in the development of the relationship of the treaty-making power of the Crown and the necessity for legislation to give internal effect to its exercise by the King. The discussion of the alleged violation of the treaty is intimately bound up with the relationship between treaties and British municipal law.

In order to understand both issues we must return to the Treaty itself. Towards the end of 1691 Irish forces were continuing to hold out against William of Orange in the City of Limerick and a number of the western counties of Ireland. William facing reverses on the continent was anxious to bring the war in Ireland to a quick end in order to release his troops for service in Europe. The Irish in Limerick, although militarily in a position to hold out until further aid arrived from France, for reasons which have never been quite clear, were also willing to bring the war to an end.[7] On 27 September 1691 the garrison at Limerick proposed the following terms to the English Commander in Chief:

"1. That their Majesties will by an Act of indemnity pardon all past crimes and offences whatsoever.

[4] For a short modern account of this war, see J. C. Beckett, *A Short History of Ireland* (revised edition, London, 1958), pp. 89-102.

[5] See Donald MacCartney, "The writing of History in Ireland, 1800-30," *Irish Historical Studies*, vol. 10 (1956-57), 347-62, esp. pp. 357-8.

[6] J. C. O'Callaghan, *History of the Irish Brigades in the Service of France* (Glasgow, no date), p. 355.

[7] For a good general discussion of the background to the Treaty see J. G. Simms, *The Treaty of Limerick* (Dundalk, 1961), and J. G. Simme, "Williamite Peace Tactics, 1690-91," *Irish Historical Studies*, vol. 8 (1952-53), pp. 303-23.

"2. To restore all Irish Catholics to the estates of which they were seized or possessed before the late revolution.
"3. To allow a free liberty of worship, and one priest to each parish, as well in towns and cities as in the country.
"4. Irish Catholics to be capable of bearing employments, military and civil, and to exercise professions, trades, callings, of what nature soever.
"5. The Irish Army to be kept on foot, paid, etc., as the rest of their Majesties' forces, in case they be willing to serve their Majesties against France or any other enemy.
"6. The Irish Catholics to be allowed to live in towns corporate and cities, to be members of corporations, to exercise all sorts and manners of trade, and to be equal with their fellow Protestant subjects in all privileges, advantages, and immunities accruing in or by the said corporations.
"7. An Act of Parliament to be passed for ratifying and confirming the said conditions." [8]

An important question to be faced arising out of these proposals is the significance of the seventh clause, providing for an Act of Parliament to confirm and ratify the earlier conditions. Was it included because the Irish understood that the King could not enter into a legal obligation in respect of the first six of their proposals without the approval of Parliament in the form of a statute? [9] It is submitted that the answer to this question is in the negative. The proposal of the Irish was that De Ginckel as the King's representative should promise that a law should be passed by Parliament in accordance with the terms of their demands, merely as an additional assurance that the promise made on behalf of the Crown would in fact not be ignored by Parliament. In the 1640's agreements made in Ireland on behalf of the Crown had been followed by Parliamentary legislation allegedly inconsistent with the terms of agreements with the Crown.[10] Blackstone, writing much later, expounded his view of the treaty-making authority of the Crown as follows:

"It is also the king's prerogative to make treaties, leagues, and alliances with foreign states and princes. For it is by the law of nations essential to the goodness of a league, that it be made by the sovereign power; and then it is binding upon the whole community: and *in England the sovereign*

[8] G. Story, *A Continuation of the Impartial History of the Wars of Ireland* (London, 1693), p. 230.

[9] This is the view expressed by T. Dunbar Ingram in *Two Chapters of Irish History* (London, 1888), p. 97.

[10] T. Dunbar Ingram, *op. cit.*, p. 117.

power, quoad hoc, is vested in the person of the king. Whatever contracts therefore he engages in, no other power in the kingdom can legally delay, resist or annul." [italics added – P.O'H.]

Holdsworth has accepted this as an accurate statement of the legal position before 1688,[12] although at the time when Blackstone wrote it was certainly subject to qualifications.[13] But these qualifications were themselves says Holdsworth "the result of the constitutional settlement effected by the Great Rebellion and the Revolution [of 1688/9]." [14] To ascribe to the Irish a view of the treaty making power of the Crown, which was a product of the events in which they were participating is to invest them with a foresight they did not possess.

To return to the Irish proposals of 27 September, De Ginckel's reply was that

"though he was in a manner a stranger to the laws of England, yet he understood that those things they insisted upon were so far contradictory to them and dishonourable to himself that he could not grant any such terms." [15]

The Irish then inquired what terms De Ginckel was willing to grant and he submitted twelve articles which subsequently were accepted by the Irish with small modifications to form the Civil Articles of Limerick. Article I guaranteed that all Roman Catholics in Ireland should "enjoy such privileges in the exercise of their religion as are consistent with the laws of Ireland, or as they did enjoy in the reign of Charles the Second; and their Majesties as soon as their affairs will permit then to summon a Parliament in this kingdom will endeavour to procure the said Roman Catholics such further security, as may preserve them from any disturbances upon the account of their said religion."

The second Article provided that all persons in Limerick and all the Irish forces in the counties of Limerick, Clare, Kerry, Cork and Mayo "*and all such as are under their protection in the said counties*" should be left in possession of their property, and should continue to be free to carry on their occupations as freely as they did under Charles II. The words italicised were the subject of much contro-

[11] *Commentaries*, 1, 266-7.

[12] "The Treaty-making Power of the Crown." *Law Quarterly Review*, vol. 58 (1942), pp. 175-83.

[13] *History of English Law*, vol. X, p. 374; vol. XI, pp. 253, 268.

[14] *Law Quarterly Review*, vol. 58 (1942), at p. 175.

[15] Story, *op. cit.*, p. 230.

versy. They had been expressly included at the request of Sarsfield, the Irish leader. They were included in the final draft agreed to, but were accidentally omitted when the final draft was transcribed for the purpose of signature.[16] William accepted that the omission was accidental and the Civil Articles as ratified by him contained an additional paragraph reintroducing the omitted clause.[17]

Other Articles made provision for particular individuals, as well as promising that persons entitled to the benefit of the Second Article (and also certain persons who were overseas at the date of the Treaty) should be entitled to carry arms. Article IX provided that the oath to be administered to Roman Catholics should be the Oath of Allegiance. Article XII provided that

> The Lords Justices and General do undertake, that their Majesties will Ratifie these Articles within the space of eight months, or sooner, and *use their utmost Endeavours, that the same shall be ratified and confirmed in Parliament.*" [Italics added – P.O'H.]

Lecky fairly commented on the Articles:

> "Such a treaty was very reasonably regarded as a solemn charter guaranteeing the Irish catholics against any further penalties or molestation on account of their religion. It is true that the laws of Elizabeth against Catholicism remained unrepealed, but they had become almost wholly obsolete, and as they were not enforced during the reign of Charles II., it was assumed that they could not be enforced after the Treaty of Limerick." [18]

Such reasonable expectations were not fulfilled. An English Act of Parliament [19] was passed in 1692 to exclude all Catholics from the Irish Parliament. Some hesitation was expressed in the English House of Lords as to whether this was not a breach of the first of the Civil Articles of Limerick. In the time of Charles II no test excluded Catholics from the Irish Parliament; to impose any new test to exclude them now would be a breach of public faith.[20] The Act further

[16] See J. G. Simms, "The Original Draft of the Civil Articles of Limerick, 1691," *Irish Historical Studies*, vol. 8 (1952-53), 37-44, and J. G. Simms, *The Williamite Confiscation in Ireland* 1690-1703 (London, 1956), chapter 5.

[17] See Appendix.

[18] W. E. H. Lecky, *History of Ireland in the Eighteenth Centruy* (London, 1892, 5 vols), vol. 1, p. 139.

[19] 3 Will. & Mary, c. 2. Despite the existence of an Irish Parliament the English Parliament could legislate for Ireland.

[20] T. B. Macaulay, *History of England* (Ed. C. H. Firth, London, 6 vols., 1913-15), vol. 5, pp. 2088-9.

required all persons practising law to take both an oath of allegiance and make a declaration against transubstantiation. This being an apparent breach of Article IX was referred to Lord Holt, C. J. for his opinion, and the bill was amended in the light of his opinion.[21] The only concession made to the Civil Articles of Limerick was found in section 11 of the Act which contained an exception in favour of persons covered by the Articles of Limerick.

It was not until 1697 that reluctantly the Irish Parliament passed an Act [22] "for the Confirmation of Articles, made at the Surrender of the city of Limerick." The first section indicated that the Act had a more limited aim:

"Whereas divers doubts have arisen on the articles made at the treaty for the late surrender of the city of Limerick, the third day of October one thousand six hundred ninety one, and concerning the true intent and meaning of several parts thereof: and whereas your Majesty hath been graciously pleased to recommend to your Parliament: That the said articles, or so much of them as may consist with the safety and welfare of your Majesty's subjects of this kingdom, may be confirmed by authority of this present Parliament; we the lords spiritual and temporal and the commons in this present Parliament assembled, having due regard to your Majesty's honour, for declaring the true sense and meaning of the said articles, and taking away all occasions of doubt for the time to come, do most humbly beseech your Majesty that it may be enacted [as follows] . . . That the second Article, in the aforesaid articles mentioned, be and is hereby confirmed and ratified in the sense and intendment following, and not otherwise . . ."

There then followed an account of the second Article but excluding all reference to the omitted clause,[23] thereby narrowly restricting the scope of that article. The Act did not refer at all to the vital general Articles 1 (guaranteeing all catholics the same liberty as in the reign of Charles II) and 9 (which restricted the oath that could be demanded of catholics to the oath of allegiance).

The argument which has since raged over the question whether the Civil Articles were violated by the conduct of the Irish Parliament, which in succeeding years passed a number of Acts [24] depriving

[21] *Ibid.*
[22] 9 Will. III, c.2 (Ir.).
[23] See above, p. 216.
[24] These Acts collectively are known as the "Penal Code." The best summary of the Penal Code may be found in *A Statement of the Penal Laws* (3 parts, Dublin, 1812-13), published anonymously but in fact by D. Scully. To the international lawyer the most interesting provision in the Penal Code

catholics of such liberty as they may have possessed during the reign of Charles II, has turned first of all on the construction of the Articles. Being in many respects ambiguous it was argued that they really guaranteed nothing to the Irish, but this flies in face of any reasonable construction of the Articles. It was sometimes even argued that there was no obligation to keep faith with catholics, they being as it were outside the civilised community.[25] But the main legal argument in favour of there being no breach was that Parliament could not be bound by an exercise of the treaty making prerogative. An echo of this argument may still be found in modern historical writing.[26]

In order to understand the legal issues involved we have to remember that in the last decade of the seventeenth century, the King still constitutionally possessed the power of refusing assent to legislation of either the Irish or English Parliament. As respects the Irish Parliament its legislative authority was severely limited.

> "No Irish Bill could be laid before the Irish Parliament which had not received the approval of the English Privy Council. No Irish Bill could become law except in the precise form which the English Privy Council had sanctioned. It was sometimes beyond the power of the English Government to induce the Irish Parliament to carry measures which they desired, though even in this case they claimed, and occasionally exercised, the power of binding Ireland by English Acts. But they had no difficulty in preventing the enactment of any Irish law which they disliked." [27]

If we add to this that Blackstone's doctrine was true at least for most of the seventeenth century, namely that any agreement made by the Crown could not legally be delayed, resisted or annulled by any power in the kingdom, the position in 1691 would appear to be that it was not constitutional for Parliament to do anything which involved a violation of an agreement made by the Crown and the Crown had the constitutional means to prevent any such legislation coming into effect. In the light of this the language used by the Irish Parliament in 1697 is significant for so far as express words are con-

was that in case of war with a Catholic country, Irish Catholics had to reimburse any Protestant who suffered loss at the hands of enemy privateers.

[25] E.g. Bishop Dopping on a sermon preached in Christ Church Cathedral Dublin. See J. G. Simms, *Williamite Confiscation*, p. 29.

[26] *Cf.* J. C. Beckett, *The Making of Modern Ireland, 1603-1923* (London, 1966), p. 149; "It might be argued, of course, that parliament could not be bound in advance by an agreement of this sort . . ."

[27] Lecky, *op. cit.*, vol. 1, p. 145.

cerned it purports for the most part merely to declare "the true sense and meaning of the said articles." On the other hand the reference to the consistency of the Articles with the safety and welfare of the country marks the emergence of the idea that constitutionally Parliament has a discretion as to the implementation of a treaty.

So long as Blackstone's doctrine was true it was not necessary to distinguish clearly between an obligation under international law, binding upon the State, and the implementation of such obligation in terms of municipal law. But it is this very distinction which is at the heart of the controversy over the violation of the Articles of Limerick, and it was only in the years subsequent to the Treaty that this distinction slowly became clear in British law. The Treaty itself reveals the germ of this distinction, in Article XII, wherein a promise is made that the King and Queen will "use their utmost endeavours, that the same [Articles] be ratified and confirmed in Parliament." The origin of this Article lies no doubt in the Irish side's desire for the utmost security, the King being far away and the Irish Parliament near at hand, and in the uncertainty of the Crown as to its relationship with Parliament. In modern terms the Civil Articles bound the Crown under the Law of Nations, but the implementation of parts of the Treaty were dependant upon action by Parliament. Again in modern terms any statute violating the Civil Articles would be valid British law, notwithstanding that it was simultaneously a violation of international law.[28]

It has been argued that the obligation of the Civil Articles in the light of Article XII was "conditional on the approbation and confirmation of the Irish Parliament, to the ratification of which . . . [they] were made expressly subject." [29] It is suggested that although there is no reason why one should not have a treaty whose obligation is conditional upon approval by Parliament, this is not the meaning to be attributed to Article XII, and indeed is inconsistent with the whole tenor of the Articles. Sir Charles Porter, the Irish Lord Chancellor, who was himself one of the signatories to the Civil Articles of Limerick, expressed the opinion in 1695 that the only provisions in these Articles that "require an Act of Parliament to make them good . . .

[28] *Cf. I.R.C.* v. *Collco Dealings* [1962] A.C. 1.
[29] T. Dunbar Ingram, *op. cit.*, p. 102.

are those which forbid any suits to be brought for any trespass during the war." [30]

In an unguarded moment Arthur Browne,[31] Regius Professor of Law at Trinity College, Dublin, a great Irish civilian, who was almost certainly the first man to teach the Law of Nations to undergraduates in Ireland [32] invoked the case of the Caudine Forks to suggest that a treaty made without authority from Parliament was not binding,[33] and quoted Grotius, *De Jure Belli ac Pacis*, II, 15 in support. Although it is true that the Romans repudiated the agreement made by leaders of the Roman troops surrounded at the Caudine Forks, there was never any suggestion that such an agreement was not binding upon the parties to it, and that the Romans who were party to it had not to make reparation for its non-performance by the Roman State.[34] But if Professor Browne seemed to imply that the Crown lacked authority to make a binding treaty without the prior authority of Parliament, this was almost certainly not his real view. This can be seen from his discussion of the problem in *A Brief Review of the Question, Whether the Articles of Limerick have been Violated?* [35] In this work Browne's answer to the allegation of treaty violation was that Parliament is

[30] *Calendar, State Papers, Domestic, 1695*, p. 36.

[31] See P. O'Higgins, "Arthur Browne – an Irish Civilian," *Northern Ireland Legal Quarterly*, vol. 20 (1969).

[32] See P. O'Higgins, "The Study of International Law in Ireland," *Annuaire de l'Association des Auditeurs ... de l'Academie de Droit International de la Haye*, vol. 29 (1959), pp. 68-73. It may be of historical interest to notice that William O'Connor Morris, Professor of Law at the King's Inns, Dublin, in 1862, in his novel *Memoirs of Gerald O'Connor* (London, 1903), based upon the life of an ancestor of his, causes his ancestor, in a fictionalised account of the events leading up to and following the Treaty of Limerick, to refer to the civil part of the treaty as having been "infamously violated before many months had passed" (at pp. 79-80). Another Irish lawyer, Sir William Shee, an expert in the law of admiralty, and the first catholic member of an English superior court since 1688, took a practically identical view, in his *Papers and Letters on Subjects of Literary, Historical and Political Interest* (London, 1862, for private circulation only), at p. 170: "... no sooner were the immediate objects attained than every promise was forgotten and every engagement violated."

[33] *A Compendious View of the Civil Law* (2nd, ed., London, 1802, 2. vols.), vol. 2, pp. 11-12.

[34] *Cf.* Coleman Phillipson, *The International Law and Custom of Ancient Greece and Rome* (London, 1911, 2 vols.), vol. 1, pp. 370-2.

[35] Dublin, 1788 (there were apparently 2 editions in that year). This work was later reissued in somewhat cruder form as *The Articles of Limerick Are Not, Were Not Violated* (Dublin, 1825), purporting to be by an anonymous writer who signed himself "Pro Aris et Focis."

never obliged to give municipal effect to a treaty made by the Crown.

"An immense power, the whole executive power is lodged in the Crown, the power of war and peace, the right of making leagues and alliances, of forming treaties with foreign states, of granting terms to the enemy, rests in majesty. To control so immense a power, parliament retains the privilege of shewing both by word and deed its approbation or disapprobation of the royal mode of exercising this power, by addresses; by refusing supplies; by not following the treaty up with such acts as may be necessary to complete it, and which are at the same time solely within their province." [36]

Because of this he argued that there was no violation.

"They [the Irish] must have known, that the Articles were accepted, subject to the risk of parliamentary disapprobation." [37]

But the fallacy in this argument is that the mere fact that under municipal law Parliament is free not to give municipal effect to an international obligation, does not affect the fact that such non-implemetation is a violation of the international obligation. Furthermore the Irish could not have been aware of Parliament's constitutional right under British municipal law to refuse to implement a treaty, because this parliamentary freedom was only clearly established after 1691; indeed the reaction of the English and Irish Parliaments in enacting municipal legislation violative of the Civil Articles of Limerick, helped to map out the new relationship between the treaty making prerogative and British municipal law.

An anonymous reply to Browne stated

"... he [Browne] remarks 'that Parliament may control this power; and may or may not ratify, any treaties which the king may have entered into.' There if I mistake not, rests the whole strength of Mr Browne's reasoning... If such a monstrous incongruity existed in the constitution, foreign powers would long since have set it to rights: the law of nations

[36] *Op. cit.*, p. 39. It is interesting to contrast this with what Blackstone had written only a few years earlier on the means of limiting abuse of the treaty-making power. "And yet, lest this plenitude of authority should be abused to the detriment of the public, the constitution (as was hinted before) hath here interposed a check, by the means of parliamentary impeachment, for the punishment of such ministers as from criminal motives advise or conclude any treaty, which shall afterwards be judged to derogate from the honour and interest of the nation" – *Commentaries,* I, 267.

[37] *Ibid.*, p. 40.

would not admit this ingenious artifice, power would soon join with justice in correcting it." [38]

The writer sees that the liberty of Parliament to ignore a treaty could involve it in action inconsistent with the law of nations, but his views, not to mention those of Browne and Blackstone, illustrate the long period which often elapses before a change in practice is given clear doctrinal recognition.

A further argument used by Browne to justify the alleged breach was that

"The Articles could not in any common intendment be interpreted without this implied provision, that they were to stand, unless some publick necessity required an alteration, or unless the Papists broke them on their part." [37]

There was in fact no concrete evidence to justify the invocation of this argument, and Browne did not advance it with much conviction.

In case the objection is raised that perhaps after all the Treaty of Limerick was not an instrument governed by the Law of Nations it may be worth emphasising that no one on either side at the time had any doubt that it was a transaction of an international legal character. Indeed on the Irish side, when the English Parliament, failed to enact legislation to ensure the free practise of their occupations, etc., to the inhabitants of a number of towns which had surrendered to the English on the basis of Articles of Peace in terms similar to the Civil Articles of Limerick, the persons concerned petitioned the English Parliament, arguing that the Articles of Peace agreed upon in their case "... are by the Law of Nations, as obligatory as any of the rest." [40] On the other side, Dr Mathew Tindal in 1693 advising the Privy Council on the legal status of subjects taken at sea while acting as privateers under commission from James II, was quite clear that so long as the Irish "had an Army in the Field, and were Masters of

[38] *The Question Considered: Have the Articles of Limerick been violated? Being Strictures on Mr Browne's Review* (Dublin, 1788), p. 12. There was a second edition of this work in 1808.

[39] *Ibid.*, p. 56. It is worth noting that much of the discussion, in T. Dunbar Ingram, *op. cit.*, of the arguments against there having been a violation of the Articles of Limerick, is merely an unacknowledged transcription of Browne's work.

[40] See *The Case of the Persons comprized in the Articles of Waterford, Bophin, Sligo, and Drogheda, in the Kingdom of Ireland* (a single folio sheet, without date, to be found in vol. 101 of the Miscellaneous Pamphlets in Lincoln's Inn Library, London).

fortify'd Towns, they were esteemed and us'd as [an] Enemy."[41] Once they ceased to function as an effective administration the Law of Nations no longer applied to relations with them.

If the Civil Articles of Limerick contributed to the development of the modern British doctrine on the relationship between treaties and British municipal law, the Military Articles played a parallel role in the emergence of the modern doctrine that the Crown cannot by treaty alter the law to be applied by British courts.[42] The Military Articles were largely concerned with the detailed arrangements for the transportation of those of the Irish forces who wished to leave Ireland and to serve where they would.[43] The bulk of them sailed to France where they formed the nucleus of the Irish brigade which was to fight on the side of France for much of the next century. Clearly the Military Articles[44] which permitted an undefeated army to depart for Britain's enemy France envisaged that the soldiers concerned should be free to fight for France against Britain. From the point of view, however, of English municipal law, such Irish soldiers would be guilty of treason for levying war against William, in English eyes now the lawful King of Ireland. Implicit in the Military Articles was the agreement that Irish soldiers permitted to leave Ireland were free to fight for enemies of the Crown, and would not be regarded as traitors for so doing. What was the legal position in fact of Irish soldiers who left Ireland under the Military Articles who were subsequently captured by British forces while serving in the French army?

Holdsworth notes[45] that as early as 1689 the chief justices of the King's Bench and Common Pleas, the judge of the Court of Admi-

[41] M. Tindal, *An Essay concerning the Law of Nations, &c* (London, 1693), reprinted in *A Collection of State Tracts, Published on Occasion of the Late Revolution in 1688 And During the Reign of King William III* (London, 3 vols., 1705-7), vol. II pp. 462-75 (See especially pp. 469-70, and 472). See also Narcissus Luttrell, *A Brief Historical Relation of Affairs from September 1678 to April 1714* (6 vols., Oxford, 1857), vol. 3, p. 183.

[42] *Walker v. Baird* [1892] A.C. 491.

[43] J. G. Simms, *The Treaty of Limerick*, p. 11. See also J. C. O'Callaghan, *op. cit.*, p. 190, who quotes a Declaration on October 5, 1691, made by Baron De Ginckel to the Irish troops, in which De Ginckel says that as between British interests and French designs, the Irish soldiers were "at full and entire liberty to chose what part they will take."

[44] It may also be of interest to note that Article III of the Military Articles provided for the mutual surrender of military deserters between the English and Irish armies.

[45] "The Treaty Making Powers of the Crown," *Law Quarterly Review*, vol. 58 (1942), pp. 175-83, at p. 176.

ralty, the Attorney- and Solicitor-General, and the Advocate-General, had in answer to a question posed by the Crown stated that a treaty could not affect the law to be applied by English courts in determining the extent of the rights of English subjects to arrest and claim their goods in prizes brought to England.[46] In 1694 a number of Irishmen, captured on board French privateers were variously charged with high treason, robbery, piracy and murder. They pleaded the Articles of Limerick as part of their defence, but still they were convicted. It is not clear from the report,[47] whether this was because the court took the view that they had not proved their status as privateers or that they had ever actually been members of the Irish forces at Limerick, or because the court believed that the Articles could not be construed as giving Irishmen who had served at Limerick the freedom to fight for enemies of the English Crown, or because the Military Articles could make no difference to the law applied by the Court. In 1707, Peter Drake, an Irishman who had served at Limerick in the Irish forces, was captured on board a French privateer.[48] In June 1708 he was tried for treason. Of this event he wrote:

> "I shall not trouble the reader with many of the particulars of this trial, which lasted above two hours and a half; and shall only say that my counsel pleaded strongly my being under the [Military] Articles of Limerick; and therefore hoped the court would grant me the benefit of them [*sic*] Articles, which they were ready to prove I was entitled to; and then called my witnesses, which were sworn; the chief of them was my Lady Tyrone, who knew me in Limerick at the time of the Surrender, and after that in France, at our landing at Brest. This, and all my defence, was overruled, and the jury brought in their verdict, guilty." [49]

Drake was sentenced to death, which sentence was commuted to life imprisonment, and then later lifted entirely by royal pardon.[50]

[46] Holdsworth refers to the actual opinion which is to be found in Marsden, *Law and Custom of the Sea* (Navy Records Society), ii, 125-6.

[47] Manuscript (MS 148) at All Souls College, Oxford. For this reference and other advice I am much indebted to my colleague, David Yale, M.A., LL.B., Fellow of Christ's College, Cambridge.

[48] *Amiable Renegade: The Memoirs of Capt. Peter Drake, 1671-1753* (ed. S. Burrell, Stanford, 1960), p. xxxv.

[49] *Op. cit.*, pp. 134-5. Professor Burrell notes (on p. 135) that a record of Drake's trial and sentence can be found in the Public Record Office (H.C.A. 1/16 f.168) and that references to the case may also be found in Narcissus Luttrell, *A Brief Historical Relation of State Affairs from September 1678 to April 1714* (Oxford, 1857), vol. 6, pp. 294, 296 and 311.

[50] *Op. cit.*, p. xxxvi.

The outcome of Drake's case appears to have established the precedent that whatever was the true intention of the Articles of Limerick, the English courts being unwilling to give them such effect as would prevent Irish soldiers captured while serving France from being convicted of treason, the only way to implement the intention of the Military Articles was by administrative action. In later years even Irish troops, who not having been at Limerick and therefore were clearly not entitled to the protection of the Articles, were treated not as traitors but as ordinary prisoners of war, despite the fact that in English law they were traitors.[51]

CONCLUSIONS

1. Until 1688 any treaty made by the Crown was binding both under international and municipal law upon all organs of the state.
2. The changed relationship between William III and his parliaments, led the latter, albeit uncertainly to claim the right under English municipal law not to give legislative effect to treaties, and even to legislate in a manner inconsistent with them.
3. Simultaneously the courts began to refuse to allow treaties to affect the law applied by them in ascertaining the rights and duties of the King's subjects.
4. The Treaty of Limerick and the legislation and litigation arsing out of it mark a decisive turning point in these developments.
5. Theoretical discussion in the eighteenth century of the question whether the Treaty had been violated did not make the modern distinction between the obligation of the treaty under international law and the question whether under English law Parliament is free to ignore the treaty, even if this involves a violation of international law. The juridical recognition of this distinction is a product of the nineteenth century.
6. The answer to the question, was the Treaty violated, is in terms both of the legal position in 1691 and of modern law, yes. The eighteenth century legal argument for there being no violation was based upon the recognition that English law did not oblige Parlia-

[51] O'Callaghan, op. cit., pp. 436-7, discussing the fate of Irish soldiers captured at sea in 1745 on their way to aid Prince Charles in Scotland, as well as Irish soldiers in the French service captured at the battle of Culloden. Irishmen, who had deserted from the English army, and later joined the French army were executed.

ment to give effect to a treaty combined with a failure to distinguish between the obligation of international law and the obligation of English law.

Appendix

Civil Articles of Limerick

Articles agreed upon the Third Day of October, 1691 between the Right Honourable Sir Charles Porter, Knight, and Thomas Coningsby, Esq., Lords Justices of Ireland; and His Excellency the Baron De Ginckle, Lieutenant General, and Commander in Chief of the English Army; on the one Part.

And the Right Honourable Patrick Earl of Lucan, Piercy Viscount Gallmoy, Colonel Nicholas Purcel, Colonel Nicholas Cusack, Sir Toby Butler, Colonel Garret Dillon, and Colonel John Brown; on the other Part:

In the behalf of the Irish Inhabitants in the City and County of Lymerick, the Counties of Clare, Kerry, Cork, Sligo and Mayo.

In Consideration of the Surrender of the City of Lymerick and other Agreements made between the said Lieutenant General Ginckle, the Governor of the City of Lymerick, and the Generals of the Irish Army, bearing date with these Presents, for the Surrender of the said City, and Submission of the said Army: It is Agreed, That

I

The Roman Catholicks of this Kingdom shall enjoy such Privileges in the Exercise of their Religion as are consistent with the Laws of Ireland; or as they did enjoy in the Reign of King Charles the II: And their Majesties, as soon as their Affairs will permit them to Summon a Parliament in this Kingdom, will endeavour to procure the said Roman Catholicks such further Security in that particular, as may preserve them from any Disturbance, upon the Account of their said Religion.

II

All the Inhabitants or Residents of Lymerick, or any other Garrison now in the possession of the Irish, and all Officers and Souldiers, now in Arms, under any Commission of King James, or those Authorized by him to grant the same in the several Counties of Lymerick, Clare, Kerry, Cork, and Mayo, or any of them; [52] and all the Commissioned Officers in their Majesties' Quarters, that belong to the Irish Regiments, now in being, that are Treated with, and who are not Prisoners of War, or have taken Protection, and who shall return and submit to their Majesties' obedience, and their and every of their Heirs, shall hold, possess and enjoy all and every their Estates of Free-hold and Inheritance; and all the Rights, Titles and Interests, Privileges and Immunities, which they, and every or any of them held, enjoyed or were rightfully and lawfully Intituled to, in the Reign of King Charles the II, or at any time since, by the Laws and Statutes that were in force in the said Reign of King Charles the II, and shall be put in possession, by order of the Government, of such of them as are in the King's Hands, or the Hands of his Tenants, without being put to any suit or trouble therein; and all such Estates shall be freed and discharged from all Arrears of Crown-Rents, Quit-Rents, and other publick Charges incurred and become due since Michaelmas, 1688 to the day of the date herof: And all persons comprehended in this Article shall have, hold, and enjoy all their Goods and Chattels, real and personal, to them, or any of them belonging, and remaining either in their own hands, or the hands of any persons whatsoever, in trust for, or for the use of them, or any of them: and all and every the said persons, of what Profession, Trade, or Calling soever they be, shall and may use, exercise and practise their several and respective Professions, Trades and Callings, as freely as they did use, exercise and enjoy the same in the Reign of King Charles the II: Provided, that nothing in this Article contained be construed to extend to, or restore any forfeiting person now out of the Kingdom, except what are hereafter comprized: Provided also, That no Person whatsoever shall have or enjoy the benefit of this Article, that shall neglect or refuse to take the Oath of Allegiance made by Act of Parliament in England, in the First Year of the Reign of their present Majesties, when thereunto required.

[52] The omitted clause "and all such as are under their protection in the said counties," should have appeared at this point. It was restored with the Crown's approval by the last paragraph of this Appendix.

III

All Merchants, or reputed Merchants of the City of Lymerick, or of any other Garrison, now possessed by the Irish, or of any Town or Place in the Counties of Clare or Kerry, who are absent beyond the Seas, that have not bore Arms since their Majesties' Declaration in February, 1688, shall have the benefit of the Second Article, in the same manner as if they were present, provided such Merchants, and reputed Merchants, do repair into this Kingdom within the space of eight months from the date hereof.

IV

The following Officers, viz., Colonel Simon Lutterel, Captain Rowland White, Maurice Eustace of Yermanstown, Chievers of Maystown, commonly called Mount-Leinster, now belonging to the Regiments in the aforesaid Garrisons and Quarters of the Irish Army, who were beyond the Seas, and sent thither upon affairs of their respective Regiments, or the Army in general, shall have the benefit and advantage of the second Article, provided they return hither within the space of eight months from the date of these Presents and submit to their Majesties' Government, and take the above mentioned Oath.

V

That all and singular, the said persons comprized in the 2d and 3d Articles, shall have a general Pardon of all Attainders, Outlawries, Treasons, Misprisions of Treason, Praemunires, Felonies, Trespasses, and other Crimes and Misdemeanors whatsoever, by them, or any of them committed since the beginning of the Reign of King James the II: and if any of them are Attainted by Parliament, the Lords Justices, and General, will use their best Endeavours to get the same repealed by Parliament, and the Outlawries to be reversed Gratis, all but Writing-Clerks' Fees.

VI

And whereas these present Wars have drawn on great Violences on both parts, and that if leave were given to the bringing all sorts of private Actions, the Animosities would probably continue, that have been too long on Foot, and the publick Disturbances last: For the Quieting and Settling therefore of this Kingdom, and avoiding those Inconveniences which would be the necessary consequences of the contrary, no person or persons whatsoever, comprized in the foregoing Articles, shall be Sued, Molested, or Impleaded at the Suit of any Party or Parties whatsoever, for any Trespasses by them committed, or for any Arms, Horses, Money, Goods, Chattels, Merchandizes, or Provisions whatsoever, by them seized or taken, during the time of the War. And no person or Persons whatsoever, in the Second or Third Articles comprized, shall be Sued, Impleaded, or made accountable for the Rents or mean Rates of any Lands, Tenements, or Houses by him or them received or enjoyed in this Kingdom, since the beginning of the present War, to the day of the Date hereof, nor for any Waste or Trespass by him or them committed in any such Lands, Tenements, or Houses: And it is also agreed, that this Article shall be mutual, and reciprocal, on both sides.

VII

Every Nobleman and Gentleman, comprized in the said 2d and 3d Article, shall have liberty to Ride with a Sword, and Case of Pistols, if they think fit; and keep a Gun in their Houses, for the Defence of the same, or for Fowling.

VIII

The Inhabitants and Residents in the City of Lymerick, and other Garrisons, shall be permitted to remove their Goods, Chattels, and Provisions, out of the same, without being viewed and searched, or paying any manner of Duties, and shall not be compelled to leave the Houses or Lodgings they now have, for the space of six weeks next ensuing the Date hereof.

IX

The Oath to be administered to such Roman-Catholicks as submit to their Majesties' Government, shall be the Oath abovesaid, and no other.

X

No person or persons, who shall at any time hereafter break these Articles, or any of them, shall thereby make, or cause any other person or persons to forfeit or lose the benefit of the same.

XI

The Lords Justices and General do promise to use their utmost Endeavours, that all the persons comprehended in the above-mentioned Articles, shall be protected and defended from all Arrests and Executions for Debt or Damage, for the space of eight months, next ensuing the Date hereof.

XII

Lastly The Lords Justices and General do undertake, that their Majesties will Ratifie these Articles within the space of eight months, or sooner, and use their utmost Endeavours, that the same shall be ratified and confirmed in Parliament.

XIII

And whereas Colonel John Brown stood indebted to several Protestants, by Judgments of Record; which appearing to the late Government, the Lord Tyrconnel, and Lord Lucan, took away the Effects the said John Brown had to answer the said Debts, and promised to clear the said John Brown of the said Debts; which effects were taken for the publick use of the Irish, and their Army: For freeing the said Lord Lucan of his said Engagement, past on their publick Account, for Payment of the said Protestants, and for preventing the ruine of the said John Brown, and for satisfaction of his Creditors, at the instance of the Lord Lucan, and the rest of the Persons aforesaid, it is agreed, That the said Lords Justices, and the said Baron de Ginckle, shall intercede with the King and Parliament, to have the Estates secured to Roman-Catholicks, by Articles and Capitulation in this Kingdom, charged with, and equally liable to the payment of so much of the said Debts, as the said Lord Lucan, upon stating Accompts with the said John Brown, shall certifie under his Hand, that the Effects taken from the said Brown amount unto; which Accompt is to be stated, and the Ballance certified by the said Lord Lucan in one and twenty days after the Date hereof:

For the true performance hereof, We have herunto set our Hands,

Char. Porter,

Tho. Coningsby.

Bar. De Ginckle.

Present,

Scravemore,

H. Maccay.

T. Talmash.

And whereas the said City of Lymerick hath been since, in pursuance of the said Articles, surrendered unto Us, Now know ye, that We having considered of the said Articles, are Graciously pleased hereby to declare, that We do for Us, Our Heirs and Successors, as far as in Us lies, Ratifie and Confirm the same, and every Clause, Matter and Thing therein contained. And as to such Parts thereof, for which an Act of Parliament shall be found to be necessary, We shall Recommend the same to be made good by Parliament, and shall give Our Royal Assent to any Bill or Bills that shall be Passed by Our Two Houses of Parliament to that purpose. And whereas it appears unto Us, that it was agreed between the Parties to the said Articles, that after the words, Limerick, Clare, Kerry, Cork, Mayo, or any of them in the second of the said Articles, the words following: Viz., *And all such as are under their Protection in the said Counties*, should be inserted, and be part of the said Articles. Which words having been casually omitted by the Writer, the omission was not discovered till after the said Articles were Signed, but was taken notice of before the second Town was surrendered: And that our said Justices, and General, or One of them, did promise that the said Clause should be made good, it being within the Intention of the Capitulation, and inserted in the Foul Draught thereof. Our further Will and Pleasure is, and We do hereby Ratifie and Confirm the said omitted Words, Viz. *And all such as are under their Protection in the said Counties*

Hereby for Us, Our Heirs and Successors, Ordaining and Declaring, that all and every Person and Persons therein concerned, shall and may have, receive, and enjoy the Benefit thereof, in such and the same manner, as if the said Words has been inserted in their proper place, in the said second Article; any Omission, Defect, or Mistake in the said second Article, in any wise notwithstanding. Provided always, and Our Will and Pleasure is, that these Our Letters Patents shall be Enrolled in Our Court of Chancery in our said Kingdom of Ireland, within the space of one year next ensuing. In Witness & c. Witness Our Self at Westminster, the twenty fourth day of February, *Anno Regni Regis & Reginae* Gulielmi & Mariae *Quarto per Breve de Privato Sigillo.*

GPSR Compliance

The European Union's (EU) General Product Safety Regulation (GPSR) is a set of rules that requires consumer products to be safe and our obligations to ensure this.

If you have any concerns about our products, you can contact us on ProductSafety@springernature.com

In case Publisher is established outside the EU, the EU authorized representative is:

Springer Nature Customer Service Center GmbH
Europaplatz 3
69115 Heidelberg, Germany

Batch number: 10830937

Printed by Printforce, the Netherlands